THE GOOD FIGHT

Spiritual Warfare and the Believer's Hope

DR. LARRY A. VOLD

3Crosses

20600 John Drive

Castro Valley, California 94546

www.3crosses.org

The Good Fight: Spiritual Warfare and the Believer's Hope
Dr. Larry A. Vold — 1st ed.

ISBN: 9781072672579

Imprint: Independently published

DEDICATION

To the many people in my life who have modeled the good fight.

Thank you for reminding me that there is no one more powerful

than Jesus.

And no love greater than His.

And no victory more sure than the one He promises.

TABLE OF CONTENTS

ACKNOWLEDGEMENTS

The book you are about to read would have never been possible without the good editing work of my personal assistant, Tracy Teyler, and the patience and fine formatting of my editor, Rick Chavez. The cover design is the creation of my daughter, Katy, whose artistic skills bring such pleasure to me.

I'm indebted also to the family of 3Crosses Church whose fight in the spiritual realm is both a source of great joy and impetus for instilling in me a greater dependence on God.

I'm also so grateful and must acknowledge without individually naming them, the host of colleagues and brothers and sisters in the faith who inspire me to live more deeply in love with Jesus my Savior, giving me courage to fight the spiritual battles that the enemy wages in my life.

Ultimately, I must acknowledge the One who one day woke me up to see the spiritual realm which was more real than I had imagined, and after seeing it, heard the voice of God to give the rest of my years to serving God by shepherding His people.

INTRODUCTION

I don't like to fight. I was born with an aversion to conflict. From my earliest memory of social interaction, I believed that fighting was wrong and should be avoided if possible. I come from a long line of men who learned to solve their problems without using their fists. My father, and his father before him never shared stories of bar room brawls where people got what they "had coming to them!" As far as I was concerned, fighting might be for some people but never for me. I was a peacemaker at heart. Throughout my childhood, I sincerely hoped I would never have to fight anyone about anything. That hope was shattered in the spring of 1970. I was in 8th grade at Ralston Middle School.

A new kid arrived at school and was introduced in my 7th period history class. From the moment of that first introduction, Paul had it out for me. I hadn't said or done anything to provoke his obvious disdain for me, but somehow he was determined to view me as his enemy. Every day for at least a week after arriving at my school, he "called me out" (the way adolescent boys announce their desire to fight someone publicly). Somehow throughout that week, I was able to deflect his persistent threats.

I'm sure this kind of bullying has taken place for as long as kids have gone to school—especially middle school where social relationships can be treacherous. It's only been in recent years that students, parents, and educators have become more aware of the dangers of bullying among young people and have taken steps to curtail such behavior. Thankfully, there are signs of improvement but we are far from eliminating it on campuses across our nation. But in my situation back then, only a few of my peers knew what was going on and none of us told anyone about it. Every night I prayed that I would arrive at school the next day to learn that Paul had been transferred to another school or had mysteriously gone

1

missing. I simply didn't want to fight him. I had no experience with fighting and was sure he would make good on his promise to hurt me.

When talking about fighting among my peers a few years later, I would jokingly say that "no one ever wanted to fight me (pretending to sound tough), *"...because everyone thought they might kill me"* (playfully reminding people that I didn't know how to fight, and probably wouldn't survive if I got into one). This would usually get some laughs, but truthfully, the thought of throwing punches and trying to protect myself at the same time seemed terribly unsettling. It just wasn't me.

So there I was, walking down the main hallway at Ralston Middle School when it happened. I noticed the other students in the hallway clearing a path like Moses parting the Red Sea. Kids around me were getting out of the way fast! I had no idea their purpose in moving so quickly was to get a good look at a fight that was about to begin—a fight that unbeknownst to me involved yours truly. Turning around, there was Paul, with his big fist coming straight toward my face! I was shocked! I ducked to the side causing him to miss and lose his balance. Instinctively, my own fist came back and connected squarely on his jaw tumbling him to the ground. The crowd cheered as if an underdog had landed a knock-out punch against a prize fighter in an early round of a boxing match.

My adrenaline pumping, I dropped everything I was carrying in my other hand wondering what would happen next. By God's grace, I was grabbed from behind at the scruff of my neck by our school's vice principal, the dreaded Mr. Haley. In a single move, Mr. Haley also wrestled my opponent to his feet, marching both of us straight into his office a short distance away. Most students at my school believed that Mr. Haley had been a prison warden in a previous career which caused much fear whenever he got involved in things like this on campus (he was probably a really nice guy). In that moment, however, I viewed him as a savior who had rescued me from certain death.

2

For the next hour, Paul and I sat in Mr. Haley's office as phone calls were made to our parents and referrals for "fighting on campus" were handed to both of us. We were offered a plea bargain. If we shook hands and said we were sorry, we could avoid suspension from school and only need to serve detention. To avoid the dreaded "suspension" we carried out our mock reconciliation ceremony. We then did our "time" after school for a few days. The funny thing about that whole incident was that after that day, Paul never bothered me again. In time, we actually became friends.

Perhaps as you read this story, you are reminded of a time when there seemed no other choice but to fight. While it's true that some people actually enjoy fighting and might even pick a few fights now and then, most of us would rather avoid conflict of any kind.

When it comes to the spiritual dimension of life, however, the Bible teaches that we are engaged in a spiritual fight—like it or not—*believe it or not*. We really don't have a choice about it. The only choice we have is whether we will use the resources God has given us for the fight that is waging against us. Every believer needs to be informed and prepared when encountering battles that are spiritual in nature. How do we know whether our battle comes from Satan or is a result of our or someone else's decision—or can both be true? I suspect that it's also true that our one true enemy, Satan, would rather all of us feel like there's no battle to be fought at all. He would love for us to assume that in the toughest seasons of our lives, when he's been working behind the scenes, it's only bad luck or strange circumstances—nothing more. He doesn't want us to see his fingerprints on the destruction he plans and carries out all around us.

Through this book, we will conduct an overview of the nature and practices of our spiritual enemy—Satan—and his demonic host that we contend with daily whether we know it or not. We will do this to gain a simple understanding of our enemy's system that he has cleverly created to discourage or derail our journey with Christ. We will enter the battlefield of Old Testament saints and discover timeless principles for engaging the enemy. We'll also examine New Testament teachings on how to effectively deal with spiritual warfare, knowing the hope we have as believers in Jesus Christ.

Our spiritual warfare is what the Bible calls, among other things, *the good fight.* When writing to his young disciple, Timothy, the Apostle Paul gives instructions so that Timothy might, **"fight the good fight" (1 Timothy 1:18).** Near the end of the Apostle Paul's life, he claimed to have **"fought the good fight" (2 Timothy 4:7).** Yes, it's a good fight to which every follower of Jesus Christ has been called.

As we examine basic truths about spiritual warfare, we are encouraged to learn that we are not fighting alone. We'll also see that the spiritual fight is not always about getting what we desire. Our great and Almighty God, the Host of Heaven's armies, is with us and for us. He's fighting our battles with us even when we can't see Him fighting. His plan for us clearly includes learning to fight our spiritual battles. His plan will always be met with resistance and even opposition from our enemy who may even mount an offensive attack on us as he did to Job which is recorded in the Old Testament book that bears his name. We must embrace this reality and arm ourselves with the spiritual armor of faith, love, truth, holiness, mercy, prayer, and all that God has given us, including the sword of the Spirit (which Paul identifies as the Word of God) and engage in the spiritual battle that is being waged every day.

It's time we put aside fear, laziness, indifference, and anything that is sinful, to engage our enemy with boldness and humility, remembering the words of the Apostle John who wrote, **"You, dear children, are from God and have overcome them, because the One who is in you is greater than the one who is in the world" (1 John 4:4).** In the context, the "one who is in the world" is a portrayal of Satan and his demonic host. Greater is the God who lives in us and does his work through us.

It is my hope that this book will help us see more clearly how to fight in the spiritual dimension and in doing so, help us be more aware of Satan's strategies and schemes in our lives so we can be victorious through trusting God and His promises. It's about time we did so, don't you think? Let's begin!

CHAPTER 1

WAKE UP CALL
Know Who You Are Up Against

The church I attended when I was college-aged had developed a robust youth ministry with local public high schools in proximity to the church. Campus After Dark (C.A.D) was the "unchurchy" name given to campus club meetings held in students' homes from each of the campuses where these clubs existed. I had been part of the birth and subsequent growth of C.A.D., and at that time, I served as a club director for Aragon High School in San Mateo. One of the kids who attended our club and showed interest in spiritual things was a small-statured, quiet kid named Bill.

Our club meetings focused on merely introducing students to the gospel of Jesus Christ. They weren't Bible studies or discipling environments, but rather a place where kids could hear about Jesus in a very fun environment among their peers. Kids who were interested in learning more about Jesus were invited to other meetings held at our church where our youth ministry provided more substantive material for growing in a relationship with Christ. After one particular club meeting, Bill decided he wanted to take the next step and show up to church but showed reluctance when admitting he wanted to come check things out. I, along with another club director agreed to meet him at the church at the upcoming Sunday meeting to help him feel more comfortable— hoping his reluctance would diminish. My co-leader, Mark, met me outside the church that Sunday evening and we waited together for Bill to show up. He came right on time.

"Hi Bill! Glad you made it! Ready to go in?" I remarked, as he approached us in the parking lot. "They won't let me go in." he replied. "Who won't let you?" we inquired. No response. Bill had this blank look on his face as if he was tuned to some other world or dimension. With a few more gentle nudges to join us inside, we could clearly see something was holding him back—he wasn't going in. "Let's just go hang out at my house" I offered quickly, hoping we could at least salvage Bill's effort to come check things out, also hoping my home might be a safe and more inviting place for Bill to open up about what was going on in his life. With little more than a nod of agreement, Bill followed us to my VW bug in the church parking lot. We got in and drove away.

Within a block from exiting the church, Mark said something to Bill about how good it was that he had showed up to check out the church meeting, mentioning that Jesus loved him. Before the words were finished coming out of his mouth, Bill let out a shriek and became physically combative as we were in route to my house. What was happening? We didn't have a clue! I made a quick U-turn and drove immediately back to the church. Just as suddenly as his negative reaction had come, it left and he seemed peaceful again. As we pulled into the church parking lot having been gone for only a couple of minutes, Bill agreed to go with us into an office to talk. What took place in that office gave me a first-hand look at spiritual warfare and the power of Jesus Christ. It completely changed my life.

As we sat there in that office, the mention of Jesus would send Bill into a fit of rage, convulsing and spewing animalistic noises and growls toward us. It was like something out of a movie. Throughout these outbursts, vulgar and abusive language came from his mouth but the strange thing is that many of the things said seemed to be aimed at both Bill as well as those in proximity to him. He became extremely combative at times and appeared to want to hurt himself by striking his own face with his fists and banging his head against a wall or on the floor when his

8

convulsions took him to the floor. We quickly realized these outbursts were not being initiated by Bill, but by some other force that was indwelling him. Clearly, these were demons who had been outed and were not wanting to give up their place in Bill's life.

We began commanding the voices speaking to us to tell us their names. As one voice shouted, "You have no right over Bill—he's ours!" we'd respond, "In the name of Jesus, tell us your name!" "Blood! My name is Blood! I want blood!" Those in the room would begin praying as one of us nearby would begin commanding the demon named "Blood" to leave Bill and to never return—that Jesus' blood was shed for Bill and only His blood could cleanse Bill from sin!" Throughout the evening, we witnessed several of these manifestations that were followed by a deep exhale and then an eerie quiet in what felt like Bill was at peace. Bill would open his eyes and ask what was happening. We'd tell him to trust in Jesus because there were evil forces trying to keep him captive. More conversation would occur and then, before Bill could ask Jesus to come and live inside him, another voice, different from the last would speak and the process would repeat itself once again.

Some of the names I remember the demons identifying themselves as that night were, "Blood," "Pain," "Murder," "Liar," and "Legion." Over the several hours that followed, I witnessed first-hand the most startling and eerie realities of the spiritual realm of Satanic influence and possession. During such a short period of time, we witnessed Bill demonstrate extraordinary feats of strength as stronger and spiritually mature men tried to prevent him from physically hurting himself. Ultimately, and more importantly, we witnessed Bill finally being set free from the evil influences that had plagued his life at such a young age. I've never forgotten that night and how it impacted my life.

I remember Bill, after finally being freed from these terrible influences that had taken residence in his body, bowing his head and asking Jesus Christ to enter his life and take the reins. He was at peace with an extraordinary sense of calm. It reminded me of the account where Jesus cast out the demons of a man who immediately afterwards, was found clothed and in his right mind (Mark 5:15).

That experience was my wake-up call regarding the reality of what the Apostle Paul called, **"...the powers of this dark world...and the spiritual forces of evil in the heavenly realms" (Ephesians 6:12b).** It was that night when I heard the call of God in my life to become a pastor. Knowing the reality of Spiritual warfare, I could do no other thing but to offer my life to God to serve Him and take the gospel of Jesus Christ to everyone needing freedom and new life. That may not have been everyone's experience in that room, but it was certainly mine.

This is a book about spiritual warfare. This isn't an easy topic for a couple of reasons. First, this kind of warfare deals with *spiritual* realities that are not seen or experienced like *physical* ones. While the experience I've just shared was clearly one that gave visibility to unseen realities, it isn't always this way. We can't always see spiritual warfare with our physical eyes, but God can open our eyes to see into the spiritual dimension through prayer and the Holy Spirit's illumination of Scripture.

It's also not easy because Satan, our enemy, wants us to be clueless about this subject. He'd love for us to stay completely ignorant of his schemes. In his book, *Kingdoms In Conflict*, Charles Colson wrote, "Military strategists know that the first rule of warfare is to know the enemy. And knowing the enemy demands naming the enemy." Satan wants us to assume that spiritual warfare is nothing more than alarmist thinking that is either made up or, if real to some degree, is blown out of proportion.

When we think this way, however, Satan's strategies appear as nothing more than setbacks in life, unexplainable tragedies, senseless evil, curious opposition or emotional frustrations—all of which can be explained on a purely human level. And often, we try to solve our spiritual problems by merely reading a book, talking to a counselor or a faithful friend, or attending a conference or seminar. These can be helpful, but often what's missing is a sense that a spiritual battle is waging, developed cleverly by Satan and his demonic host. This reality requires a completely different approach for the one who might withstand Satan's attacks and strategies.

On the other hand, we can be confident that Satan delights in those who carry the theme of spiritual warfare too far, assuming all their problems are a direct result of some kind of Satanic attack. So when the car breaks down we might wrongly assume there's a demon of battery failure. Or when we lose our job it's because somewhere in the spiritual realm, Satan somehow made the boss terminate our employment. Or when our kids act out in disobedience or rebellion, we are sure they've become possessed by an evil spirit (if you are a parent, it may feel this way sometimes!). Or, if we don't have money to pay our bills a demon must be interfering with our cash flow. The bottom line is that when things don't go well for us, we're quick to assume we are under Satanic attack, when in reality, we may be merely encountering life in a broken world. Yes, the brokenness of our world can be traced back to Satan's attack on humanity right there in the garden, but not all problems we encounter have a direct connection with him. Sometimes it's merely our own bad choices or the bad choices of others that bring us difficulties. Satan often is given far too much credit for bad or difficult things that happen in our lives.

I will point out however, at the onset of this book, that if we take this subject seriously and really want to learn and grow in our understanding of spiritual warfare, we just might encounter more opposition from Satanic forces than we anticipated. Satan hates it when God's people are informed of his schemes and choose to stand firm when under spiritual opposition and attack. In this sense, I'm inviting us into a fight—one that we must learn and engage in properly, one that is worth fighting, one that we are called to fight. But even better, one in which we are guaranteed victory!

The Apostle Paul gave the church at Ephesus a wake-up call reminding them that spiritual forces were often at work behind the scenes, and to therefore, *"Put on the full armor of God so that you can take your stand against the devil's schemes" (Ephesians 6:11).* Like the Ephesians, we tend to see more plainly the struggle we have with unruly coworkers or a neighbor with whom we have a hard time getting along. But the struggle that is more real is one against the forces that exist in the spirit realm. Paul affirms this as he continues his instruction: *"For our struggle is not against flesh and blood, but against the rulers, against the authorities, against the powers of this dark world and against the spiritual forces of evil in the heavenly realms" (Ephesians 6:12).* Clearly, believers must recognize that there is an elaborate network of spiritual forces and beings who wish to bring havoc in this world—and in our lives.

We are comforted knowing that the extent of the havoc these forces may have on our lives is determined by God's Sovereign rule—and that nothing that comes our way in this life has not first passed through the loving determination of Almighty God and His purposes for us. This allows us to rehearse the question Job asked in the aftermath of the news of losing his family and possessions when his wife considered it better for him just to curse God and die: *"Shall we accept good from God and not trouble" (Job 2:10)?* And in similar fashion, King Solomon wrote, *"When times are good, be happy; but when times are bad, consider: God has made the one as well as the other" (Ecclesiastes 7:14).* We conclude that God allows both blessings and trials in our lives—and those trials sometimes stem from forces that exist in the spiritual realm.

Who is Satan?

Let's begin by taking a candid look at Satan, our spiritual enemy. To do so, we'll let Scripture offer us principles about him so we can know what we are up against. These are the basic principles every believer needs to know about Satan who is our true adversary. And I might add, *he would rather you didn't know these things about him.* We will focus on four things we really must know and truly believe about him if we are going to have victory over the battles he wages against us.

Satan is real

Do you believe this? The question arises from the fact that as a spiritual being, he can't be seen in the physical dimension. This leads some people to believe him to be merely a fictional character that represents all the bad things that happen in our world or to us personally. Images of Halloween costumes featuring red flannel and someone holding a pitchfork, work against our need to acknowledge this formidable enemy. The Bible, however, speaks clearly to this question affirming that Satan is a real being—and one with whom we must deal with in our lives as followers of Jesus. Some people think that believing in God is the only thing that matters. Believing Satan is a real being is important, too. To believe in one and not the other simply isn't Biblical.

The Apostle Peter writes about this in his first epistle: "*Be self-controlled and alert. Your enemy the devil prowls around like a roaring lion looking for someone to devour. Resist him, standing firm in the faith, because you know that your brothers throughout the world are undergoing the same kind of sufferings*" *(1 Peter 5:8-9).*

Peter is sending a strong warning and wake-up call urging us to action. Why? Because we have an enemy who prowls around looking for someone to *devour.* No matter how you interpret that phrase, it warns of a dark and dangerous reality that can bring spiritual disaster to any one of us. To be devoured by Satan is to be under his dominion, and him having his way in our lives. Remember, Jesus said that Satan's mission is to steal and kill and destroy (John 10:10a). That's something we'll see again before the end of this chapter.

13

Who would choose to be devoured by Satan? Yet it happens to countless people every day, even believers. This battle is more real than any national or world conflict. And what makes it worse, it's personal, impacting every person who doesn't heed the warning.

Martin Luther's great hymn titled, *A Mighty Fortress* captures this reality: *"A mighty fortress is our God, a bulwark never failing; our helper He, amid the flood of mortal ills prevailing. For still our ancient foe, doth seek to work us woe; His craft and power are great, and armed with cruel hate, on earth is not his equal."* As Luther rightly points out, our God is a mighty fortress in whom we find refuge and never-failing help. But it's also true that we wage war against an enemy that loves to wreak havoc in our lives. Both truths, God's powerful help in the midst of our struggle against Satan's relentless attack must remain clear in our minds.

When we read Peter's warning of the devil prowling around like a roaring lion, we should keep in mind that he is writing to believers. He warns us to be on alert, knowing that our enemy seeks to devour us. It's easy to see that Satan often has his way with more than a few of us who follow Jesus. And this is not merely because he has more power than we have or that we must always yield to his influence or temptation. He may have his way simply because we don't believe he's real or are ignorant of his schemes, or we are not staying alert. In boxing, the punch that knocks you out is usually the one you didn't see coming.

Throughout the Bible, Satan is presented as a real being, not a metaphor for all the evil in the world. He is not an impersonal force. He has personhood. He is a living being. We first meet him on the pages of Scripture in Genesis 3:1 where he is called **"the serpent"** and **"one more crafty than any of the wild animals the Lord God had made."** We know that the reference to the serpent in Genesis 3 is actually referring to Satan in the form of a serpent since in the book of Revelation, John writes, **"…the great dragon was hurled down—that ancient serpent called the devil, or Satan, who leads the whole world astray…" (Revelation 12:9).**

We see only a few other direct references to him in the Old Testament, such as his attack on Job after the cosmic wager made in the heavenly realm (see Job 1:8-9), or when he incites King David to number his troops in direct opposition to the will of God (1 Chronicles 21:1), or in his attempt to derail the divine purpose of God through Joshua the high priest in Zechariah's day (Zechariah 3:1-2).

Let's get a little more specific about Satan's real existence. Sometimes when considering his diabolical nature, we forget that he is a *created* being. He had a beginning like everything and everyone in all of God's creation. Satan's origin can be traced to God's creation of angelic beings. According to Scripture, Lucifer (who would later be known as Satan), was God's highest ranking angel in all the angelic host. Lucifer, whose name means, *"morning star"* or, in Latin, *"light-bearer,"* held the highest position over all of God's angelic beings. If you know your Bible, then it's no surprise to you that something dreadful happened within him. The highest ranking, most beautiful, and perhaps most powerful of all God's angelic host decided to rebel against God. Wickedness was found in him and God removed him from his once lofty place.

There are two specific places in the Old Testament where we read of Lucifer's fall from his position as God's highest ranking angel. Both are found in the prophetic sections of the Old Testament. The first we will look at is Ezekiel 28:11-14. In both prophecies we have at first, a reference to an earthly king, followed by prophetic descriptions of another type of ruler obviously not of this world. It is interesting how Old Testament prophecies often do this; while speaking of an earthly character, another being (and in this case, Lucifer) is introduced or described. The nature and descriptions of the latter ruler leads students of Biblical prophecy to deduce these sections of Scripture as depicting the one we have come to understand as Satan himself.

In Ezekiel's prophecy, the earthly person introduced is the king of Tyre (Ezekiel 28:1-2), which historically would likely be Ethbaal III. But notice the obvious change that occurs in the text as the prophet is commanded to take up a lament concerning this king of Tyre: *"You were the model of perfection, full of wisdom and perfect in beauty. You were in Eden, the garden of God; every precious stone adorned you: ruby, topaz…on the day you were created they were prepared. You were anointed as a guardian cherub, for so I ordained you. You were on the holy mount of God; you walked among the fiery stones. You were blameless in your ways from the day you were created till wickedness was found in you" (Ezekiel 28:11-15).* It's obvious to the reader that the object of Ezekiel's lament is someone with far greater importance than the human ruler of Tyre. He's describing the darkest and most diabolical ruler in all of God's creation. Bible scholars believe this prophetic lament is aimed at the fallen angelic being we know as Satan, or the devil.

Another key prophecy which offers insight into the once glorious, but fallen creature that Ezekiel introduced to us is found in the book of Isaiah. The prophet pronounces judgment on the king of Babylon (probably Sennacherib) when suddenly the narrative changes as if speaking of someone eerily similar to the human king, but whose nature is obviously different. The prophet speaks of this other-worldly creature giving enough detail to help the reader understand just who is in view: *"How you have fallen from heaven, O morning star, son of the dawn! You have been cast down to the earth, you who once laid low the nations! You said in your heart, I will ascend to heaven; I will raise my throne above the stars of God; I will sit enthroned on the mount of assembly, on the utmost heights of the sacred mountain. I will ascend above the tops of the clouds; I will make myself like the Most High…"* (Isaiah 14:12-14).

In the Ezekiel text we learn of the once beauty and lofty position of this fallen being, while from Isaiah, we learn why this once cherished being had been banished from his high position. The Isaiah passage

16

reveals the five *"I will's"* of Satan's pride which led to his downfall. In the New Testament, the Apostle John records what appears to corroborate with Isaiah's prophecy. He offers insight that confirms that along with Lucifer's rebellion and fall, he seduced a host of angelic beings who were then swept into judgment, too (Revelation 12:9).

Before leaving the Isaiah passage, notice that each of the "I will" statements are an ascending declaration of pride and full of imagery that culminates in the final boast: *"I will make myself like the Most High" (Isaiah 14:14).* Satan's ultimate purpose is to gain authority over everything God has created and even God Himself! But since God allows no rivals to his Sovereign rule, Lucifer and a host of angelic beings are cast out of heaven. While this reality holds a great deal of mystery to human understanding, it does provide the framework for our understanding of this very real being who opposes God and the children of God at every turn.

It's important to point out here that while Satan is God's arch enemy, he is not an eternal counterpart to God. In contrast to Almighty God, Satan is merely a subordinate. His nature and capacities while great from a human perspective, fall infinitely short of God's power and Sovereign rule.

Satan is our true enemy

It sometimes appears that we are surrounded by enemies. Someone has it out for us at work. A disgruntled employee is threatening litigation. A neighbor doesn't care that his music keeps us up at night. Someone has taken advantage of us financially. But are these people *really* our enemies? I'm not suggesting having human enemies isn't possible but I am saying that out of all our enemies—real or perceived—Satan is *truly* our enemy.

Jesus warns us of his insidious nature, recorded in John's gospel for all to hear and understand. *"The thief comes to steal and kill and destroy…" (John 10:10a).* Satan would love nothing more than to rip us off every way he can, cut our lives short and destroy everything we've ever developed for good. He hates us because he hates God. And because God's Spirit lives in those who belong to Him, we are a desirable target to him. If we only knew just how much he hates us and the lengths he will go to upset and hurt us for following Christ, we would likely be far more quick to take up our spiritual armor to do battle against him rather than just being passive or happily ignorant of his tactics.

When the Apostle Paul wrote to the Ephesians, he wanted them to be aware that their struggle in this life found its origination in the struggle that occurs in another realm. Our struggle, Paul says, *"...is not against flesh and blood—but against the rulers, against the authorities, against the powers of the dark world and against the spiritual forces of evil in the heavenly realms" (Ephesians 6:12).*

Often our struggle seems pitched against or among those around us— a boss, a neighbor, a co-worker, a classroom bully, a family member, etc. True, these relationships may have a negative impact on us or might even be used by Satan to whittle away at us. Paul says the *real* struggle, the one that is truly behind all the others, is our struggle against the spiritual forces of evil in the heavenly realms. It is also true that we have a Savior who has conquered Satan and all spiritual forces of evil through His blood shed for us on the cross.

Later in this book, we'll examine more closely exactly what these evil forces seek to bring against us and more importantly, the resources God gives to us to fight back—and win. But it is important at this point to have a firm resolve in our hearts and minds that we have an enemy who really does have it out for us. Satan works hard at harassing and accusing God's beloved children day and night (Revelation 12:10). It's also important to remember he is one being, not omnipresent like God. While his elaborate system of attack effects all of us, very few of us will ever have the misfortune of being attacked personally from this menacing spirit being. So we must not forget that while God is Sovereign, there is

18

a realm in which Satan has control over this world. As such, he is named the ruler of the kingdom of the air (Ephesians 2:2) and he would love to put you in spiritual darkness, confusion, depression or delusion—whatever he can do to discourage your faith.

There's not a week that goes by that I don't encounter individual followers of Jesus who feel particularly worn out over what appears to be some kind of spiritual attack being waged against them. This is why Peter urged his readers to remain alert (1 Peter 5:8) and by extension, so must we.

Thankfully, those who belong to Jesus Christ have a hedge of protection around them that is none other than our precious and powerful Savior! Where would we be without Jesus? And seen in contrast to the enemy of our soul who comes to steal, kill and destroy, our Savior Jesus comes to give us life and have it to the full (John 10:10).

A timely question for you at the beginning of this book is to ask yourself if you are under Jesus' protection? Do you have his light and power in your life? If you do, you need not be intimidated or fearful over the enemy's plans for you. You are more than a conqueror (Romans 8:37)! You fight knowing that the victory is yours and that nothing will separate you from the love of God—neither death nor life, neither angels nor demons, neither the present nor the future, nor any powers, neither height nor depth, nor anything else in all creation, will be able to separate us from the love of God that is in Christ Jesus our Lord. Not trouble or hardship or persecution or famine or nakedness or danger or sword, not death or demons, present or future, nor any powers are able to separate us from God's love. Nothing in all creation can separate us from the love of God that is in Christ Jesus our Lord (Romans 8:38-39).

Satan has many followers

This is a difficult truth for people to hear. If you don't believe in Christ and have not submitted your life to His Lordship, you might feel like you are in a place of neutrality—neither owned nor possessed by Satan or Christ. But the truth of the matter is this: If you don't belong to Jesus Christ, you belong to Satan and you are following him. He owns you. He has rights over you. If you are in a place where you still reject Christ's Lordship, don't feel you are merely neutral on spiritual things. You belong to Satan. Only the believer has been transferred from the kingdom of darkness and brought into the kingdom of the Son He loves (Colossians 1:13). Then, and only then, can you be sure you are possessed and protected by our great and loving God.

Once as Jesus was being questioned by a group of religious leaders over the issue of his true identity, he made a claim that those religious leaders were actually sons of Satan. Though religious, they had never entered into a covenant relationship with the only true God. But those who hear and follow Jesus are assured that God is their Father. However, those who cling to religion but reject the personal presence and invitation of Jesus Christ have a different father. Jesus said Satan is the true father of any who have not yet believed in Him as the Son of God. And when Jesus informed these religious leaders who their father was, or course they didn't like it at all. And if this is upsetting to you for my having pointed this out to you, I understand how offensive it sounds. It's a strange reality, indeed. But it's true. Either God or Satan is your father. Who is *your* father?

Jesus describes the devil as ***"...a murderer from the beginning— not holding to the truth, for there is no truth in him. When he lies, he speaks his native language, for he is a liar and the father of lies" (John 8:44).*** Satan's method of keeping people under his rule and possession is to lie to them. He loves to deceive. It's just his nature to do so—according to Jesus. He is the king of liars and all he speaks are lies. He will lie about where true meaning and fulfillment is found—telling people the meaning of life is found in possessions, money, sex, power, status or relationships. He will lie about where truth is found—in the stars, one's horoscope, palm reading, psychics, spiritualism, philosophy, or even religion that doesn't embrace the person and work of Jesus Christ. In this way he keeps more people under his tight-fisted reign because those who don't acknowledge Jesus Christ can often still be very religious.

Underneath all of these things, he nudges our pride, knowing that this is the way he gets to all of us. We have his seed in our hearts because of the first Adam who was beguiled by the lie of the serpent: *"Don't you know that when you eat of this fruit your eyes will be opened, and you will be like God..." (Genesis 3:5).* The Serpent's (Satan) ploy with Eve sounds eerily familiar to his own self-talk recorded in Isaiah's prophecy: *"I will make myself like the Most High" (Isaiah 14:14).*

In response to these things, I've heard people say, "I don't get it. All of this talk about Christ and my need for Him is foolish and purely a religious overreaction! I don't see anything special or worthy in Christ which would compel me to offer my life to Him—and besides, I'm a good person. Why do I need Jesus?" If you're feeling this way, listen to what Paul said about Satan's deception over those who belong to him: *"The god of this age has blinded the minds of unbelievers, so that they cannot see the light of the gospel of the glory of Christ, who is the image of God. For we do not preach ourselves, but Jesus Christ as LORD, and ourselves as your servants for Jesus' sake" (2 Corinthians 4:4-5).*

I enjoy people-watching. There are so many interesting people in our world! When I'm traveling through an airport, I like sitting at the gate and watching the masses coming and going. If I have the chance to go to a Golden State Warriors game, I like looking throughout the arena taking in the sight of forty-thousand fans gathering to cheer on their team. In these moments a question often comes to my mind: *How many of these people actually belong to Jesus Christ?* The Biblical answer is, very few. Jesus said, *"...small is the gate and narrow is the road that leads to life and only a few find it" (Matthew 7:14).*

21

It's always a sobering reminder to hear the voice of the Spirit remind me that the vast majority of people all around us are on their way to an eternity separated from God's loving presence. And I'm reminded again that Satan loves it that way. His grip is strong and it doesn't help that our nature as rebels to God makes for a perfect prescription for keeping a lot of folks in the dark about who Jesus is and how to know Him personally.

Satan is a defeated enemy

It should be mentioned before we close this chapter that as serious and true that our enemy prowls around seeking someone to devour, it's also true that he's defeated. Jesus Christ's death and resurrection dismantled his strength and prowess. Of course, he would love it for people to stay ignorant of this truth causing them to yield to his power even though they don't have to anymore. Do we still yield to these so-called powers? Yes, sometimes we do. But we do so out of sheer rebellion, blind ignorance, fear, or a host of other reasons. The point is that we don't need to yield to our enemy any longer. When the resurrected Christ comes into our lives, he sets us free! Jesus said, **"If the Son sets you free, you will be free indeed" (John 8:36)!** The Apostle Paul reminded the believers at Colossae, that the cross of Christ has disarmed the powers that once had power over us (Colossians 2:13-15). The New Testament is filled with reminders that Christ's finished work at the cross sets us free. Paul reminded the believers at Ephesus that, though at one time they were under the captivity of Satan, they need not live this way anymore. Describing their former way of life, he writes, **"As for you, you were dead in your transgressions and sins, in which you used to live when you followed the ways of this world and of the ruler of the kingdom of the air, the spirit who is now at work in those who are disobedient" (Ephesians 2:1-2).** But he continues by describing the amazing work of God in our lives as believers: **"And God raised us up**

22

with Christ and seated us with him in the heavenly realms in Christ Jesus, in order that in the coming ages he might show the incomparable riches of his grace, expressed in His kindness to us in Christ Jesus" (Ephesians 2:6-7).* If you belong to Jesus Christ, you have been raised up with Christ and seated in heavenly realms. This is describing your identity and position as a follower of Christ. You are no longer under Satan's authority or dominion. In *The Collected Letters of C.S. Lewis,* he writes, "The enemy will not see you vanish into God's company without an effort to reclaim you" which gives fair warning that he won't easily give up his assault, though he no longer has no claim over us.

As Jesus was nearing the time when he would be going to the cross to pay for our sins, he foretold the doom of his [and our] enemy: *"Now is the time for judgment on this world; now the prince of this world will be driven out. But I, when I am lifted up from the earth will draw all men to myself" (John 12:31-32).* Just a few chapters later, *"...in regard to judgment, because the prince of this world now stands condemned" (John 16:11).* These statements are Christ's declaration of the victory won at the cross and the beginning of the end of Satan's rule for all time. What this means for us right now has some powerful implications, not the least of which is knowing and acting without being bound by His devices.

Satan's final banishment will be the lake of fire. On that last day of judgment, Matthew records that the King *"...will say to those on his left, 'Depart from me, you who are cursed, into the eternal fire prepared for the devil and his angels..." (Matthew 25:41).* We forget that while he is already defeated, Satan's punishment is still in the future. John writes about the apocalypse: *"And the devil who deceived them, was thrown into the lake of burning sulfur, where the beast and the false prophet had been thrown. They will be tormented day and night for ever and ever" (Revelation 20:10).* After this, those who rejected Christ and tried to earn their way to heaven, whose names were not written in the book of life, were all thrown into the lake of fire (Revelation 20:15).

Here at the close of this first chapter, I think it's important to know what's coming with regard to Satan's judgment. Satan will soon no longer influence and rule as he does in so many lives today. His judgment is near. It happened in the spiritual dimension when Christ died for our sins and rose again from the grave, but it will happen in the physical dimension on the day of God's fierce and righteous judgment over Satan Himself and all evil in the world.

My hope is that you will be on alert, knowing our enemy is out there, and what you are up against. And that you will be more discerning over the nature of events and circumstances in your life. I hope you will draw nearer to Christ, knowing that through Him, you are protected and victorious. I hope you will come alongside others who are in this fight in hopes of helping them be victorious. Most of all, I hope that you will fight the good fight all the way to the end of your life.

Before turning the page, if you need a new life, let the beauty of Scripture and the power of the Holy Spirit awaken you from death to be brought to life through faith in Jesus Christ right now! May Satan's blinders come off as you hear the voice of the Spirit of truth calling you to come to Jesus and trust him alone to forgive your sins and make you his child. And then, may you submit your entire life to Him. May you leave anything sinful and rebellious and run hard after the transformation God has in store for you. It's time to wake up and live.

CHAPTER 1: WAKE UP CALL
DISCUSSION QUESTIONS

1. Which of the four realities about Satan impacted you the most? Why? Of the four, which one(s) are least understood by those with whom you are sharing the good news of Jesus Christ?

2. Considering the relationship which existed between Lucifer and God before his fall, what to you, is the most striking flaw in Lucifer's character? (See Isaiah 14:13-14) What evidence do you see of this flaw also manifested in humanity's fallen state?

3. In what specific ways are Lucifer's and humanity's falls similar? Read Ezekiel 28:13-16 and draw some comparisons with Genesis 3:1-24.

4. Why is it impossible to assume one can be neutral concerning allegiance to Jesus Christ? Why are non-believers unable to see that, in refusing to submit to Jesus Christ, they are choosing to follow Satan? (See Matthew 12:30; John 8:44)

5. How is knowing that Satan was defeated through the death and resurrection of Jesus Christ helpful in dealing with his schemes and attempts at bullying us into fear, doubt and even disobedience?

6. How does Matthew 25:41 and Revelation 20:10 refute the wrong assumption held by some that hell is a place where Satan rules and evil is celebrated?

7. What encouragement do you find in Jesus' warning and promise found in John 10:10?

CHAPTER 2

DELIVER US FROM EVIL
The Role of Demons in Spiritual Warfare

I was working late one night at church when someone knocked at my office door. When I opened it, someone I didn't recognize had a very worried look on his face urging my cooperation; *"Pastor, we need you downstairs right now! There's a woman in the lobby who wandered in tonight wanting to talk to someone, but we can't seem to help her."*

I followed him downstairs wondering what I was getting myself into. There, in the dimly lit lobby of our church sat a woman speaking to a few others who, I was told later, were leaving their evening Bible study when they met this woman at the door as she came in looking for help. I approached her gently. "Hi, I'm Pastor Vold. Can I help you?" I asked, as I sat down next to her. "I feel tormented" she admitted—her face sullen and her eyes cast down while getting a little agitated. "How so? What's going on?" I asked, hoping to assure her she was in a safe place to talk. She told me and the others who had summoned me that she couldn't get away from voices inside of her who told her disturbing things. As she spoke, her facial expressions would change as if to present a completely different countenance throughout each transition in her story. I felt an evil presence. It made the hair on the back of my neck bristle as I listened to her, asking God for wisdom. As she looked at me, I felt as if someone from inside her was looking directly at me. It was creepy. As she began to open up a little, words like "blood" and "hate" and "torture" were woven into her explanations and concerns. I felt it was time to ask an important question.

26

"Can you tell me about your relationship with Jesus?" As soon as the name, "Jesus" left my lips, her countenance changed again—to one even more disturbing. She became extremely agitated, confused and started mumbling incoherent sentences. This went on for a while as I considered how to help her. She seemed to go in and out of lucidity. Suddenly, she shut down and wouldn't even speak. I offered to pray for her and she nodded in agreement. I prayed (with my eyes open!) that Jesus would join her in this moment of desperation and that she would call on Him to give her the life she needed and to free her from whatever was tormenting her. The others around us in the circle affirmed my petitions with lots of "Amens." I knew only Jesus could deliver her if she was being harassed by one or more evil spirits. After my prayer, she seemed calm and had a semblance of what seemed like normal interaction for a brief moment before she suddenly decided it was time to leave. She thanked us for our time and quickly walked towards the door. We offered to continue speaking with her or to meet with her again and invited her back for a church service. She walked away from us, and into the night as if another force were guiding her away.

I wish I could tell you that this woman experienced the power of Jesus delivering her soul from the powers of evil. I also wish I could tell you with certainty whether or not this woman was demon possessed, mentally ill, or both. There were moments that clearly seemed we were encountering a person under the influence of demonic forces, but she could have struggled with some kind of mental illness, too. Mental illness is, at times, connected to demonic influences, but I don't think one can always link the two together. It's a complex issue.

In chapter one we focused on Satan, the chief enemy of our souls. In this chapter we will examine biblical truth concerning his army of spirits, known commonly as *demons*. How much do you know about demons? Do you ever wonder if you've encountered one? Have you ever wondered when observing someone if they might be under the control of a demon?

Do you believe demons are real and are actively involved in our world just as they were in Biblical times? Do you ever worry you might become the object of a demonic attack? What effect can demons have on Christ-followers? Have you ever wondered if one of your children might be under the influence or possession of a demon? My guess is that we all have our questions about demons.

It would be great if we could find one passage of Scripture that would answer all our questions concerning demons, but this is a topic that requires a little wider Scriptural exploration. In this chapter, we'll explore what the Bible reveals about this interesting and somewhat difficult subject about demons. If you are going to fight the good fight of spiritual warfare, having a basic understanding of demonic influence and possession is important.

Demons are real

We've already shown that Satan is a real being. For that reason alone, we can safely assert the reality of demons, too. The Scripture presents demons as spirit-beings that are able to possess human bodies. God didn't create demons. Demons were once angelic spirits that were seduced by Satan himself to rebel against God. Therefore, they are also fallen angels in the same fashion as Lucifer carrying out his bidding in the heavenly realm.

The Apostle Paul writes, "***For our struggle is not against flesh and blood, but against the rulers, against the authorities, against the powers of this dark world and against the spiritual forces of evil in the heavenly realms*** *(Ephesians 6:12).* While many never arrive at understanding this, our primary struggle is not against the flesh (our own or someone else's), but against the beings who live in the spirit realm. These descriptive monikers, "rulers, authorities, and powers" seem to point to levels of power and influence in the spirit realm. While Biblical writers show Satan's position among all fallen angels as being the highest in rank, this text appears to reveal a tiered hierarchy of leadership among these beings. The Ephesian text is one of those places that provides insight into this truth through the use of different Greek words describing what appears to be the various positions that spirit beings hold. First, there are "rulers" (Gr., *archoi*, cosmic powers), followed by, "authorities" (Gr., *exousias*), and then, "powers" (Gr., *kosmokrator*). According to the Apostle Paul, demons are not only real, they apparently exist within an organizational hierarchy.

Let's dig a little deeper into the origin of when these angels actually became the minions of Satan. I've already pointed out that demons are fallen angels as was Satan. They were once angelic beings who were corrupted by Satan's influence and chose to align with him in his rebellion mentioned in Ezekiel 28 and Isaiah 14. Because of their rebellion, God removed them from their original position of worship and service to Him (See 2 Peter 2:4; Jude 6; Revelation 12:4) and they became as it were, those whose goal is to advance Satan's interests and hinder the work of God. They know who God is. And they believe in Him—though not with the kind of belief that results in salvation. And surprising to many, they also fear God, too. Remember when the Apostle James asked a group of professing believers, *"You believe there is one God? Good! Even demons believe that—and shudder" (James 2:19)*.

Demons clearly recognize they are subject to Almighty God and will one day be punished in eternal fire. And in the Gospel of Matthew we read, *"When He [Jesus] arrived at the other side in the region of the Gadarenes, two demon-possessed men coming from the tombs met him. They were so violent that no one could pass that way. 'What do you want with us, Son of God?' they shouted. 'Have you come here to torture us before the appointed time'" (Matthew 8:28-29)?* Yes, demons fear the Almighty, and in this text, their fear is revealed when being confronted by Jesus. They know their time is short and that their demise will take place during the time when God judges the world.

In the previous chapter, I shared a story about a young man who demonstrated possession of demonic spirits. Because matters of this nature aren't always cut and dry, it's difficult to be dogmatic about the exact nature and characteristics of demonic possession. But taking Scripture as our guide, it's not difficult to see some basic things of how demonic possession manifests itself in a person's life. For Bill, the young man I described earlier, the mere mention of Jesus' name was enough to send him into a fit of rage. I had never witnessed this first hand, until that surreal experience one evening in the basement of the church where I began following Jesus. Being a witness to how these entities interacted both with Bill and the person of Jesus Christ made it easy to see their disdain for Jesus and those who follow Him. This was also true in the experience a few of us had with the woman who wandered into the church one evening looking for help. I've witnessed this truth in many other settings and situations where it's obvious that an evil spirit is harassing or possessing someone.

These experiences and many others over the course of my pastoral ministry has given me much clarity about the power and authority that Jesus has over everything—including demons. The torment I could see in Bill's eyes that evening as raspy voices shouted blasphemous names at Jesus, gave proof they were clearly not the ones really in control—but they seemed to know who was. Jesus was the one truly in control. As we quoted the very words of Jesus and his love for all of us, in those settings, demons would recoil and retreat behind their blasphemy and hate. On many occasions over the years, I've experienced individuals who've reacted vehemently to the name of Jesus, or become very submissive after an outburst of some kind simply by invoking His Name. The gospel record and personal experience have both affirmed that when demons are active, there's almost always a demonstrative hate for Jesus and what He desires as well as a clear submission to Him when His Lordship is called upon.

This is seen in Mark's gospel, where we read about Jesus going into the synagogue at Capernaum and beginning to teach. As people were marveling at Jesus' teaching, Mark records that, *"Just then a man in their synagogue who was possessed by an evil spirit cried out, 'What do you want with us, Jesus of Nazareth? Have you come to destroy us? I know who you are—the Holy One of God" (Mark 1:23-24)*!

It should not surprise us to see that demons show great fear as well as deference to Jesus. Demons know who Jesus is and they even show specific knowledge of those who carry out ministry with His authority. This is shown in a fascinating story recorded in Acts 19 where we learn of seven sons of a Jewish priest named Sceva who had been watching the Apostle Paul performing extraordinary miracles and casting out evil spirits. The sons of Sceva decide to try their hand at exorcism, too, and one of the sons did so on a man whom he believed was demon possessed, saying to him, *"In the name of Jesus, whom Paul preaches, I command you to come out.' And the evil spirit speaking through the man possessed answered, 'Jesus I know, and I know about Paul, but who are you'" (Acts 19:15)?* The man possessed by the evil spirit proceeded to jump on the brothers and gave them a fierce beating!

Be warned

This story should at least give pause to anyone simply wanting the power to go looking for demons in order to cast them out of people. The spirit realm isn't something with which to play games. Dealing with demons is serious business and it's always best to trust Jesus' power rather than our own when confronting them. Referring again to the incident with Bill, all who were present that evening were completely astonished by the unusual physical strength he manifested when the demons living inside of him made themselves known. Bill was a short, thinly built high school kid who, while lying flat on his back with two grown men holding him down, raised up effortlessly. I thought my eyes were playing tricks

31

on me.   These men were restraining him because when the demonic voices would spew their vitriolic rage, Bill's body would turn against itself with arms swinging and fists punching.   At first, those close to him thought his rage was turned outward toward them but it soon became evident they were taking aim at him!   A human body possessed by a demon places the person possessed and those nearby in peril.

A few observations

The reality of demons and their influence over humans are found throughout the New Testament Gospels where we find no less than thirty-two references to "demons" and nine to "evil spirits." Jesus confronted demons driving them out of people by His word, but he also empowered his disciples to drive them out as extensions of His own authority. Even so, the disciples were not always successful in delivering the one plagued by demonic forces (see Matthew 17:16 and Mark 9:18).

The book of Acts offers a half dozen references to the expulsion of demons and demonic activity that opposed the work of the Apostles. Even in our experience that night with Bill, and other similar experiences in my role as a pastor over the years of my ministry, it is interesting how relatively easy it is to command these demons to leave a person alone and they obey.   As long as there is a clear confrontation with a spirit and an honest and passionate command in Jesus' name for it to leave; it does, most of the time.   Why some demons seem to leave someone who has awakened by God's grace to resist and call on the name of Jesus for deliverance and others are more stubborn, isn't altogether clear.

When demons leave someone's body in whom they've occupied for some time, the person may feel weak or appear to be sleeping. The energy drain of a demonic presence finally removed must be the reason for this sudden and noticeable change in one's demeanor.

In summary, the Apostles wrote of the future of the church and even the last days, and warn believers to beware of the activity of demons and their teachings. To suggest that demons are not real is to be ignorant of Scripture and in full denial of what it proclaims concerning spiritual warfare.

Awareness of demonic activity is important

We've discussed the reality of demonic activity. Now let's consider the relevance of being aware of them for our own good. God wants us to be aware of demonic activity so we are not caught off guard by Satan. The Apostle Paul wrote of this when dealing with someone in the congregation who has sinned but needed restoration. Paul affirms his own forgiveness of the man asserting to the Corinthians, *"...in order that Satan not outwit us. For we are not unaware of his schemes"* (2 Corinthians 2:11).

In the Old Testament, God warned His people against any participation in Spiritism (which is the worship of evil spirits), promising that one's participation would be punishable by death. God's moral law clearly condemns this kind of activity among his people: *"I will set my face against the person who turns to mediums and spiritists to prostitute himself by following them, and I will cut him off from his people"* (Leviticus 20:6). God continues to warn his people through Moses saying, *"A man or woman who is a medium or spiritist among you must be put to death. You are to stone them; their blood will be on their own heads"* (Leviticus 20:27). Later, in the second giving of the law, God says to the people through Moses: *"Let no one be found among you who sacrifices his son or daughter in the fire, who practices divination or sorcery, interprets omens, engages in witchcraft, or casts spells, or who is a medium or spiritist or who consults the dead. Anyone who does these things is detestable to the LORD, and because of these detestable practices the LORD your God will drive out those nations before you"* (Deuteronomy 18:10-12).

Under the old covenant, God required strict obedience to matters of his moral law. The punishment for refusing to obey was severe. While these practices today are just as morally reprehensible to God, his own Son paid our penalty so that even those who would violate these commands might be shown mercy through faith in Jesus Christ. But neglecting to come for his mercy today eventually brings the same result in the end: death and separation from God.

Examining the New Testament, we read the Apostle Paul's warning to the Corinthians who were apparently on occasion, celebrating at feasts where foods eaten had been first sacrificed to idols. Paul addresses this issue in his first letter to the Corinthians: ***"Do I mean that a sacrifice offered to an idol is anything, or that an idol is anything? No, but the sacrifices of pagans are offered to demons, not to God, and I do not want you to be participants with demons"*** *(1 Corinthians 10:19-20).*

Paul says to be careful not to engage in those things that are connected to demonic worship or activities. Stopping at a meat market for something to throw on the BBQ rarely if ever would bring a caution to our hearts about the meat being previously used in some kind of evil ceremony devoted to demonic worship. But I've met people over the years who speak about visiting psychics or wanting to participate in psychic phenomena, clairvoyance, tarot card reading, palm reading, astrology, horoscope, fortune tellers—and even hoping to call on spirits of the dead through mediums. While this is not an exhaustive list by any stretch, many in modern society participate in and seek these experiences eagerly. There is absolutely no area of modern society were demonic activity can't be found. Demons infiltrate mainstream vices within our society including parts of the entertainment industry, drug and alcohol addiction, and pornography. The list is endless as to where their influence can be found. When people indulge themselves in activities where demonic influences are obvious, they put themselves in a jeopardous situation. Considering Bill's story, as recounted earlier, it was affirmed to all of us that before our encounter with him, he had demonstrated a clear fascination with the occult and paranormal experiences—even calling on spirits to give him powers he wanted. Bill had literally invited these forces into his life. It was the grace and mercy of God that delivered him that night as he was surrounded by loving people who ministered to him in Jesus' powerful name.

Demons have their methods

How do demons work? Let's keep in mind that demons are *spirit* beings. You can't hear their voices audibly. I'm not denying that some people hear demonic voices in their mind, but their voices can only be heard audibly when they are speaking through a person. Most people are thought to be mentally ill when they claim they hear voices in their heads. There may be some forms of mental illness where the person suffering hears inner voices that are difficult to explain. But when voices in someone's head direct physical pain, suffering or death on themselves or someone else (or a group), this is clearly evidence of demonic spirits being involved through either harassment or possession. Every time I hear the news of an active shooter with mass casualties, it seems to align with the methods of demonic spirits.

What the Bible teaches us about a demon's routine is that they *must* embody someone for maximum influence. The only demons we know about in Scripture are those who had taken residence in someone's body. So the biblical answer to how demons generally operate is *"embodiment."* They possess someone to influence and direct them for their purposes.

There's an example of this in Matthew 12:43-45. Get ready, this is wild stuff. Right in line with our topic, Jesus says: ***"When an evil spirit comes out of a man, it goes through arid places seeking rest and does not find it. Then it says, 'I will return to the house I left.' When it arrives, it finds the house unoccupied, swept clean and put in order. Then it goes and takes with it seven other spirits more wicked*** *than itself, and they go in and live there. And the final condition of that man is worse than the first."*

What I want you to see here is that the way demons express themselves and influence people is through taking up *residence* in them. The Bible doesn't give us absolute clarity on *how* this happens; just *that* it happens. What's even more unsettling about what Jesus says about demons taking up residence in someone is that apparently even when a demon leaves, it's possible for him to return and bring along other evil spirits to take up occupation there again making the latter condition of the person even worse than formerly.

I'm imagining the following kind of scenario might lend to what Jesus presents in Matthew 12. Suppose a person has had an evil spirit that introduced him to drug use and eventual addiction. Over time the person gets fed up with the life he is living and decides it's time to change. But it's not easy to change. Addiction ravages a person in every area of life: family relationships, friendships, work, financial management, health, etc. But through the help of his family, and a good support system, he finally overcomes his drug addiction. But now, having overcome the addiction, he still has his house unoccupied—that is—an evil spirit has been overcome and can't find traction in his life anymore, so it moves on. But the once addicted person doesn't fill his house (body) with the one who alone can guarantee him a new and vibrant life he's never known before through the Holy Spirit. He feels free and in command of his life, yet his life is still vulnerable to different types of evil spirits to come occupy his body even along with the original evil spirit who had vacated. Some of these evil spirits might champion self-help, or any number of "saviors" for his initial breakthrough from addiction, but the fact remains, until the God who created Him comes to reside in his heart, he's still vulnerable to be influenced or possessed by evil spirits.

I've met people who have overcome terrible addictions and obstacles but still haven't experienced new life through faith in Jesus Christ. The latter condition of their lives can, in some respects, be worse than the former. Not worse in the sense of quality of having overcome the addiction, but worse in the spiritual dimension since even though they are freed from the addiction, they are still not completely delivered. Think about it. Does it really matter if a person's life is cleaned up for a short time, but upon death, be eternally separated from God? This is one of the great tactics of the enemy—to concede defeat in one area of someone's life only to keep them in a lost state of being spiritually dead.

How might someone unwittingly open his life to an evil spirit in the first place? While Scripture doesn't directly answer this question, it seems that evil spirits look for some kind of opening in a person's life where they can enter easily and without detection. Unbelievers who give themselves to evil repeatedly and desire in their hearts to do more evil are inviting malevolent spirits in though they are likely unaware of this. Establishing patterns of sin with little thought or care to the damage it causes are ways demons find entrance.

There are even those who openly pray to Satan, asking for his help to do what they want such as immoral or illegal acts, hateful, hurtful acts or doing wicked things in this world. It's easy to imagine that people who are empowered by demonic entities can be involved in virtually all strata of culture: politics, the entertainment industry, education, and even religious institutions that propose unorthodox teaching concerning God and the meaning of life. In virtually every arena of life, actions, words and motives can be inspired and supported by demonic entities. This is at least in part, what the apostle Paul had in mind when reminding the Ephesians the origin of their true struggles (Ephesians 6:12).

Whenever people open themselves up to sin or look for true contentment outside of a relationship with the one true God, they openly set themselves up for the enemy's influence. Ever wonder why the world is such a mess? There are people everywhere who are being influenced by demonic forces without even knowing it. In contrast to the ignorance of those outside of God's family, believers are not unaware of Satan's schemes (2 Corinthians 2:11).

Demons are at work in our world just as in Biblical times

I often hear people articulate suspicion over whether evil spirits are active in our world today as they appear to be in Biblical times. In the global north, (the modernized nations of the northern hemisphere), evil spirits and their work are often mistakenly explained away by medical issues, a psychological diagnosis or something attributed to chemical or hormonal imbalances. I'm not suggesting that any of these conditions always point to demonic involvement, it's just that we seem to find it easy to view spiritual realities with an interpretive lens void of spiritual realities. Even at a more basic level, people might observe the direct manifestation of an evil spirit and simply attribute it to behaviors that are at best, merely socially unacceptable, or worse, egregious and malevolent. Yes, demons are just as active today as in Biblical times even if not as easily recognized.

There are still cultures in the world where an awareness of demonic activity is normal and in those places the similarities between those manifestations and what's written in the gospel accounts are unmistakable. The result of demonic influence and possession are often the antecedent to drug addiction, immorality, a spirituality apart from being in relationship with Jesus Christ, rebellion against authority, injustice, hurt, hate, hubris, murder, and suicide. The list is endless. These forms of wickedness and evil abound in every culture and always behind them are the nudging, prompting, and possession of evil spirits.

It seems from the Biblical record that there are seasons when evil spirits and the work of Satan become intensified. The synoptic gospels all introduce Jesus' public ministry by informing the reader that immediately following His baptism, the Spirit sent Jesus into the wilderness to be tempted by the devil. We'll examine that beginning salvo between Satan and our Savior in the next chapter. Here, I simply want to point out that both at the beginning and end of Jesus' public ministry, the enemy comes after Him in order to derail Jesus' mission. He comes after us this way, too. When making a commitment to Jesus or deepening our walk with him, often comes the attack of the enemy.

The Apostle Paul informs Timothy that in the days just prior to the return of Jesus Christ, there will be a resurgence of Satanic opposition. He writes, *"The Spirit clearly says that in later times some will abandon the faith and follow deceiving spirits and things taught by demons. Such teachings come through hypocritical liars, whose consciences have been seared as with a hot iron. They forbid people to marry and order them to abstain from certain foods, which God created to be received with thanksgiving by those who believe and who know the truth..." (1 Timothy 4:1-3).*

When Paul wrote this letter, the reigning heresy was Gnosticism, the ascetic practices of abstaining from things God called good for obtaining a perceived holiness. Many observe this same kind of practice today, wrongly assuming they can be made right with God by merely abstaining from certain things. Is it any wonder that many people in our culture have adopted a church-less, cross-less, godless, even Christ-less, unjust or hateful Christianity, while presuming all along, their view is correct? This is the work of Satan and it points to a rising crescendo of demonic activity as the return of Christ draws near.

Believers and demonic possession

What restrictions do demons have in terms of access and possession in a believer's life? There are some who believe that followers of Christ can be possessed by demons. There are deliverance ministries that believers turn to for help in expelling demonic forces that have, in their belief, possessed them. They argue that when believers struggle with addictions, mental illnesses and various immoral behaviors that this is evidence that a demon has possessed a believer.

When examining the Biblical record, however, one would be hard pressed to find any Scripture that would validate a believer becoming possessed by Satan or demons. Those who advocate the possibility of a believer being possessed by a demon make their case by citing Judas, one of Jesus' disciples, whom "Satan entered" just prior to his betrayal (Luke 22:3; John 13:27). But Jesus made clear that Judas, while clearly a part of his inner circle, was not one of his true followers. As Jesus was washing his disciples' feet during the last supper, he claimed that they were *"...clean, though not everyone..."* while the apostle John continues with an important clarification, *"For he knew who was going to betray him, and that was why he said not everyone was clean" (John 13:12b, 13).* Of course, Jesus was referring to Judas. Being religious or having some form of spirituality doesn't protect anyone from demonic influences and even possession.

Furthermore, we are told that when Jesus died on the cross, he disarmed Satan's spiritual arsenal against us. *"And having disarmed the powers and authorities, he made a public spectacle of them, triumphing over them by the cross" (Colossians 2:15).* How might something disarmed have the gripping power of the enemy over the believer's life and witness? Most importantly, Paul makes sure that the Corinthian believers understood that their bodies were now under the rule and possession of Christ. *"Do you not know that your body is a temple of the Holy Spirit, who is in you, whom you received from God? You are not your own; you were bought with a price. Therefore honor God with your body" (1 Corinthians 6:19-20).*

The Apostle John reminds his readers that while many false spirits exist in the world, Christ-followers are from God, *"You, dear children, are from God and have overcome them, because the one who is in you is greater than the one who is in the world" (1 John 4:4).* The "world" (Gr., kosmos) is the realm in which Satan rules and carries out his wicked plans.

Jesus prayed for his disciples **to be protected from the evil one (John 17:15).** If Jesus prayed for us to be protected, I think it's safe to assume we are protected! Therefore, it doesn't seem plausible for those who belong to Christ to be possessed by evil spirits though they may be *badgered, tempted, harassed, taunted, accused or influenced* by them.

I met a young woman one Sunday after church (I'll give her the name, Monique) who asked if she could speak to me privately about a problem she was having. When inquiring what she meant, she confided to me that every night when she went to bed, she felt the presence of evil spirits that would literally crawl into her bed and attempt to suffocate her. She wanted to discuss how she could find freedom from these dreadful and terrifying experiences. I agreed to meet with her a few days later, asking if she would allow another young woman to join us whom I considered to be strong spiritually and could perhaps provide a female perspective that might be helpful. Knowing my friend's spiritual wisdom and love for prayer, I knew it would be good for Monique and also provide her with a new friend in which to confide if she wanted. She heartily agreed to the three of us sitting down to discuss the matter and pray together.

We all got together about a week later. After nearly an hour of Monique describing her situation, we started asking her questions. Through the discussion that followed, Monique admitted that earlier in her life, she had experienced some physical abuse from a family member that could have easily been a pathway for evil spirits to gain a foothold in her life. We affirmed her identity in Christ and his protection over her, also reminding her that Satan is a defeated enemy and has no real power over a believer's life. We spent considerable time praying for Monique to find freedom from this harassing spirit who had been tormenting her.

Monique found a new sense of freedom that day and over the weeks that followed, things continued to improve. Through the power of the Word of God, the loving prayers of God's people, along with the support of her new friend who met with her that day, Christ delivered Monique.

41

He can deliver anyone who comes to Him, believing his powerful Word. This is a great example of how a believer may be tormented by an evil spirit but not necessarily possessed by one. Some of the literature on this topic refers to this aspect of demonic influence and harassment as *demonization,* intimating the difference between a believer being demonized (harassed, attacked) and possessed (indwelt).

We aren't immune from temptation, sinful habits or even addictions just because we belong to Jesus. But neither are we captive to the whims and desires of our spiritual enemy, Satan or his demonic forces. That's because we are possessed by the Spirit of the true and living God and have an arsenal of God's protective armor always available if we choose to wear it. Keep in mind that even with demonic attack or influence, **"He will not let you be tempted beyond what you can bear. But when you are tempted, he will provide a way out so you can stand up under it"** **(1 Corinthians 10:13).**

The judgement of demons

A day is coming when all Satanic power and his demonic host will be vanquished forever. Satan knows his time is short. We read in Revelation 12:12 that when Satan is expelled completely from the heavenly realms and sent to earth during the day of great tribulation, he is *filled with fury, because he knows that his time is short.* Demons know this, too. On one occasion in Jesus' public ministry, he confronts two men who were demon possessed. When meeting Jesus, they shout, **"What do you want with us, Son of God? Have you come here to torture us before the appointed time" (Matthew 8:29)?** The "appointed time" seems to indicate the demon's recognition of coming judgement. Knowing demons recognize a future judgement should cause us to be zealous for fighting the good fight knowing we are on the winning side.

Fast forward to the end of the age. Jesus describes a scene where the righteous and unrighteous are brought before the judgement: **"Then he**

will say to those on his left, 'Depart from me, you who are cursed, into the eternal fire prepared for the devil and his angels'" (Matthew 25:41). On this day, the devil and his angels (demons) will be cast into the lake of fire. The lake of fire is synonymous with hell. It's a tragedy that people are sent to the lake of fire when originally, it was the final judgement place for fallen angels. Note that Matthew tells us that the lake of fire was *prepared for the devil and his angels,* not for people. Yet, people will be sent to this terrible and unrelenting place of judgement. This means if you have not yet turned your life to Jesus—believing in Him as your only savior and Lord—it isn't too late for you to do so and thus avoid being included in that vast number of souls who will be separated from a loving God; apart from truth, light, beauty and freedom for all eternity.

Perhaps God has been speaking to you in this chapter in order to pull you out of the darkness and into the light. Won't you give your life to Jesus now? Won't you come to him now and trust that he will come into your life and take up residence in your soul? Those who do, enter the good fight and are promised certain victory.

CHAPTER 2: DELIVER US FROM EVIL DISCUSSION QUESTIONS

1. How conscious are you about the role demons play in our struggles? Do you feel equipped to deal with demonic forces and the realities they present to believers? If not, what do you feel would help you most?

2. Under Old Testament law, Israel was commanded to avoid all contact and involvement with demonic influences. Take a moment to review these prohibitions found in Leviticus 20:6, 27 and Deuteronomy 18:10-12. Where do you see similarities to these activities in our culture? What do these prohibitions reveal about God's desire for His children?

3. Why must demons find a person in whom they can occupy to carry out their work? What does Matthew 12:43-45 reveal about the ways evil forces plague some people?

4. Where do you see evidence of demonic activity within our culture? (For additional insight, examine 1 Timothy 4:1-3.)

5. Some people believe that a Christ-follower can become possessed by a demon(s). In your opinion, is this belief supported in Scripture? What is the difference between being possessed by an evil spirit and being harassed by one?

6. What does God's future judgment on demons reveal about His character and patience? How does this affect the way you prepare for, and engage in spiritual warfare?

CHAPTER 3

A KEY STRATEGY OF THE ENEMY
Dealing Effectively with Temptation

Temptation is one of Satan's strategies that plays a significant role in spiritual warfare. This behooves us to know how to deal with temptation when it comes our way. All of us face temptation. It comes in all shapes and sizes. Sometimes our temptations are not all that consequential while other ones are. Examples of inconsequential temptations might include things like considering eating at *In-N-Out Burger* when you know a more nutritious meal would be better for you; or whether to skip out on that meeting at work knowing you could be on the golf course instead. Many of the temptations we face don't play a huge role in shaping our lives one way or another however, if you eat at *In-N-Out* too much, you can count on a different "shape" if you know what I mean!

But there are far more consequential temptations; like when an attractive co-worker comes on to you in the break room; or you are out of town on a business trip and the boss invites you to dinner as she intimates her inappropriate desire for this time with you. Maybe your boss offers you some special perks if you will just stay quiet about the unethical practices of his business. When preparing your taxes for the IRS, the under-the-table income you earned this past year may not, in your opinion be something you need to declare. While none of these temptations alone are consequential, our giving in to them certainly is. There's no end to the kinds of temptations both small and big that we deal with every day.

Some of us are reaping the results of giving in to temptation. Your marriage may be failing. You might suffer from an addiction. You could be in financial ruin. Your health may be in a compromised state. The initial temptation that led you to where you are today might have occurred months or even years ago, but now you are suffering from that moment of weakness. Trapped. Addicted. Bankrupt. Morally ruined. Many of us suffer in the wake of giving in to temptation.

The temptations we've given in to may not have landed us in a terrible or despicable condition yet. They may simply be creating a foothold for an even greater assault on our spiritual well-being or planting a besetting sin in our lives that keeps us from being the person we know God wants us to be.

God wants us to be prepared to confront temptation knowing it is a big part of the enemy's strategy to win in our engagement in the good fight. What we need to do, therefore, is take a closer look at the subject of temptation to know how to deal with it when it comes our way.

What we should know about temptation

Most people (even believers in Jesus) tend to misunderstand temptation. If we don't get some basic things straight about temptation, we're in trouble from the get-go. Let me offer a few very basic, but critical truths about temptation.

It isn't a sin to be tempted

I'm amazed at how many people immediately feel guilty simply because they experience temptation. The rationale behind feeling guilty stems from assuming godly people should not be tempted in the first place. Thinking this way, we feel guilt over being in a place where we struggle with a moral or ethical choice. The enemy somehow infuses this kind of thinking into our minds knowing that if someone already feels guilty over the apparent struggle, giving into it is likely the next step.

I've spoken to people who tell me this directly; that because they were already feeling so guilty over being tempted with something, the next step of giving in to it didn't seem like any big leap—so they just gave in. Scripture never condemns a person for being tempted. Even our Lord Jesus was tempted—something we will look at more closely later in this chapter.

The writer of Hebrews speaks of this very thing as a reminder for why any of us can find help and guidance when being tempted by going straight to Jesus, our true high priest: *"For we do not have a high priest who is unable to sympathize with our weaknesses, but we have one who has been tempted in every way, just as we are—yet was without sin" (Hebrews 4:15).* If Jesus experienced temptation, but never sinned by giving in to it, why do we feel guilty over the mere temptations themselves? We should not feel guilty just because we are being tempted. Furthermore, we should not sin by giving in to them.

God never allows us to be tempted/tested beyond what we can bear.

This is a Scripture that everyone needs to commit to memory: *"No temptation has seized you except what is common to man. And God is faithful; he will not let you be tempted beyond what you can bear. But when you are tempted, he will also provide a way out so that you can stand up under it" (1 Corinthians 10:13).* Isn't that amazing? Let's break this down a little more to explore its meaning.

First, Paul reminds the Corinthians (and by extension, all of us) that whatever temptation we might face isn't unique. The exact kind of temptation that we may struggle with finds company among many others as well. One of Satan's key strategies in all of this is to make us feel we are the only one struggling with the exact temptation happening to us in the moment. He whispers in our ear, "No one else struggles with this…and you shouldn't be struggling with it either!" For some, he may use the route of rationalizing the temptation by suggesting it isn't a sin to give in to it. Most often, however, he causes us to feel we should not struggle with a certain temptation in the first place, keeping us isolated and removed from getting help. It's hard for us to get help from things we feel we shouldn't be struggling with in the first place.

I met a man (I'll call him Tim) after church one Sunday in the parking lot. He mentioned his concern over a struggle he was having but was reluctant to share any detail. I invited him to share his struggle with me so we could pray together. He reluctantly agreed and we set a time to meet that week to have a conversation. When he showed up to my office, I could tell he was nervous. He had shame written over his countenance and could hardly look me in the eyes as he began to talk. As he stumbled over his words and rambled along for a few minutes, I stopped him and said, "Tim, nothing you say to me will leave this office. Unless you have committed a felony or are in some way in danger of hurting yourself or someone else, whatever you share, is between you, me and God. But if you want help, you need to be honest and open up." Somehow that opened the door for him to begin telling his story.

He began by sharing some experiences he had as an adolescent and that during that time in his life, he was exposed to some pretty heavy doses of pornography. He went on to tell me that since that time, he's continued to struggle with pornography and knew it was an addiction in his life. He felt ashamed as a husband to a godly woman, a father of two amazing young boys and a respected leader in his workplace that this was his problem and that he hadn't found a way to overcome it. Underneath his shame and regret, it was clear he felt uniquely impacted by this problem and honestly doubted if anyone else could possibly be in the same dilemma—especially any fellow believers.

I quickly assured him that he was not alone. I candidly informed him that during that particular week, two other brothers in Christ had confessed to me their struggle with pornography, asking for prayer and resources to help them overcome. I also confessed to Tom my own experiences and struggle of being exposed to pornography as a young man and some ways God helped me make healthier choices. Having heard he was not alone, Tim was quickly energized with a new resolve to overcome this struggle in his life. Tim was on a pathway to healing and over the months that followed, found deliverance and wholeness from his addiction—something that had plagued his life for years. This began when Tim realized for the first time that his struggle was not unique.

The second thing 1 Corinthians 10:13 reminds us regarding temptation is that God is faithful. Let that sink in for just a moment. *God is faithful.* We aren't always faithful, but God certainly is. Always. What specifically is God faithful to do regarding temptation? The text tells us. He's faithful to do two important things.

First, he won't allow us to be tempted beyond what we can bear. That means, he will make sure that there are boundaries to the kinds of temptation that comes our way. I'm grateful knowing this. When I experience temptation, I can be assured that God, in his omniscience, knows exactly at which point I no longer am able to resist. Whenever a temptation arises that comes from our enemy, we can be assured even the enemy has orders from "on high" that he must respect. We get a little window into this when reading the story of Job. In that story, God limits Satan's scope of bringing disaster to Job's life—all in his attempt to tempt Job to curse God to his face.

What gets a little complicated here is that not all temptation comes directly from Satan. Some temptation comes merely from our own flesh—or the world that Satan has set up to dismantle our integrity and godliness. These aspects of temptation originate from our fallen world and our sinful flesh. This may be why Jesus taught his disciples to pray, *"...lead us not into temptation, but deliver us from the evil one" (Matthew 6:13).* Jesus knows that our human nature tends to drift toward things that are not good for us. Metaphorically, we enjoy coming close to the edge of the cliff to see the view. Some get too close and fall over the edge. But that's not necessarily because Satan had anything directly to do with it. We sometimes just get distracted by our own human

49

nature and before we know it, we fall into sin. Mother Theresa was known for saying, *"I know God will not give me anything I can't handle. I just wish he didn't trust me so much!"* Sometimes we feel that way, too.

God is not only faithful to put parameters around how invasive the enemy can be in our lives, but he is also faithful to provide a way out for us so that we don't have to give in to a temptation. He provides a way out! This is amazing! It isn't that God is going to provide a supernatural escape like a fighter jet pilot pulling his ejection lever as his aircraft is spiraling to the ground. Some escapes will be far more laborious and demand a few more strategic steps to insure victory. But the good news is that God will help us escape the temptation if we are looking for the pathway out.

The story of Joseph in the Old Testament book of Genesis serves as a good example of this. When tempted by the repeated seduction of Potiphar's wife, one day Joseph is trapped in her grasp as she said to him, ***"Come to bed with me" (Genesis 39:12)!*** Assuming this woman had physical traits that made her attractive (otherwise there is really no temptation here to overcome), we see quickly how Joseph handles this delicate situation. The text says that he literally leaves his garment she had wrestled from his body in her hand, and runs out of the house (Genesis 39:12). For Joseph, the means of escape was his purely removing himself from the location of temptation. Sometimes, it's that simple. We just need to walk away (or run!). Other times, it's a little more complicated. But the fact remains, a way of escape is there, if we are looking for it.

A young man (I'll call him Craig) confessed to me inappropriate use of a social media app and how it was likely going to destroy his marriage. Part of his dilemma was that this app was part of maintaining his responsibilities at work. After we discussed the situation, he decided to disclose what was happening to his boss, respectfully informing him that if he was expected to continue to use this app for work, he'd have to move to another department where it wasn't necessary or he'd have to quit his job. Thankfully, his boss showed understanding and granted his request. For Craig, his escape started with creating healthier boundaries with a tool that was commonly used in his workplace.

Another young man I know once told me that when he was out of college, he began working for one of the largest beer manufacturing companies in the world. He was on the fast-track for management which included visiting many of the large distribution sites for this company throughout the country. At one location, he was curious about the destination of some of the larger shipments of beer leaving the plant. The supervisor over this part of the project jokingly told him that those large quantities were headed to Indian reservations since people living there loved to drink beer so much.

This young man understood immediately that one of the largest profit makers for this company was from among a people group who had needs in education, jobs, social support services, etc. not alcoholic beverages. He explained that in that moment of awareness, he could either continue down the path which promised a high likelihood of big money and an advancing career, or he could leave it behind to pursue something more beneficial to society. Within a month, he had quit this job and began pursuing a career in teaching. While earning his teaching credential, he spent two years serving as a high school math teacher on an Indian reservation in Arizona.

Often, temptation is an indirect attack from the enemy

Contrary to what many believe, very rarely, if ever, will anyone experience a temptation directly sent from Satan. While Satan may very well be behind the various kinds of temptation we encounter, he can only be in one place at a time, so the odds of entertaining a direct hit from him is slim. Satan's dominion is the world and he knows the weaknesses of humanity. He has worked hard to establish an elaborate *system* that pulls at humanity's weaknesses holding us captive to things that are unhealthy and destructive.

The Apostle Paul refers to this idea when he writes, *"As for you, you were dead in your transgressions and sins, in which you used to live when you followed the ways of this world and of the ruler of the kingdom of the air, the spirit that is now at work in those who are disobedient. All of us also lived among them at one time, gratifying the cravings of our sinful nature and following its desires and thoughts" (Ephesians 2:1-3a).* What Paul is eluding to here is that the vices of this world have their origin in the enemy's master plan for this world and that before God rescued us from his clutches, we were all following his ways and probably without even knowing it.

We get another glimpse of this from the Apostle John when he writes, *"Do not love the world or anything in the world. If anyone loves the world, the love of the Father is not in him. For everything in the world—the cravings of sinful man, the lust of his eyes and the boasting of what he has and does comes not from the Father but from the world" (1 John 2:15-16).* The world, according to John isn't the physical planet, but the system that the Evil One has set up to trap the unsuspecting and to harass and accuse God's children.

The Scripture affirms that the source of temptation can be attributed to one of three things: the *flesh*, the *world* or the *devil*. I'm simply pointing out that our temptations aren't likely to be a direct attack from Satan, though this is possible of course. They are more likely to have come from the world (Satan's dominion) or our own flesh.

Temptation comes from within and without but never from God

The Apostle James makes this clear when he writes, *"When tempted, no one should say, 'God is tempting me.' For God cannot be tempted by evil, nor does he tempt anyone; but each one is tempted when, by his own evil desire, he is dragged away and enticed. Then, after desire has conceived, it gives birth to sin; and sin, when it is full-grown, gives birth to death" (James 1:13-15).* This truth often places the real issue of who is responsible for temptation squarely on our own shoulders. How many of us are dragged away and enticed by our own sinful flesh?

James offers such a powerful word-picture as to how this process works. He helps us picture sin as that which our own flesh is drawn toward at times in our lives. Notice that he makes clear that our temptation often originates by "our own evil desire" (v. 14). Once the desire has conceived, James points out it gives birth to sin.

I picture this to be somewhat similar to the way a fisherman baits a hook in order to entice a fish to bite. Fishing is full of adventure and fun and it yields good food when the fishing is successful. My favorite place to fish is in the ocean off the Mendocino coast. I sit in my kayak with a sturdy fishing pole and drop a very tantalizing jig about 40 feet where I bounce it along the bottom hoping to attract the vicious and predator instincts of the Pacific Lingcod. Every time I pull one of those monsters from the deep to put in my kayak, I wonder if it ever dreamed that by going after what looked like a perfectly delicious meal would end up with him providing the delicious meal for my family! No, I know fish don't reason like humans do, but it still strikes me as sad (but not sad enough to release it!) that this was his fate.

I have been myself, not unlike a fish drawn toward a shiny but deadly object that, if it could, would undo every vesture of virtue in my life. There is no end to the entanglements that have shipwrecked so many in life—even believers. Things like the love of money, selfish ambitions, the quest for fame, sexual pleasure outside a marriage covenant between a male and female, popularity, illicit relationships…all of these things and more have been the downfall of humanity.

There is someone who can help us when we are tempted

This, among all the things I've shared so far about what we need to know about temptation is the most important. Two little sections in the book of Hebrews provide such beautiful encouragement to us about temptation. *"Because he himself suffered when he was tempted, he is able to help those who are being tempted" (Hebrews 2:18).* And the other, *"For we do not have a high priest who is unable to sympathize with our weaknesses, but we have one who has been tempted in every way, just as we are—yet was without sin" (Hebrews 4:15).*

Jesus was tempted in every way as we are, but never gave in to any temptation. Considering how often we give in, this should be a big part of our approach to the good fight in which we are engaged as believers in Christ. There is a section in the gospel record that actually offers a short series of temptations that Satan presented to Jesus and how he dealt with each one of them. This will work as a form of encouragement and equipping for the battle we are in right now. I want us to be aware of Satan's *strategies* and also how Jesus *countered* these strategies. Remember, Jesus' encounter with Satan *was* direct—ours is unlikely to be so. However, we can see that Satan's direct assault on Jesus parallels the *indirect* assault he levels on us every day through *the world and our flesh*. So let's take a closer look.

We can overcome temptation by following the example of Jesus Christ

The synoptic gospels (Matthew, Mark and Luke) all make reference to the temptation Jesus encountered by Satan following his public baptism as the Spirit of God sent Jesus into the wilderness for forty days. Matthew and Luke offer significant detail about this encounter. Mark only mentions that it happened. Let me point out a couple of observations from Matthew 4:1-11 where the narrative of Jesus' temptation is found.

First, observe the *proximity* of Satan's assault to Jesus' actual baptism. Jesus' baptism was the official beginning of the mission which the Father had sent Him to accomplish. Immediately after this significant event the text tells us that the Spirit led Jesus into the wilderness to be tempted by the devil (v.1). Don't ever think it's mere coincidence when you are starting out to do something God has called you to, that the Spirit of God allows the enemy to tempt us in some way. The enemy wants to derail your efforts or energies while the Spirit wants to use this experience to fortify them. It stands to reason that the moment we decide to get serious with God in any area of our lives, we can count on the adversary waging some kind of battle against us.

Let's look a little more closely at the Spirit's role in all of this. Matthew 4:1 states, *"...Jesus was led **by the Spirit** into the desert to be tempted by the devil."* Mark's account of this event translates the English word, "sent" from the Greek word, "ekballo" which really means something more like *"to thrust or push out"* (Mark 1:13). This shows us that the Father knew that this confrontation between Jesus and Satan at the beginning of his ministry was *necessary*. It's a good reminder that while God doesn't tempt us, he allows temptation as a means of *testing* what is inside of us—making us stronger and more fit for kingdom work. Here is something worth thinking about: Testing *builds* character but also *reveals* it. How we handle temptation says a lot about our character.

I would also point out that the location of the confrontation between Jesus and Satan is the *desert*. The desert was a place of testing for Israel, remember? They spent forty years in the desert! When the people witnessed the glory of God on Mount Sinai manifested through thunder and lightning, and heard the trumpet and saw the mountain in smoke, they trembled with fear. But Moses said to the people, ***"Do not be afraid. God has come to test you, so that the fear of God will be with you to keep you from sinning" (Exodus 20:20).*** So we see that like Israel, the desert was a place of testing for Jesus, too. Israel was tested for forty years; Jesus was tested for forty days.

The desert can be considered a place of testing for us. While Jesus encountered a literal desert, for us, the desert is a good metaphor for times when things are not as we think they should be; when comforts are sparse, or we are without things we think we need; when we feel alone or are in distress. Some of us are dwelling in a desert-like experience where the oases of comforts or assurances to which we've become accustomed are missing. If that's the situation you are in, then realize you are truly in a time of spiritual testing.

In Matthew's narrative of Jesus' temptation, he points out, *"After fasting forty days and forty nights, he was hungry" (Matthew 4:2).* It's time now to reveal Satan's strategy in his attempt to make Jesus fail this test. We can learn so much from both how Satan approaches Jesus and how Jesus responds to him as a means of our own equipping and readiness for the temptations that are likely to come our way in life.

Keep in mind that Satan will never come to any of us and offer the same temptations he offered to Jesus. These temptations apply only to Jesus because none of us have the supernatural power to make bread from stones, or to presume God's rescue if we stepped off a cliff. Nor will any of us be offered the kingdoms of this world because none of them can or will be ours in the first place. No, these are all temptations specific to Jesus Christ alone. My desire, however, is to show how the strategy that Satan uses on Jesus can be used on us, too. For that reason, we can learn a lot about handling temptation by how Jesus handled it when he walked the earth.

Essentially, I see three specific strategies that Satan uses with Jesus—which his system uses on us as well.

Instant Gratification

In Matthew 4:2b-4 we discover that after being in the desert for forty days and nights, Jesus was hungry. The tempter comes to Jesus and said, "If you are the Son of God, tell these stones to become bread." Satan is simply leveraging the obvious—that hunger might move Jesus toward choosing to gratify a natural urge apart from trusting in the provision of God. There would have been no sin if Jesus wanted to make bread out of stones any time he chose. The issue here is that as the Spirit had led Jesus into the desert without any food, he could be trusted to provide it for him when the time was right.

Notice the pitch Satan uses with this strategy. It's found in the little word, **"If." "If you are the Son of God..."** Satan isn't challenging the deity of Christ. He's merely planting a seed of entitlement. Jesus being God's Son *deserves* to be satisfied. And if food would satisfy him, then he should wait no longer. He's insinuating that the Son of God has no business being hungry in the first place! Satan knew that for Jesus to make stones into bread, he would have to do something completely inconsistent with his earthly mission. He would have to step aside from total dependency on His heavenly Father and supernaturally provide something for himself. *This, Jesus would not do, for it would violate his trust in his heavenly Father's provision* while in his humanity. Satan is saying, "You deserve this. C'mon Jesus, you're hungry. You're the son of God. Fix your problem by making some food for yourself."

Let's draw some analogies to the way Satan uses this strategy in our lives. He loves to use normal and healthy appetites to tempt us toward self-gratification apart from the provision of God. It goes like this: If you are hungry for something in this world, then go after it *right now.* You deserve certain things—and why not go after them now instead of waiting for God's provision. The "don't wait, get it now" suggestion is a common temptation of the enemy and our flesh is all too eager to satiate itself, making it a high probability kind of temptation that results in brokenness and guilt when acted upon.

Our appetites often lead the way to disastrous decisions. We have an appetite for food. But there's something healthy about waiting to eat at the proper time. Our fast food culture has created the problem of obesity as few of us show the kind of self-control needed to plan our meals more effectively and to eat healthier. The appetite isn't to blame—but the flesh that always wants to be satisfied. For most of us reading this, we might not consider this to be a huge problem or certainly not one worth bringing up here in a book aimed at helping us fight our spiritual battles. The problem of overeating and maintaining an unhealthy diet is a major spiritual problem for many people. The Bible teaches us that our bodies are the temple of the Holy Spirit; that we are no longer our own and so we must glorify God with our bodies (1 Corinthians 6:19). For many, this is a serious issue.

We all have a God-given appetite for physical intimacy. God created our sexuality to be enjoyed within the context of a marital covenant made with God between a physically born male and female. But our appetites for physical intimacy have led many people to choose a path where there is no restraint resulting in ungodly and immoral lifestyle choices. Behind all of this is an enemy of our souls who, like with Jesus, loves to plant the suggestion of entitlement. He whispers, "If you are God's creation, don't you think you should have whatever you desire?" Or, "God made you the way you are; explore your desires and choose the path that is best for *you.*" The problem with this kind of thinking is that it feeds into one of Satan's oldest strategies: instant gratification.

This can be true with our money and possessions. We feel we deserve a comfortable life so we listen to that voice that says, "You deserve this— *buy it now.*" We don't really have the money for it so we buy it on credit and go into debt and this becomes a repeating pattern that eventually produces great loss and anguish in life. I think you get the picture. Satan, or the system he has set up in our world, presents us with something that we subtly feel we *deserve* and if we are not wise and discerning, we pay a huge price.

Notice how Jesus counters this strategy. He does so with Scripture! Quoting Deuteronomy 8:3, Jesus proclaims to Satan that his appetite wouldn't be bullied into doubting God's provision for satisfying him at the right time and with the right means. Make note of this: Our purpose and meaning are not found in always doing something to satiate our desires, especially if it means being inconsistent with our character as Christ followers. More importantly, in Jesus' response, he is declaring that living obediently to God and His Word is far more important and ultimately more satisfying than merely gratifying our cravings.

Perhaps you are currently dealing with this kind of temptation. There is an urge for you to set aside your convictions as a follower of Jesus and go after something that you know is not God's desire for you. Consider Jesus' words here in Matthew 4:4 and like him, trust what God says rather than the enemy's message to you. There is something far more meaningful than just satisfying your appetites; it is *knowing and doing the will of God in your life.* John Piper, a noted theologian and pastor speaks of our need to counter the devil not by arguing with him, but by declaring as Jesus did, "It is written." He writes:

> **Stand upon it, and if the devil were fifty devils in one, he could not overcome you. On the other hand, if you leave 'It is written,' out, Satan knows more about reasoning than you do. He is far older, has studied mankind very thoroughly, and knows all our weak points. Therefore, the contest will be an unequal one. Do not argue with him but wave in his face the banner of God's Word. Satan cannot endure the infallible truth, for it is death to the falsehood of which he is the father." (John Piper, How Redeemed People Do Battle with Sin, Decision, January 1990.)**

Putting God to the test

Let's look at another strategy that the enemy uses to tempt Jesus. The Jewish Midrash (commentary on the Ancient Scriptures) supported the belief that when Messiah arrived, He would prove himself by leaping from the pinnacle of the temple. Satan, using this commonly held belief about Messiah during the time of Jesus, tempts Jesus to consider performing a "Messiah-proving" miracle which would summon angelic protection and God's intervention. He baits the trap by quoting from the Psalter (Psalm 91:11-12) which promised the supernatural protection of the angelic host over the promised Messiah's life and ministry.

Satan's deceit lay in misapplying Scripture to trap Jesus into forcing the Father to do something to *prove* His care for His Son. Had Jesus followed this temptation, he would have forced the Father to rescue Him from death. Notice that Satan even uses Scripture with this temptation. Few of us realize that Satan knows the Bible better than believers do, but his use of it always is to distort the truth. Remember, he is the father of lies and he has no truth in him (John 8:44f). Nevertheless, Satan's citation from Psalm 91 suggests that Jesus prove to himself and everyone around him that He really is Messiah and do so by making God step in and do something miraculous to prove it.

The way this works in our lives is when we suddenly have the thought that it's okay to *put yourself in a situation where God must come through for you in some miraculous way in order to prove He is God.* Ever hear something like that yourself? God promises to take care of you so do what you want to do!

In the first strategy, temptation is leveraged by our *appetites*. Here, the temptation is leveraged by *presuming* on God for something He must do in order to prove that He loves you. We start thinking things that are ridiculous—but have behind them, an ill-fated belief that God will step in if He needs to and make everything alright in the end. What's wrong with a little recreational drug use? If we take too much or too often, won't God just take this desire away? We don't have to discipline our children; let them do what they want! After all, God will come through for us at some point and get them back on the right path, won't He? We can enjoy illicit relationships now and then; God won't let us hurt ourselves or someone else in the process. He loves us too much for that, right?

Debt, immorality, bad relationships and personal addictions can often be traced back to this kind of temptation—*make God prove His love for you by bailing you out of your rebellion or stupidity.* Just presume that God will take care of it. Many people who should really know better, listen to the enemy and take the bait.

Note how Jesus counters this strategy. He states that though we know God's promises, we must never put Him to the test. Jesus quotes Scripture again to counter its misapplication by the enemy. He draws from the book of Deuteronomy: ***"Do not test the Lord your God" (Deuteronomy 6:16).*** When looking at the context of this verse, we discover that Israel tested the Lord by complaining to Moses that there was no water for them to drink. They put Moses in the unenviable position of needing to do something on his own instead of trusting what God had promised. So Moses struck the rock.

When we argue with God over not meeting our needs or when we rebel against his promises or commands, we are putting Him to the test. It's like we are trying to force Him to step in and do something supernatural to prove His care for us. Whenever we do this, we are *testing* God. Jesus would not have any part of this, nor should we. Some of us are always wanting God to prove His love for us in some supernatural way when He already has. He has proved his love for us when He sent His Son to the cross to die for our sins. If you are looking for a "sign" that proves God loves you, look at the Cross of our Lord Jesus Christ where his amazing and merciful love is proven for all humankind.

Short-Cut Christianity

We don't know how or where Satan took Jesus to show him all the kingdoms of the world and their splendor. Matthew 4:8-10 simply says that he "took him to a very high mountain." And there, Satan offers Jesus all of what could be seen if he would bow down and worship him just once. This shows a little of Satan's narcissism.

I call this the **short-cut** strategy because Satan is offering something to Jesus that was already *promised* to him from the Father, but would not be received until after his mission was completed. Satan is not offering Jesus something that he will never have, he's simply offering him what he should have; yet, Jesus was already promised the kingdoms of the world. During the Great Tribulation the seventh angel sounds his trumpet and the voices in heaven said, ***"The kingdom of the world has become the kingdom of our Lord and of His Christ, and he will reign forever and ever" (Revelation 11:15).*** But in the time of Christ's incarnation, and until the judgment of God falls on earth during the Great Tribulation, Satan was and is the ruler of this world.

But if Jesus would have worshiped Satan in that moment, he could have had right then, what the Father had promised him later. But this would have meant that Jesus would have received his inheritance without the suffering and pain that the Father required of him to obtain it. For Jesus, this was intolerable and, therefore, must be rejected.

This strategy is still used by the enemy in our lives today. His system is set up to cause us to believe *we can arrive where God wants us to be by neglecting or rejecting what God requires.* Satan tells us, you can have what God promises by doing things another way. Satan and his system loves to promise things to us that are eerily similar to the very promises of God—but the difference is how they are obtained. All religious systems promise elements of what the Bible promises to those who follow Christ—without following him at all! No sin, no hell, no need for surrender to Jesus. No need to die to self, to sacrifice for kingdom work; no need to love, give or serve. By contrast, he promises salvation to people if they will work hard for it; never needing to trust God's grace or see how undeserving they are.

Our culture has heard this strategy and taken it hook, line and sinker. You can have a relationship with God apart from what God requires: faith in the life and work of Jesus Christ. In our culture, we are witnessing a brand of Christianity that bears no cross; where following Jesus is without sacrificial service or discipleship. It is a self-styled faith that promises all the goods apart from the person and work of our Lord Jesus Christ. This is the essence of *religion* without *relationship*. We choose our lifestyle and then form a religion around it in hopes that someday we will have what our souls were created for and promised if we simply follow God's Word and trust Him to provide it all for us in his perfect time.

Don't kid yourself. Satan knew he really couldn't fulfill his promise to Jesus but hoped it would be enough to rock him off His allegiance to His Father's will and plan for Him. Note Jesus' counter to this strategy. He quotes Scripture and affirms the cardinal truth of all of Christendom: ***"Worship the Lord your God, and serve him only" (Deuteronomy 6:13).*** Jesus is simply saying that having what God has decreed for him comes only through worshipping God fully and serving him passionately.

I see all these strategies that Satan used on Jesus in our culture and world today. He uses them on God's people just like he did on God's Son, Jesus Christ. My hope is that this will put all of us on alert and that when we are tempted (and we will be) by these strategies, we will respond as Jesus did; with Scripture and surrender to Christ.

As an addendum, I like how this passage in Matthew 4 concludes. The devil leaves Jesus (Luke's gospel says, ***"until an opportune time" 4:13)***, and angels came and *attended him.* My bet is that they brought Jesus some bread to eat. What do you think?

There is nothing more deflating to our Christian journey than when we fall to temptation. Nothing more exhilarating than when we stand up under it. The good news is that if we belong to Christ but realize we have fallen for one of Satan's strategies, we can confess this right now and He is faithful to forgive and cleanse us from all unrighteousness (1 John 1:9). For those who realize they are being held captive by Satan's evil system and want to be free, you can believe in Jesus today and follow Him wholeheartedly beginning right now.

CHAPTER 3: A KEY STRATEGY OF THE ENEMY
DISCUSSION QUESTIONS

1. What are the ways Satan uses to leverage temptation in Christ-followers?

2. Is temptation a sin? How might temptation build character in a believer's life? What key instruction and promises does 1 Corinthians 10:13 give to the believer regarding temptation?

3. Why does Jesus instruct his followers to pray that the Father would not lead them into temptation?

4. What do Hebrews 2:18 and 4:15 offer the believer going through temptation? Share some personal examples when you have found encouragement and victory through the truth of these Scriptures.

5. Give one or two examples of how Satan's strategies when tempting Jesus are similar to the way we are tempted?

6. Which of the three strategies that Satan used on Jesus is most significant to you? Why?

CHAPTER 4

FIGHTING IN THE DARK
Standing Firm When You Can't See Your Way

Regina is one of the sweetest Christ-followers I've ever meet. A couple of years ago, she and her family began to experience some challenging circumstances. While on vacation, her husband was severely injured when losing control of the ATV he was riding. His injuries were life-threatening and for a period of weeks, he was hospitalized in an ICU near where the accident occurred. After several surgeries, he slowly began to stabilize. Regina drew strength from the many prayers being offered by church members who knew of her situation. Due to her husband's injuries, he couldn't work which put their family into a financial crisis that seemed overwhelming. It seemed like a dark cloud hovered over them.

Eventually, her husband recovered and it appeared things were finally starting to turn around for them. Shortly after her husband's recovery, Regina went to the doctor because of a persistent headache and, after running some tests, doctors discovered she had a brain tumor. Once again, Regina's life was turned upside down. Many prayers went up for her and thankfully, doctors successfully removed the tumor and she began to recover. She was sensing some relief around this time, but then her father had a stroke which landed him in the hospital for several weeks. Throughout these inexplicable circumstances, Regina's faith never wavered. She calmly handled each experience by asking the body of Christ to pray for her and her family and for God to be glorified through what happened.

During that season in Regina's life, my wife and I would pray each day for her and her family. We sometimes remarked that Regina was having what looked to us like a "Job" experience—though we couldn't necessarily connect these tragedies with a wager being made between God and Satan over the sincerity of Regina's faithfulness as a worshipper of the one true God. In Job's case, that was, in fact, what was going on behind all the carnage being leveled against him.

Most of us are familiar with the curious Old Testament story of Job. Regina's troubles weren't anywhere close to the catastrophic losses that Job encountered. Yet, when people experience trials that come with rapid succession with the kind of severity that Regina experienced, it's not difficult to see a comparison to the story of Job.

Maybe you have been through, or are currently going through a season in life that has caused you to wonder if Satan has worked out a deal with God to test how sincere your love for God really is. The true story of Job recorded in Scripture is a great source of encouragement for anyone who is dealing with tragedy and loss and might be wondering if God has left them to deal with these things on their own. Whenever we find ourselves fighting in the dark, not knowing what is really going on, or fearful we may never understand, we are likely experiencing the kind of spiritual warfare Job faced.

While it is difficult to say with absolute certainty where and when Job finds his place in human history, the internal evidence of the book and a few places in Genesis point to Job living around the time between Noah and Abraham (1700 BC). The land of Uz (not to be confused with the land of Oz) appears to be the area known as Edom, east of the land of Canaan, in the same general region as Ur of the Chaldees. Some speculate (with good reason) that Job may have been the king of Edom, a man of great renown in that area and time.

Some believe Moses wrote the book we know as Job, while others believe that the narrative points to one of Job's friends, Eliphaz as the writer. The area of its origination, historical timeline, its references to creation and even sacrifice, without referring to Mosaic law, the tabernacle or the temple, seem to place the events of the book of Job in the Patriarchal age. This makes it one of the *earliest* sections of Scripture, along with the first five books of the Old Testament otherwise known as the Pentateuch.

I believe that Job is a historical figure, not, as some have proposed, a fictional character or allegory that presents an interesting story with only hidden or spiritual meaning. It is a *true story* about a man of great honor whose life is turned upside down by decisions made in the spiritual realm that he knows *nothing* about. Whatever Job's spiritual battles consisted of at the time, none of them could compare with the season of his life that we read about in the prologue of this book. If you are unfamiliar with this story, strap in and get ready for an account of a man's life that is truly mind-blowing.

The story of Job and by extension, our own story, reflect this truth: *There are times when we simply can't see or understand fully the spiritual battle in which we are engaged.* During these times we are fighting in the dark like Job. There is a mystery to the kinds of challenges and suffering we read about in the life of Job. We often simply don't know and might never know what's really going on in some forms of spiritual warfare. It's remarkable to see in the story of Job, that God never tells Job what's really going on. Job gets his moment of clarity near the end of the book—but it's not clarity about the enemy he's been fighting, it's about God's plan and Sovereignty over all things, both the good and the difficult.

Perhaps a good place to start in trying to determine if this is the kind of battle we are encountering, is to suggest some signs or indicators that point to our struggle being devised by our unseen but very real enemy, Satan. These indicators would simply point to (though they don't prove) the fact that we might be, like Job, *fighting in the dark*. We'll consider some *truths* found in Job that should *encourage* us *if we are fighting a similar fight*. We'll also consider some *action points* worth taking if our fight has found an uncanny similarity to Job's.

If you have ever engaged with the devices of the enemy without really knowing it at the time, the following things are likely true of your experience.

Confusion

This is an observation only; the text doesn't say that Job was confused by what was going on when everything started unraveling in his life. But when you read Job 1:1-5, you are struck by the fact that Job was a godly man, a good father who seems to be doing all the right things in life. *"He was blameless and upright; he feared God and shunned evil" (v.1).*

Knowing what we know about Job and God, and reading what happens to Job just doesn't seem to make sense. Most of us don't believe that if we live a good life we won't have bad things happen to us. The role of suffering even among godly people is clearly found in the pages of Scripture. But in Job's story, the difficulties he encounters seem so intense and happen in rapid succession.

Job is a man doing virtually everything right in his life. He's a godly man and one whose attention and devotion to his family is notable. He's got his kids on his mind and has done well in showing care for their spiritual lives, too. He's a godly parent, wanting his kids to do well spiritually and doing all he can (within the context of this dispensation) to insure they are walking with God. This was his regular custom (v.5b).

Add to all of this the fact that Job is a very prosperous man. Prosperity isn't the proof that God is pleased with one's life but I want to point out that God had blessed Job with many good things. Job's life and experience leading up to this season of disaster, would only have affirmed that things were as they should be in his life and walk with God. But little does Job know, a storm is about to break out over his life—and boy did it ever break!

Maybe there is a sense of confusion right now in the circumstances you are facing. You are having a hard time connecting the dots between what is going on and how God might use this to sharpen or build your character or glorify His name. If that is true for you, it MIGHT indicate that you are in or approaching a Job-like experience.

Destruction

The backstory of Job's experience recorded in Job 1:13-17 tells us that Satan approached God and accused Job of a false loyalty. Job, according to Satan, is faithful only because God has blessed him with an easy and prosperous life. In what feels to the reader as a divine misjudgment, God gives Satan permission to take some shots at Job's life; to touch him where it will hurt. This is one of the mysteries revealed in Job. The thoughtful reader of the book of Job can't help wondering if God has, or will ever do this in our lives, too. This can feel a little unsettling for most of us, nevertheless, that is what we discover in Job's story and we need to accept it.

One day, Job experiences a rapid-fire succession of bad news. First, one of his servants brings him news that while he and the other servants were out caring for some of Job's livestock, a marauding band of tough guys overcame them and stole much of Job's livestock; even killing a few of Job's servants in the process. Then, no sooner than this report is made, another servant runs in with the news that a grass fire has killed off more of his livestock and workers. Before that servant is finished sharing the report, another comes in saying that there were three raids that carried off his prize livestock of camels and killed more servants! This is horrible! Job is counting up his losses as each servant comes through the door and it is for Job a dark day, indeed.

These raids and unfortunate events were all too common in ancient times against men of considerable wealth. Had these inexplicable events happened over the course of Job's life, it would have been one thing, but having it all happen in such a short period of time is what makes this story so incomprehensible. Life can be that way sometimes, especially if there's an intentional spiritual attack being leveled against us.

If you have ever had something of value taken from you, there's a sense of being violated that hurts to the core. When someone takes what isn't theirs and just walks off with it, it's traumatic. And when these things are taken by force, it is even more traumatic! Have you been a victim of a violent crime? Mugged or robbed at gun point? Beaten? Attacked? We read about these types of events in the news every day. They usually happen to "others" but sometimes, we fall victim as well. Could it be that these experiences are the results of something happening in the spiritual dimension that is orchestrated between our enemy *and God?* Here it appears that the battle is being waged against Job, but the truth is that it's being waged between Satan and God. This is both amazing and mysterious.

What follows is even more challenging for the one fighting in the dark.

Escalation

Up to this point, Job's emotional baseline is clearly being challenged but he hasn't snapped. When someone messes with our stuff we react but we soon realize it's only *stuff.* We can replace our stuff. In Job 1:18-19 and 2:7-8 the scene changes dramatically. Job is about to learn that his losses are not just material possessions. The third servant has just caught his breath and opened the door for yet another to enter, bearing some horrible news: ALL of Job's kids were killed when a storm caved in the home in which they were all gathered for a party.

I can't read this text without considering the level of anguish and emotional shock this had to have produced in Job's heart. Serving as a chaplain in the local fire department, I've had the unfortunate experience of presenting a death notification to a family member who had no idea what was coming. The shock, disbelief, utter anguish and unrelenting pain

71

is difficult to watch as the words, "Your loved one is dead" enters their mental and emotional understanding. I've seen people in these moments flop on the ground and roll around screaming in torment. It's difficult to witness. I can hear the cry, the gasping unbelief, the screams, the wailing of a mom or dad in such raw moments. It is nothing short of horrific. There's a hopeless and awful awareness of what those moments mean for the ones receiving this kind of news.

In typical Eastern fashion, Job gets up, tears his robe, shaves his head and falls to the ground crying out to God. I know there are people reading this who have lost a child to sickness or a tragic accident. We are told that the grief of losing a child is the most difficult and emotionally challenging event a person can experience in life. Many simply can't endure it. Losing a child often means terrible things for the future of a family—separation of parents lost in their grief and not able to console each other; divorce, blame, shame, emotional problems, sibling rebellion and much more. The loss is unrelenting and consuming. And worse, it's permanent.

I know this is shocking, but we learn that in Job's situation, his children's deaths came at the hand of Satan who had received permission from God to perpetrate this terrible loss. This is part of what D.A. Carson calls the difficult doctrine of the Love of God—that a loving God allows the death of one or more of our kids is one thing, but to know that, at least in Job's case, God was proving something to Satan makes all this a little difficult to swallow. It gives us pause. *What do we think about a God who allows this kind of suffering for the sole purpose of proving his point to Satan?* We don't know if there were other lessons God had in mind for Job to learn, aside from proving to Satan that his servant Job was faithful for the right reasons. With what we do know, it seems a little unsettling to say the least.

Maybe your loss has led you to question God's goodness. It may be the loss of a loved one or something very precious to you. Your emotions have been rocked with the foreboding news of what's taken place. This is what I mean by *escalation*. The losses are no longer just material, they are personal and seemingly unrelenting. We'll come back to how Job deals with his anguish in a remarkable way but first, let's consider another aspect of this escalation.

For a second time, Satan and God discuss Job's life and God gives permission to Satan to touch Job's health, with the proviso that Job's life is spared. Job contracts a skin disease that creates boils all over his body. It's nasty and ugly and very painful. He's in physical torment. He's suffering the emotional anguish of losing his kids and now the anguish of physical disease; the light is slowly fading for Job. He's spiraling down with no end in sight. This is something that some of us have felt in our lives, perhaps not with the same severity as that of Job's circumstances, but something happens to make our vision of God seem blurry and His purposes unclear. We find ourselves adrift in a sea of confusion and doubt. In those moments, we are tempted to give up and throw our once held spiritual convictions aside.

Sometimes in life's darkest moments, we must realize that the nature of what we are going through isn't any different than what Job encountered. God is *allowing* something terrible to come into our lives and the disappointment may feel overwhelming. That's the way it feels when we are fighting in the dark.

Isolation

Job's circle of support is getting smaller and smaller and then Job's wife asks, **"Are you still holding on to your integrity? Curse God and die" (2:9)!** Wives, allow me to suggest this isn't a very good way to encourage your husband when times are hard! Keep in mind that in ancient times, skin diseases were viewed as a kind of curse and it always meant separation from the community. Job is out in the community dump, sitting among the smoldering ashes of the town's refuse. He was a castaway. No washed linen and soft comfortable bed for Job. He's taken himself to the edge of town, sat himself down in the ashes and is scraping the sores that are all over his body with broken pieces of pottery. What a terrible scene this is! Job's wife might merely be hoping for an end to his pain and sorrow; or more likely, it may be her pain and sorrow speaking. Remember she had losses, too, which brings up the matter of how Job's spiritual attack affected more than just his life.

There's a trickle-down effect on those who suffer under the attack of the enemy. No one suffers alone. There is a circle of relationships impacted when anyone comes under the attack of the enemy. If a husband falls to temptation and commits adultery, his wife is impacted, and perhaps more, his children if he has any. When the health of a mom declines and she succumbs to the disease, her children are impacted for the rest of their lives. When the enemy takes over the evil thoughts of a person open to fueling his revenge, individuals or even large numbers of people may suffer—or worse—pay with their lives. The impact of travesties of this nature can be exponential, and they bring a terrible sense of isolation on those impacted by them.

On October 1, 2017, Stephen Paddock fired over a thousand rounds from his suite on the 32nd floor of the Mandalay Bay Hotel in Las Vegas, killing 58 people and injuring 851 others (400 by gunfire and hundreds more by the panic that immediately followed the shootings) who were attending a music festival taking place across the Las Vegas Strip. Three firefighters from the fire department I serve as Chaplain happened to be in the crowd when the shooting started. They heroically treated many gunshot victims while helping others to safety all while under gun fire.

I was part of an initial critical incident debriefing with these firefighters as a means of mental health support to assess their ability to resume their work stations. Their descriptions of what they experienced were horrific. Firefighters are trained to deal with critical incidents and this was certainly one for the books. Over the weeks and months that followed, I kept in touch with some of those who had been personally impacted by these events. A common form of discomfort and uneasiness came from a sense of isolation among those who were impacted most. Survivor's guilt is what people often experience in these kinds of experiences—the gnawing question of why you survived and others didn't. This sense of isolation can be psychologically damaging when experiencing trauma.

Perhaps you feel all alone in your pain and loss, and the misery of it all is consuming your life. If you feel isolated, it's another sign that your fight is similar to Job's.

Condemnation

Job's friends show up and at first appear to be helpful in their approach. They have come to mourn and sit quietly for a week because they see Job's pain. During this time, each one is sizing up Job's predicament and assessing all that has happened. Their deduction is that Job is in his situation because of some secret sin or indiscretion in his life. *Job's hiding something. Job's up to something. Job's not where God wants him to be.* All of this is a terrible assessment of what is really going on—a spiritual battle that Job knows nothing about. Job isn't innocent of sin but he is completely innocent of why any of this has happened to him. He hasn't a clue. Chapters 3 through 36 contain the various arguments that Job's friends use to explain the reasons for what Job is going through. Apart from just one of Job's friends, they all categorically throw him under the bus.

Make a note: Be careful who you listen to when it comes to what is going on in your life! It would have been better had these friends said nothing to Job rather than offer him what they felt were the issues he needed to confront. Sometimes the best comfort and ministry we can offer someone in pain is simply our *presence*.

Maybe you're being worked over by someone who thinks they have figured out why you are in the mess you are in. If so, keep in mind this isn't so rare when we find ourselves fighting in the dark. This was Job's story; it might be yours as well.

If you've experienced an unusual sense of *confusion, sudden destruction, escalation, isolation and/or condemnation,* then perhaps like Job, you, too, are fighting in the dark.

But there's hope! As we read through the book of Job and what took place in the aftermath of his suffering, there are some hopeful things we can learn and apply to our lives when we are fighting in the dark. Let's find some encouragement from a few of these things.

What to Trust When Fighting in the Dark

God never leaves us to fight our battles alone. Whatever our fight happens to be, we can find encouragement from knowing and believing a few important things. We see them things come up in Job's personal experience, too. Consider the following.

God is Sovereign

In Job 1:6a, we read that the angels and Satan himself come to present themselves to the Lord. Clearly, the one in charge is God, not Satan. Satan and his minions are all in subjection to God Almighty. This sets the backdrop to the inexplicable things Job was about to experience. Job had not known of this mysterious meeting in the spiritual realm, but what Job did know was that the God he knew and followed was in complete control over everything going on in his life. This was one of the reasons Job was so mystified by the events that were unfolding for him. *How could God allow all this to happen to me?* Questions like this come from the base understanding that God alone directs the course of our lives and allows certain events to transpire for his purposes alone. In the end, whatever has happened to us, we must conclude that God has allowed them. While this doesn't always settle our hearts completely, it is crucial for maintaining hope when the support pieces of our lives seem to be compromised.

God sees Job's belief in his sovereignty. Notice God asks Satan, *"Have you considered my servant Job? There is no one on earth like him; he is blameless and upright, a man who fears God and shuns evil" (Job 1:8).* Embedded in God's commentary of Job is a picture of Job's understanding of God's sovereign rule, noting he is *"...a man who fears God..."* which points to God's supremacy over all other powers. The fear of the Lord is truly the beginning of wisdom (Psalm 111:10). To revere God above all, is to recognize His rightful place. It's Job's knowledge of God's sovereignty that begs the question of what is happening in his life. The Psalmist declares, *"The angel of the Lord encamps around those who fear Him, and he delivers him" (Psalm 34:7).* Job saw God as Sovereign over all things. His understanding of God's nature kept him leaning in when circumstances were devastating.

We see this in another Old Testament character. King Jehoshaphat prayed when he had heard of the armies of Moab and Ammon coming against him: *"O LORD, God of our fathers, are you not the God who is in heaven? You rule over all the kingdoms of the nations. Power and might are in your hand, and no one can withstand you"* *(2 Chronicles 20:6).* Jehoshaphat could stand strong in the face of a vast army coming against him because of one thing: He knew God was in charge. Do we?

God is sovereign. Job knew this, as should we. Perhaps right now, amidst enormous difficulty and challenges it would be helpful for you to assess your own understanding and conviction of God's sovereignty. If you truly believe He is sovereign over everything, then whatever the dilemma or disaster confronting you, trust God is going to work it out. Because God is sovereign, *"We know that in all things God works for the good of those who love him, who have been called according to his purpose" (Romans 8:28).* I find no greater assurance in the entire Bible as to what we can count on when things seem to have gone terribly wrong in our lives, especially when the disaster can't be traced to something we know we've done to cause it. That assurance stems from the knowledge and belief in God's sovereignty.

Perhaps the single most important thing for you right now is to simply rely on God's power and control over what you are facing—even if it feels odd that he's not changing anything just yet. Trust that He knows what's best for you and has a bigger picture in mind than you can see or comprehend yourself.

God sets limits

It may seem a bit unnerving knowing that God at times, allows Satan or his demonic beings to mess with us, our family, friends or our circumstances. Keep in mind that Job had no idea of this cosmic tribunal taking place in the spiritual realm of which he was the center of conversation. To be honest, I'm grateful I'm not privy to these kinds of conversations. If I knew God and Satan were discussing the core issues of my heart and God was willing to prove His point by testing me, I'd be a nervous wreck! Thankfully, by God's grace, we're not given this kind of insight or knowledge.

But I find encouragement knowing that when it does happen (if it does), God sets limits on what Satan and his messengers can do and the extent they can "tinker" with my life. Satan can never just have his way with me—or you. As with Job, God says exactly how far he can go in his attempt to cause Job to deny Him. In Job 2:6, God gives permission to Satan, "Very well, then, he is in your hands; but you must spare his life." Praise God for this! If Satan is messing with us, we can be encouraged knowing that God has ordered it and set the boundaries to accomplish His purposes for us. Knowing this at least helps us look at our predicament or problem as only a means for God to gain glory. Our part is to trust and move through the situation in a submissive and even joy-filled manner. James had this in view when he writes, ***"Consider it pure joy, my brothers, whenever you face trials of many kinds, because***

you know that the testing of your faith develops perseverance"
(James 1:2-3). Choosing joy when undergoing testing is a grace that God
gives to His children.

If God were not sovereign, then we would have no hope that God
could limit the enemy's activity or the extent to which he would go to
cause us to despair or curse God. It's His sovereignty that guarantees the
limitations placed on our enemy when he comes after us. Let's not forget,
Satan's desire is to destroy all of us. He comes to **"steal, kill and
destroy" (John 10:9).** Were it not for the boundaries that God places
around us, we'd not have a chance. God graciously allows only what he
knows will serve his purposes in a more magnificent way.

God redeems

Granted we don't see this in the prologue of this book but we do learn
at the end of the story that God redeems the broken pieces in Job's life.
We need to remember there is a difference between God *replacing* things
and God *redeeming* things. God sometimes *replaces* things that get broken,
but his specialty is to *redeem* them—which is so much better.

When I was serving as a college pastor in my local church, one of my
students was eager to have a ministry that introduced people to Jesus
Christ. Matt was a talented piano player and vocalist and whenever he
played and sang, it seemed that God may have plans to use him in
ministry. Matt was counting on this and spoke to me about it often.
Then, at the end of the school year, Matt had a terrible accident. He was
enjoying a day at the beach with friends when he dove off a rock into the
ocean where it was unexpectedly shallow, breaking his neck instantly.
Matt was airlifted to a local trauma center for treatment. Unfortunately,
Matt's neck had broken in a way that made him a quadriplegic. From that
day forward, Matt had no use of his arms or legs. He went through several
surgeries and months of rehab teaching him how to sit up and manipulate
his unresponsive body while in his wheel chair. Matt was a part of our

student leadership team and his fellow students rallied to help Matt find some semblance of normalcy in his new and difficult reality.

Matt's life span was drastically shortened due to the compromise his organs experienced from his accident. Yet, over the months and years that followed, Matt lived a courageous life sharing his story with others. I'm sure Matt prayed for God to heal him instantly after hearing the news of his paralysis. We all asked God to do this for Matt, too. But God didn't answer our prayers in the way we had hoped.

Joni Erickson Tada, who suffered her own diving accident in the 70s and, who became a champion for those with disabilities visited Matt at a critical time in his recovery. With the loving attention of godly people like Joni, Matt's physical family and his spiritual family, his testimony became strong and many found encouragement from his story. Some people came to know Jesus Christ through his life and message. Matt had several years of sharing the gospel in various settings. God didn't choose to heal Matt, but he did redeem Matt's accident by providing a platform for a greater ministry than Matt could have ever had otherwise. Then, as a relatively young man, God took him home.

From a purely human perspective, Matt's story is tragic, but from God's perspective and eternal realities, Matt's story is triumphant. God doesn't always replace, but he does redeem. If you are facing a difficult season in life or you feel something precious is broken beyond repair, take courage knowing that God is a redeemer. He has plans to use this in your life and for His glory.

You are in good company

If the story of Job is your story, then guess what, you are also in the same company as our Lord Jesus, whom the Father allowed Satan to harass, persecute, tempt, bring adversity to and ultimately even betray to the point of death! If God allowed this to happen to His Son, why are we so shocked when He allows things that are difficult to happen to us? We should be honored to suffer in the same way Jesus has for us and, share in the life experience of Job as well. The Apostle Peter wrote, *"If you suffer for doing good and you endure it, this is commendable before God. To this you were called, because Christ suffered for you, leaving you an example, that you should follow in his steps. He committed no sin, and no deceit was found in his mouth. When they hurled their insults at him, he did not retaliate; when he suffered, he made no threats. Instead, he entrusted himself to him who judges justly" (1 Peter 2:20-23).*

Let these truths take deep root in your life when you encounter a season where you are fighting in the dark.

Best Practices When Fighting in the Dark

It's one thing to identify this kind of spiritual battle. It's another thing to choose beliefs and convictions about important realities to get you through it. There's something else even more important that we need when fighting in the dark.

We need to worship God

Look at Job's response when the crushing news of his children's death arrives: *"He fell to the ground in worship and said, 'Naked I came from my mother's womb, and naked I will depart. The LORD gave and the LORD has taken away; may the name of the LORD be praised" (1:21).*

81

Job made a conscious choice about how he would respond to the terrible news of losing his kids. No one is saying this is easy. We only have two options: we can rebel against God, or we can worship Him. Job's choice, along with ours, is never going to be easy but it does make sense. Let me explain why. First, worship is simply acknowledging that God has made us and that we have come into this life completely dependent on Him alone and will leave this life the same way. *Naked I came; naked I will depart.*

Second, worship is acknowledging that God gives and takes away and throughout, He is to be praised. Nothing belongs to us, it is all his: our children, our houses, our cars, our bank account. Everything we call our own really belongs to God. He allows us a short time to steward these things for His glory. In plenty or in want, God is to be praised. This is the greatest advertisement to the world, that our hope isn't in our stuff or even in our relationships. Everything we think we possess today will one day be gone or we will be gone. We often see the professional athlete who wins the contest give praise to God but how about when he loses? Is it the same? I don't think that is seen very often. "I just want to give God glory for my defeat today; He is worthy to be praised!" I'd love to hear that more often, wouldn't you? When something isn't going well in our lives, we praise God regardless. This honors God and makes the world take notice. This is the kind of worship that is precious to God and why the writer of Hebrews says to bring the *"sacrifice of praise--the fruit of lips that confess His name" (Hebrews 13:15).*

Worship in church each Sunday should be passionate because the praise is being cultivated in the difficulties of life. Our praise should rise in view of the trouble and hardships we face. When it does, it is powerful. My first time back in church after my mom had passed was marked with unusual praise from my heart. It was the sorrow and brokenness that was pouring out to the one worthy of all praise. When people suffer and come together for worship, the power is palpable and inspiring. Some of the most enthusiastic praise services I've been in has been among those who have suffered severely. I'll never forget meeting with a group of fifty Chinese house church pastors, nearly all of whom had been imprisoned and beaten for their belief in Jesus. They raised the roof on the little makeshift church we used for our meeting.

We'll come back to this in a later chapter to see how important choosing to worship is when we are in spiritual battles, but this is important to mention here, too.

We need to embrace God's mystery

This too, is part of how we worship God when experiencing spiritual battles, but something very practical needs to be included. In moments of great confusion, the temptation is to know exactly why we are going through something dreadful. The real aim, however, is to simply acknowledge that there are things we will never know about God or this life; He sends both good and trouble to his servants. Let that settle in your heart for a moment. Mike Mason, reflecting on this section of Job's story writes, *"To accept trouble from God implies the acceptance of a certain illogical dimension to life, a dimension so totally beyond human understanding that even faith, by its own secret and darkly luminous wisdom, cannot really comprehend it. Here we need the kind of faith whose God is so big as to be not just unmanageable, but to a large extent unknowable" (The Gospel According to Job, p. 47).* Paul writes, **"Who has known the mind of the Lord, or who has been his counselor" (Romans 11:34)?**

Right now, we must embrace what's happening in our lives regardless of our understanding as to why something has happened or even knowing the purposes God may have for us because of it. Let me suggest that in doing so, we can be liberated to a new and stronger position in our faith-journey.

We need to be honest with others and especially with God

If there is something that Job's story helps us see is that we rarely go through deep valleys in our lives without a running dialogue with our friends and with God. This is normal. God loves honesty when we are in the mess of life. This is where our relationship with God deepens—when we share honestly what we are experiencing. Some people say it's unspiritual to say too much when we are troubled—we should just button down and keep quiet, but God wants us to pour out our hearts to Him.

If you take a close look at the psalms of lament, you'll discover just how honest this kind of dialogue should be. An example might help show you what I mean. *"How long, LORD? Will you forget me forever? How long will you hide your face from me" (Psalm 13:1)?* The psalms are filled with lament. Honest communication between people and God. What are you doing God?

In his insightful and compelling book, "A Praying Life," Paul Miller writes about the power of lament: *"The Israelites lamented because they longed for a better world, the way the world is supposed to be. They believed in a covenant-keeping God, one who keeps his word. That's what makes laments so passionate, so in-your-face. When you lament, you live simultaneously in the past, present and future. A lament connects God's past promise with my present chaos, hoping for a better future."* During times of challenge or even unparalleled chaos, keep talking to God! He wants to hear your honest heart. Authenticity is what creates intimacy with God. Don't be afraid. He loves you. We don't always hear God speak to us as quickly as we'd like, but he will. It's his nature to communicate—to reveal Himself just like he did with Job. Fast forward to the end of Job. God speaks, and after He is finished speaking and gives Job a chance to talk, Job decides it is better to put his hand over his mouth. Job cries out, *"I am unworthy—how can I reply to you? I put my hand over my mouth" (Job 40:4).* We should all learn from this!

Where would we be in life's darkest moments if the book of Job hadn't been written for us? It tells us so much but it also leaves much to the mystery of God and His glory for allowing evil in this world. Remember, there is a day coming when God will completely and finally and utterly make all things right. But we must wait for it. Looking forward to that day we say, along with the Apostle John, *"Even so, come quickly Jesus" (Revelation 22:20).*

CHAPTER 4: FIGHTING IN THE DARK DISCUSSION QUESTIONS

1. Why does it feel incongruous to be in a close relationship with God while having serious problems at the same time?

2. Has there been a time in your life when you couldn't understand why God was allowing you to experience such difficult circumstances? How did you respond to God during this time? What were some of the lessons you learned?

3. If Job was your friend, how would you encourage him in view of his devastating losses? If you were Job, how would you want someone to encourage you?

4. What is the most difficult thing for you to reconcile between Job's story and what you believe about God?

5. How easy is it for you to repeat Job's words recorded in Job 1:21 and 2:10 when you experience difficulties and hardships? Why are these statements important to embrace when going through trials and difficulties?

6. How does Job remind us of the person and work of Jesus Christ?

7. Why is it important to worship God when in the midst of difficult situations?

CHAPTER 5

YOU'RE NOT ALONE

What God's Presence Means to Those in the Fight

One of the things I've discovered about spiritual warfare is that there are basics to learn about the Christian life that are just as critical as engaging in the details of the spirit realm. Essentially, this book is meant to inform how our spiritual enemy works and how to counter his schemes and attacks with the truth of God's Word. It isn't meant to scare you or to make you paranoid about some kind of attack from Satan. To the contrary, I'm hoping it will serve to point out the reality of spiritual warfare in our lives and to equip us to be men and women of faith so we can stand firm in the midst of our struggle and the invisible war going on all around us.

One of the most insidious ways our enemy attacks is the indirect attack of making us feel *abandoned* or *forgotten* by God. It is one of his oldest tricks and the system he has set up often leaves us feeling that God has taken a break and isn't concerned about our lives or our struggles. If he can make us feel abandoned by God when we face the enemy's opposition, it won't be long until we have given in to fear or any number of things that defeat us.

God wants all of us to escape his trap and have confidence that He is with us and will never abandon us. When Israel was entering the promised land and charged with conquering God's enemies, Moses gave clear instructions to the priests as to what to tell Israel's army: *"Hear, O Israel, today you are going into battle against your enemies. Do not be fainthearted or afraid; do not be terrified or give way to panic before them. For the LORD your God is the one who goes with you to*

87

fight for you against your enemies to give you victory" *(Deuteronomy 20:3-4).* God being "with" his people is a refrain throughout the Scriptures. God said it to the patriarchs of Israel, Abraham and Isaac and Jacob; to Moses when he was called to deliver his people; and to Joshua who would take over Moses' place of leadership. He said it to judges and kings and to prophets, not to mention the many times He simply reminds His people en masse that they could always count on His presence. Here are a few of my favorites, which I go to often when I feel this indirect "hit" of the enemy that suggests I'm alone in the fight: *"So do not fear, for I am with you; do not be dismayed, for I am your God. I will strengthen you and help you; I will uphold you with my righteous right hand" (Isaiah 41:10).* And, a couple of chapters later: *"When you pass through the waters, I will be with you; and when you pass through the rivers, they will not sweep over you. When you walk through the fire, you will not be burned; the flames will not set you ablaze" (Isaiah 43:2).* Before His ascension, Jesus promised His disciples, *"And surely I am with you always, to the very end of the age" (Matthew 28:20b).*

The promise of God's presence is meant to anchor us in times of opposition or difficulty. Our enemy knows this, so he works hard at causing us to question if God is really there when we need him most. If we doubt and question God's presence, as some of us might be doing right now, then we are in peril of losing the ground war in the spiritual battlefield. Let's see what we can learn about trusting God's presence from what Scripture reveals to us.

I've chosen a story from the Old Testament that illustrates our struggle with regard to seeing and believing in God's presence at *all times* in our lives. It's one of many stories in Scripture that illustrate the importance of trusting God's presence. It is the story of *Gideon* found in Judges 6-7.

In this story, there are three specific action points that flow from the narrative and interface with the issue of trusting God's presence; really believing that *God is with his people always.* In the story there are no less than three corresponding movements which all have to do with believing God's presence in our lives and the battle that sometimes takes place in our hearts and minds to really believe this.

Fessing up to our flaws

The first movement is found in Judges 6:1-16 where, if we observe that for Gideon to experience a greater awareness and confidence in God's presence in his life, he needed to own up to some things that weren't right. In the backstory of Gideon's experience, we learn that Israel had gotten into trouble because they hadn't removed some practices that were not right in their worship of Jehovah. They hadn't come clean, named, identified, or called out the corrosive influences that subtly led them into places where they could no longer feel God's presence in their lives. It was a slow spiritual erosion that was limiting their spiritual vitality. Let me explain.

At this time in Israel's history, there was a slow but notable drift into pagan worship, replacing the pure worship of Jehovah with that of worshipping the god, Baal and his wife, Asherah. They had built altars to Baal and, as a complementary action, a distinctive Asherah pole that usually stood alongside of the altar to Baal. It's hard to imagine that only one generation after Joshua led Israel into the promised land, the people did evil in the eyes of the Lord and served the Baals (Judges 2:11). The book of Judges reveals this distinctive flaw of God's people from generation to generation; a slow drift from what God prescribes for His people in order for them to participate in the full measure of His blessings. Whenever this happens, the price we pay is losing our sense of God's presence.

John sat across from me in the cafe one early morning. He stared into his cup with a frown and slowly began to tell me all that was wrong in his life. He'd dabbled in pornography before, but lately it had become out of control. He had stopped reading his Bible. Stopped praying. He had nearly stopped all means of connecting with God except dropping in to church just to see if he might encounter God. What John missed most was a sense of God's presence in his life. When John felt the presence of God, he was strong in faith and was subduing his fleshly desires. He wanted all this back. But how?

The answer to John's predicament was simple—but he had trouble seeing it. Confession and repentance was necessary if John was to feel the presence of God again in his life, but the enemy had confused him to the point of questioning if this was even possible. This is the way the enemy works. He baits us into small compromises that slowly diminish our sense of God's presence while more spiritual damage takes place until it seems we can't turn back. We feel stuck and doomed. That's what John was experiencing as we sat together that morning in the cafe. God used me to help John see that it wasn't too late to turn away from the sins that were keeping him from sensing God's presence again in his life. After a time of prayerful repentance, John felt lighter in his spirit and hopeful for what was ahead.

Thankfully, under the New Covenant, God's presence in our lives isn't dependent on how well we obey. Let's be clear about the gospel—God's promises of both our salvation and his attending graces are based solely on Christ's perfect life and sacrifice, not our own. This is where the enemy works hard to play into our flesh to create a merit system by which God's presence is dependent on how well we do. The evidence of his strategy comes in the aftermath of compromise in our lives when we choose to sin rather than obey God. When this occurs, it's natural to feel as if God has turned His back on us. We know we have done wrong and the enemy leverages this to suggest that God will no longer accept us or be with us.

In the Judges 6 passage, under the Old Covenant, God allowed Israel's oppressors to wage war with them for seven years simply because of the people's *unrepentance*; they were *not fessing up to their flaws*. When harvest time arrived, the evil Midianites swooped down and pounced on all the goods, including the animals, ravaging the land and impoverishing Israel to the point of desperation. The people fled to the high country and lived in caves and used wine presses as their threshing floors simply because of their fear of the Midianites.

Israel cries out to Jehovah and in response to their cry, God sends them a prophet who tells them their problem: *"I said to you…I am the LORD your God; do not worship the gods of the Amorites, in whose land you live.' But you have not listened to me"* *(Judges 6:10).*

This happens to us, too. When we get off track spiritually and the enemy baits us to get comfortable with sin and waywardness, God is still with us—but we don't sense his presence because our hearts have moved away from Him. We feel alone. Our enemy relishes it when this kind of scenario gains momentum in our lives.

Along comes *"the angel of the LORD"* *(Judges 6:11)* whom Bible scholars believe is a theophany, or a manifestation of the pre-incarnate Christ. What does the angel of the LORD say to Gideon doing his work in the shadows of the wine press so as not to be noticed by the Midianites? He says, *"The LORD is with you, mighty warrior"* *(Judges 6:12).* If there was ever a place where I see humor in the Scriptures, it is here. I imagine Gideon looking around and wondering, "Where's the mighty warrior?" Gideon was the last guy to feel worthy of being called a mighty warrior!

Gideon no doubt had a heart for God but he and his family were part of the sinful setting of spiritual prostitution committed against God, deep into the idolatrous worship of Baal and Asherah. Gideon's response shows his own disbelief in that moment in the presence of God: *"If the Lord is with us, why has all this happened to us? Where are all his wonders that our fathers told us about when they said, 'Did not the LORD bring us up out of Egypt?' But now the LORD has abandoned us and put us into the hand of Midian" (Judges 6:13).* The response from the angel of the Lord shows His commitment to go with Gideon: *"Go in the strength you have and save Israel out of Midian's hand. Am I not sending you" (Judges 6:14)?*

When we've lived with spiritual compromise long enough, it's hard to see ourselves the way God sees us. Gideon's response expresses his diminished view of himself: *"How can I save Israel? My clan is the weakest in Manasseh, and I am the least in my family" (Judges 6:15).* Furthermore, when spiritual compromise has been our experience for too long, our vision of God's presence is likewise diminished. Everything looks so difficult and all we see are our problems and the obstacles of finding a way out.

Our struggles should lead us to turn to God for help. We see this in the text, *"...the Israelites cried to the LORD because of Midian" (Judges 6:7).* If you are in a place where the Holy Spirit is showing you where you have gotten off track and by God's grace you want to turn around, then cry out to the LORD. God loves it when we come to him— no matter what our condition. Many of us think we must wait until we can clean up our lives before crying out to God. This isn't scriptural. We turn to God and then HE cleans us up. This is the same for anyone needing to come to the LORD for salvation. We don't first clean up our lives; we simply come and trust God to do the cleaning. Sure, He won't clean us up without our making certain decisions and changes, but it's His power at work in us to do it (Philippians 2:12).

At this point in the narrative, notice the assurance Gideon receives from the angel speaking to him: *"I will be with you, and you will strike down all the Midianites together" (Judges 6:16).* Judges 6:11-16 reveals that no matter how weak or insignificant we may see ourselves in the midst of our struggle, the difference maker is God's presence in our lives.

Fueling our faith

In the next movement of the Judges narrative (Judges 6:17-40), Gideon is going to fuel his faith just like you and I need to, especially if we are going to pursue a greater awareness of God's presence in our lives. How does Gideon fuel his faith? How do we fuel our faith?

We fuel our faith by choosing to worship God regardless of our apprehension or insecurity

In Judges 6:17-24, Gideon is not entirely sure that he is speaking with the LORD of glory. He's not sure he is experiencing the presence of God: *"If I have found favor in your eyes, give me a sign that it is really you talking to me. Please do not go away until I come back and bring my offering and set it before you" (Judges 6:17-18a).* We've all had moments when we've felt what Gideon is feeling. Is this really you, God? Is it you speaking to me?

Gideon wants proof. He wants to believe God is speaking to him and assuring him of his presence, but he needs a little help. He says to the angel in v.18a: *"Please do not go away until I come back and bring my offering and set it before you"* (which is code language for worship). The Angel of the Lord responds to Gideon: *"I will wait until you return" (Judges 6:18b).*

If you are questioning God's presence, not sure if you are really hearing or seeing him in some situation in your life, learn a lesson from Gideon. Ask Him to meet you in worship, which doesn't necessarily always mean at church. You can take a walk, a drive, or go into a quiet room in your home, and bring Him the offering of your heart and allow God to minister to you through his presence.

The offering Gideon brings is consumed at the touch of the Angel of the Lord's staff and suddenly Gideon realizes it is the Lord! He gets a glimpse of God's presence and realizes that God has visited him. By the way, whenever this happens, it is both scary and beautiful all at the same time. To know you are in God's presence is both terrifying and comforting all at once. There is always a beautiful tension between a holy fear and blessed familiarity when coming into God's presence. Be wary of those who only view God like a buddy but rarely see or value the beauty of His presence resulting in a holy fear of who He is. For Gideon, the tension starts to slide toward the "fearful" side of this experience before God intervenes: *"Peace! Do not be afraid. You are not going to die" (Judges 6:23).* This moves Gideon to build an altar, calling it, *"The LORD is Peace" (Judges 6:24).* The peace (Hebrew, *shalom*) of God is what we most need when we encounter the enemy. Shalom is God's gift to his children who seek His heart no matter what is taking place in their lives. Wholesome completeness is the shalom of God for His people.

This is beautiful. When we choose to worship God despite our apprehension, He loves to break through with His peace! We know it is Him because His peace comes into our hearts. I wonder if the great Apostle Paul was thinking of Gideon's story when writing to his friends in Philippi: *"The Lord is near. Do not be anxious about anything, but in everything, by prayer and petition, with thanksgiving, present your requests to God. And the peace of God, which transcends all understanding will guard your hearts and your minds in Christ Jesus" (Philippians 4:5b-7).*

We fuel our faith when we choose to commit to God's will in our lives

What comes next in the narrative (Judges 6:25-32) is really important for understanding how we pursue a greater awareness of God's presence in our lives. We move from worship to action. The Lord tells Gideon, *"Tear down your father's altar to Baal and cut down the Asherah*

94

pole beside it. Then build a proper kind of altar to the LORD your God on the top of this height. Using the wood of the Asherah pole that you cut down, offer the second bull as a burnt offering" (Judges 6:25-26).

God tells Gideon that the way back for he and his people is to put God back in his rightful place. Tear down the idols that have allowed spiritual stagnation! He tells Gideon to prepare a burnt offering (which is an offering of repentance for sin) by tearing down false gods and idols standing between them and God. It is amusing that Gideon complies but he does it at night so he doesn't have to deal with those who would disagree with what he is doing. God seems okay with this, as if to tell Gideon, "I don't care how or even when you do it—just do it!"

Shortly after, the people living near Gideon notice what has happened and want to punish whoever did this. One thing you learn real fast when you start knocking down false gods in your life is that others don't always go along. Once you have decided to do God's will, plan on being challenged by those who are still stuck in their sin or unbelief and try to turn you back to your old ways. This is the way the enemy works. He wants you to second guess and to be intimidated so you will return to the sin you left behind. Satan works at bullying us this way. He does so knowing that once we've regained our senses and see clearly and realize God has never left us, he's lost us again! If you commit to action—to doing God's will, count on being tested! Satan never releases his influence or domain without a fight.

Use moments of desperation to galvanize your conviction to obey the Lord

We can fuel our faith by harnessing desperation as a means to see God work. In this section of the narrative, we read of Gideon's "fleece" experiment with God. We'd agree that setting out fleeces isn't probably the best way to go about discerning God's will. Admittedly, Gideon is

95

showing his desperation by asking God, not once but twice, to confirm His presence and power by showing him something with the dampening of a fleece.

Whatever you believe about the validity of fleeces, you have to at least acknowledge that God honors what Gideon does. I'm not suggesting that this is the best way to ascertain God's involvement in what He's calling you to do. God sees into our hearts and knows what we need from Him in those moments of hesitation when we're standing on the precipice ready to jump into what we think He has called us to. God meets us there in those moments, and gives us what we need, just like he did with Gideon.

We might learn from this that God isn't bothered when we come to him honestly about our concerns or hesitations, wanting to know for sure He is behind what we feel He wants us to do. God is plenty big enough to give us what we need to help us follow Him. He's so gracious to do this for us.

A few years ago, our church was planning to begin a building project that would cost several million dollars. The aim was to add some "connection" space for our people to gather informally before and after services. Of all the great aspects of our facility, simple connection space was scarce. I remember our board working with the architect, discussing plans and going over costs. At the same time, there were other areas of our facility that had become "tired" due to the wear and tear over the years. More concerning was the lack of secure space we had for our children's ministry. There was no way to limit the exposure to classrooms and entryways in our children's ministry area without doing a major renovation of the space.

One encouraging reality was that over the years, we'd been careful with our expenses, setting aside money that would one day be needed for a project like our new connection space. That time had arrived and we had substantial finances ready, but not for both the connection space and the renovation needed in our children's ministry area. While we had been planning to build the connection space first, we felt God tell us to do the renovation first and trust him for the extra several million that would be needed for the connection space afterwards. I remember thinking, "Is this you, God?" After a series of prayer meetings, discussions at the leadership level and a fair amount of personal moments of desperation with the Lord, I felt peace in moving forward with the renovation and to trust God for the remainder of the project.

We put our promotional materials together and an overview of the project so that our church family could be informed and encouraged to invest substantially in what would be a multimillion-dollar outlay for both the renovation and connection space. Little did we know, that in the time approaching our kick off, our country would enter a serious recession. 2008 for many of our members was a sheer disaster financially. People lost jobs. Some who owned businesses suffered substantial losses. Everyone was hit by this crisis. Should we pull the plug on what we felt God was telling us to do?

Because we felt that God had clearly spoken to us, we proceeded with prayerful enthusiasm. What God did was amazing. Every part of each phase of the project started and finished in the black. Near the end of the total project, we took out a line of credit which was completely paid off in less than five years from the project's inception.

To this day, our church is thankful that God made clear what He wanted us to do. Having heard from Him, it was exciting to take action and not fear what might happen even when our country went into a financial tailspin. During this time, we didn't have to cut back on our giving to our global mission's partnerships nor reduce the number of paid staff in our local ministry. Our children's area is a blessing and our connection space turned into the most amazing destination café that is filled to capacity throughout each day. On Sundays and throughout the week, both spaces are used and enjoyed by our members and these spaces are tremendous tools to reach people with the gospel of Jesus Christ. God meets us in the moments of our desperation and if we're listening, he'll show us what to do.

We've seen our need to fess up to our flaws, fuel our faith and there's something else in Gideon's story that is helpful in understanding how to protect our awareness of God's presence in our lives especially during the attack of the enemy.

We need to face our fears

In the next movement of Gideon's story (Judges 7:1-25), we read of the obvious fear that Gideon and all Israel had toward the dreaded Midianites, Amalekites and other eastern people opposing Israel. Experiencing the presence of God will always mean that we face our fears and see what God is going to do.

There are a few common fears that always seem to come up when going forward in the will of God, especially when we are questioning God's presence.

Our fear might have something to do with our provision

This is the heart of this story. Gideon assembles an army to go up against all the raiding armies of the East. He musters 32,000 soldiers from Israel. He knew that even with the size of Israel's army, they were far outnumbered by the armies surrounding them. Bible scholars estimate that the number of their oppressors totaled somewhere around 120,000 which means they were outnumbered 4 to 1 in the upcoming contest. But God was on their side and if God is for us, who can be against us, right?

Then God does something to make matters feel worse for Gideon. He tells Gideon, *"You have too many men for me to deliver Midian into their hands. In order that Israel may not boast against me that her own strength has saved her, announce now to the people, 'Anyone who trembles with fear may turn back and leave Mount*

Gilead" (7:2-3). Whenever I've read this part of the story, I think to myself, "I'd probably be one of those who trembled with fear so I would be going home." I discover I wouldn't have been alone. Twenty-two thousand Israelites decide they are too afraid to fight, so they go home! Gideon is down to ten thousand soldiers and so the fighting ratio has risen to about 12 to 1.

God isn't finished. "Still too many!" God tells Gideon. He prompts a little test to weed out more of Gideon's army and by the time the test was over, Gideon is standing there with only 300 men for the battle. Now the odds are mathematically ridiculous. Do you know what God loves to do? He loves to show us that it doesn't matter what we think we bring to the table; it's all about Him and what He brings to the table! This is because in the end, God wants all the glory.

If you are fearing that you don't have enough for what God is telling you to do, don't be afraid. If God is in it, this is all that matters. God doesn't need a strong economy to build a connection space in the local church. He doesn't need anything from us besides our willing obedience. In fact, it's more exciting when there seems to not be enough at the outset. Like the fish and loaves, just watch what God can do with the little we have at the beginning. But you better be sure God is in what you are attempting to do, or your presumption can lead to disaster.

Our fear might have something to do with our poise

How do we maintain confidence when things look so overwhelming? People who really know God's presence seem to be unflappable when the chips are down. Show me someone who is dealing with a frightening situation without the confidence of God's presence and I'll show you someone totally freaking out! I know because I've been in both scenarios. If I believe God is with me, no problem. If I think I'm alone, it is a whole different story.

It's so easy to become unraveled and lose our poise. In Judges 7:9-15, God knows that Gideon needs to be confident and keep his poise because he's the leader of the 300 member special ops team. God tells him that "if you are afraid to attack, go down to the camp with your servant...and listen to what they are saying." God knows a way to put poise into Gideon's charge to battle. He's going to do this by letting the army do a little eavesdropping on a conversation in the enemy's camp. Gideon and his servant sneak down to the outskirts of the camp and he overhears someone say, *"I had a bad dream—and it means that God has given Midian into the hands of Gideon"* (see Judges 7:13-14).

Gideon regains his poise and is now ready to roll. Pack up, assemble the troops, devise a strategy and head out to battle! Right? Wrong! The first thing Gideon does is worship God. God knows the times in our lives when we need to hear things that only he can arrange so we will give Him glory.

Our fear might have something to do with our plan

I like how Gideon springs into action and quickly divides his men into three companies. His plan is a basic "surprise" attack with a lot of extra noise added by smashing jars and blowing trumpets. In ancient times, trumpets were used to signal troops for battle. Three hundred trumpets blasting all at once would have told the enemy that they were about to be pounced on by an innumerable force. The crashing of the jars no doubt added to the sound sensation. Even with these ideas, let's remember that the Sovereign God was on the move—and when He moves, there's no stopping him.

God didn't tell Gideon how to do all this; so he creates a plan he feels will work. I don't want to stretch this too far, but sometimes when we fear, we dwell much too long on our plan, tweaking this and that, hesitating until everything is perfect. Going to battle requires one fundamental thing: Moving out! Showing up! Knowing that God shows up to reveal his power and glory. Whatever Gideon might have felt about his plan; he knew that God Almighty was with him. The Lord of heaven's armies would meet him in the fight.

God loves to reveal his power simply as we commit to just showing up to face our enemies. See what it says in Judges 7:21, *"Each man held his position around the camp, all the Midianites ran, crying out as they fled...when the three hundred trumpets sounded, the LORD caused the men throughout the camp to turn on each other with their sword..."* Only God could do something like this. It wasn't because Gideon was so clever and figured out what to do. God came alongside of Israel's plan and as they showed up, He did, too. The battle was won by God's power not Gideon's plan.

I want to challenge and encourage those of you who are in a spiritual battle and have gone to the drawing board again and again, revising your plan many times but are still in the same place as you were previously without any victory. Your plan is not as important as God's power. We show up knowing God will, too.

The Bible calls this faith. The writer of Hebrews puts it this way, *"Now faith is being sure of what we hope for and certain of what we do not see" (Hebrews 11:1).* We fight our spiritual battles with faith and belief in God's presence, just like Gideon did, even though it took him a while to be sure of this. If we feel like we've struggled too long, at least be encouraged by what we learn from Gideon's story. God is showing us through this short season of Israel's history that experiencing the presence of God is crucial for the spiritual battles we face.

CHAPTER 5: YOU'RE NOT ALONE
DISCUSSION QUESTIONS

1. Why does our sense of God's presence diminish when we choose to sin and are unrepentant?

2. How does confession and repentance of sin open the door for our awareness of God's presence in our lives? Has there been a time in your life when confessing your need for Him opened a new understanding of His presence for you?

3. In the midst of Gideon's practical dilemma and wanting to be assured that God's presence was directing him, he brings God an offering and he chooses to worship. How does this inform the way we must seek a greater awareness of God's presence when we encounter seasons of trials and adversity—even when those trials result from our own sin?

4. What does Gideon's charge to destroy the altar of Baal in order to build a proper one to God (Judges 6:25-27) tell us about how we are to leave our idols and follow Him as a means to a renewed awareness of His presence?

5. Gideon seems to need extra assurance that God was with him. How is this similar or dissimilar to the way you follow the Lord daily?

6. Why is it important to face our fears rather than run from them? How is this seen in Gideon's example? How is this seen in your life?

CHAPTER 6

THE POWER OF PRAISE
The Role of Worship in Spiritual Warfare

The high school I attended had an amazing football team. As is the case in many high schools, the most popular kids on campus are athletes. And for Carlmont High School where I attended, this was true, too. While there were other notable athletic programs at our school, football was ranked highest in popularity among most students who attended there—at least from what I observed. Football players carry themselves in ways that appear intimidating to non-athletic types. Wearing their football jerseys alone carried a kind of emblem that seemed to open social doors of popularity among their peers. There were a few players on our team that were eventually drafted into the NFL. These guys were physically strong, determined, full of self-confidence and if you ever found yourself on the wrong side of some issue that was important to them, you were in trouble.

I suppose that also meant that if you found yourself on the right side of some issue that was important to them, you had it made. For most of us, high school was a place where if you were in the right crowd, you were safe. If not, all bets were off. Remember?

I was in the school band. I started learning to play the trumpet when I was in third grade and enjoyed the instrument very much. From middle school through high school, my course electives always included band. In middle school it was called concert band. In high school, it was symphonic orchestra and for those of us who played the needed instruments and had enough talent, it was jazz band. I had the privilege of playing in both symphonic orchestra and jazz band throughout all four years at Carlmont High School.

103

Our band would faithfully accompany our football team to their games. As they made their way onto the field to prepare to do battle with their opponent, we'd make our way to the bleachers, and prepare our instruments to play our hearts out. We viewed our contribution critical for the team's success. Everyone knows that a school's pep band is the key to winning football games! Somehow the football players never viewed us in quite the same way. In my four years of going to every game and screaming out high notes to popular fight songs, I never heard one of our players after a game say to any of us in the band, "Thanks...we couldn't have won that game without you guys!"

Among fellow musicians, we saw each other as being pretty cool, but among the other subcultures of our high school campus, we were considered nerds. There's just something about being in the band that, at least at the time I was an adolescent, didn't muster the same kind of social platform as being on the football team. That was back then; maybe things have changed.

Perhaps you know exactly what I mean because you were either in band or an athlete or perhaps you were both in high school, or you're just skilled at making observations. You recognize the differences that students see in each other on a high school campus. Even if you aren't tracking much with this comparison between band people and the football squad, you probably can understand how counterintuitive it feels to assume worship somehow plays a significant role in obtaining victory on the spiritual battlefield. For reasons we will examine briefly in this chapter, God seems to use some forms of worshipful expressions as a key element for gaining ground and ultimately having victory in our spiritual battles. This chapter will examine the role of worship as a means of addressing spiritual warfare, and specifically, the power that praise to God demonstrates when encountering our enemy.

I realize I may have just lost some reading these words when suggesting the role of worship and praise to God has a place in spiritual warfare. If I've lost you, or am losing you right here, it may be because some of us simply equate worship with musical themes exclusively. Because many people aren't very musically minded, the argument may not seem relevant. We may not be able to play an instrument and when it comes to singing, we can't carry a tune. If this is you, it might even be that your view of singing in church is generally unimportant even if you enjoy hearing others participate musically.

I grew up in a church where the pastor called the musical worship portion of the church service *preliminaries*. The main event for him was the preaching element and, don't get me wrong, I think preaching is important, too, but is worship and musical praise less important or even unimportant to God when it comes to public worship? Is there any connection between our public worship and the victory we need when fighting spiritual forces? I would suggest that worship (whether musical or simply praise from the heart) is not only important, it's essential. Many of us have never really seen or understood from Scripture, the importance of worship. That's what I'd like to explore with you now.

When I say that worship is essential, you should also know what I don't mean. I don't mean that music alone or the style of the music or the era in which it was written is essential. Music and style may have some bearing on how quickly or fully I might engage in some expressions of worship, but it really isn't the most important thing about it. I also don't mean that one's *ability to sing* is critical to engaging in true worship. Your vocal ability may be of benefit to the person standing near you, but in the bigger picture, and certainly from God's point of view, your vocal ability is irrelevant to the point I wish to convey. One of my favorite verses concerning musical worship from both an instrumentalist and one who does like to sing is *"Make a joyful noise to the Lord!" (Psalm 66:1; 95:2).* Not everyone can sing beautifully, but we can all make some noise. Sometimes as our worship services would commence in the church where

I've pastored, I would feel my spirit wanting to shout, *"Let's make some noise and put the enemy to flight!"*

A couple of chapters back I mentioned a house church pastors' gathering in China where a fellow pastor and I had the privilege of attending a few years ago. There were fifty or more leaders who had traveled a long distance to come to a little compound for training. We stayed for a couple of days, tucked away inconspicuously in a remote village so as not to draw attention from the authorities, and, in addition to spending time studying the Bible together, we sang praises to God. I can still remember the power of our times of praise with those pastors! I couldn't understand a word they were singing nor were any of the melodies recognizable to me. For the most part, there were no standout vocalists among them. But without any amplification, their vocal chords raised the roof on this little compound. Off key, loud, and all over the place musically, but oh my, it was amazing! The praise was so passionate and unbridled. It was so beautiful; it brought tears to my eyes! I can't imagine how beautiful this must have sounded to God. I can only imagine how intimidating it would have been for any evil spiritual forces listening in that day. Tears, weeping, joy and laughter, with the kind of adoration that frankly made me wonder if I had ever before praised God this way. There is something very powerful about musical worship.

Praising God through musical worship is a powerful weapon whenever we find ourselves engaged in spiritual warfare. I want to offer six reasons why this is true. These come easily to me when I think of places in Scripture where there seems an obvious connection between worship and praise to God, and the spiritual battles in which people in these Scripture stories were engaged.

Praise to God realigns our hearts to His character

Our brief examination takes us first to the psalms. The book of Psalm is essentially a collection of hymns, written primarily by King David in response to the spiritual battles he faced as a shepherd boy, a leader in the making and finally, as the King of Israel. Others contribute as well to this amazing section of Holy Scripture such as Solomon, Aseph, Sons of Korah, Ethan, Moses and a few others. In total, there are 150 psalms, (or hymns) from which God's people have used to realign their hearts to God under the most extreme circumstances—not the least of which—when encountering some form of spiritual warfare. Today's praise songs reflect a lyrical content very similar to themes that the psalms bring to a worshipper.

Notice David's call to worship in Psalm 8: *"O LORD, our Lord, how majestic is your name in all the earth" (Psalm 8:1)!* As he continues we get a glimpse of the importance of song in extolling God's character but also the intended purpose in doing so: *"From the lips of children and infants you have ordained praise because of your enemies, to silence the foe and the avenger..." (Psalm 8:2).* When David suggests that declaring God's majesty will *silence the foe and the avenger..."* he's inferring that invoking this truth is to arm oneself for spiritual battle. Praise to God silences the spiritual opposition that seeks to bring havoc in our lives.

David, the biggest contributor to the Psalms, often repeats his anticipation of how God will use his worshipful praise to do amazing things. For example, listen to David's anticipation of this as recorded in Psalm 40: *"I waited patiently for the LORD; he turned to me and heard my cry. He lifted me out of the slimy pit, out of the mud and mire; he set my feet on a rock and gave me a firm place to stand. He put a new song in my mouth, a hymn of praise to our God. Many will see and fear and put their trust in the LORD" (Psalm 40:1-3).* David realizes that it's God who puts the song in his heart to sing back to him in praise, and he anticipates many discovering the worthiness of God and putting their trust in Him.

Throughout the book of Psalms, one is reminded of God's character and the value of focusing on Him throughout each day. Praise and worship to Almighty God must not be relegated to twenty or thirty minutes in a worship service on Sunday. There's power in praise throughout each day. See this in Psalm 92: *"It is good to praise the Lord and make music to your name, O Most High, to proclaim your love in the morning and your faithfulness at night" (Psalm 92:1-2).* Proclaiming God's love and faithfulness is good to do throughout each day. The Psalmist suggests that it's good to do while making "music" to [His] name" (v.1).

In short, psalms are simply lyrics of songs that we can sing to the Lord in any situation. Considering our theme, many hymns and contemporary worship songs emulate the same kind of trust, hope, waiting, expecting, honoring, glorifying and extolling God's character as they did back then. Hymnody, unless using the very words of God, doesn't carry the same weight as Scripture, but are still powerful ways to put the enemy to flight. We should appreciate the great hymn writers, both past and present, who have helped us do what the psalms have done in worshippers for millennia: to align (or realign) our hearts with God's character when we feel the enemy lurking.

When we drive in our car (or wherever we enjoy singing) and sing along with praise songs, we are helping guide our hearts back to the sweet center of God's character. We are reminded that God is good even when our circumstances are not. We are reminded that with God there are true riches. He invites us to eat from his abundance when we are hungry and famished from the emptiness of our world. Sometimes as I listen to praise music as I go about my day, I'm overwhelmed by God's love for me, His purposes through Christ and His mercy and grace. It's often that I'm overwhelmed by emotion.

108

When things are difficult or challenging, as they can be for any of us, we have a great opportunity to simply offer our praise and worship to God through song. Don't stay away from praise. Give it to God with your words and your song in prayer and praise and you will discover beauty and power in it. The writer of Hebrews proclaims, *"Through Jesus, therefore, let us continually offer to God a sacrifice of praise—the fruit of lips that confess his name" (Hebrews 13:15).* To continually offer God the sacrifice of praise shows the importance of building this expression into the rhythms of each day.

This should happen in church, too. When we participate in musical worship we're not just passing time or trying to create an emotional response where human influence can shape our view of life. Rather, in this precious time together as a spiritual family, we are realigning our hearts to God's character. We rehearse his acceptance of us through Christ His Son and are reminded of his longing and delight for us to know and walk in His ways.

Praise to God reinforces some fundamental convictions we need when we are in a spiritual battle

I love the story of King Jehoshaphat. It's found in 2 Chronicles 20:15-22. In fact, I love this story so much I'll be coming back to it in a later chapter when we start working on building our confidence for fighting in the spiritual realm. The story takes the reader through the highs and lows of dealing with opposition and desperate situations, and along the way, it points out some fundamental convictions needed when we are in spiritual battles. I find in this story three things that are so important to hold on to when facing a spiritual attack. Let me give you a quick background to the story and then I'll suggest these things on which we need a tighter grip.

King Jehoshaphat hears of an invasion that is coming from a vast army—a people whom Israel had shown mercy when entering the promised land. King Jehoshaphat is terrified along with everyone else in

109

Israel. The king calls everyone to fast and pray. It's amazing what we are willing to do when we face desperate situations. King Jehoshaphat prays an amazing prayer extolling God's character (much like we find in the psalms) and God's Spirit lands on a man named Jahaziel who gives the King and the people a direct message from God; and don't forget, by extension, is a direct message for us as well. In this message, we find the three things that need a tighter hold in our lives when facing spiritual attack.

God's stake in the battle is far greater than our own

Read the prophet's challenge: ***"Do not be afraid or discouraged because of this vast army. For the battle is not yours, but God's"*** *(2 Chronicles 20:17).* When we face spiritual battles, we need a tighter grip on believing that the battle we are in belongs primarily to God. We're involved. We have responsibility, but God's stake and portion is far greater than our own.

All spiritual battles are fundamentally a part of a much bigger picture. In the end, our battle is a mere reflection of the greater and more substantive battle that is being pitched between God and Satan. It isn't easy for us to understand the purpose God has in allowing the enemy to wage war against us as he does, but we can take courage knowing that the biggest stake holder in all of what happens is God himself.

Once I see and believe that what's happening in my life is a mere extension of what's happening in the heavenly realm between the Almighty and Satan, I can relax a little knowing that I'm on the right side of things. After all, God's win column is stellar. I may lose some of the skirmishes that arise, but the victory will be God's in the end because I belong to the One who will judge all unrighteousness and wickedness and cause whatever I'm dealing with to work out for my good and His glory (Romans 8:28).

It's our job to stand at our post and it's God's job to deliver

As I've already pointed out in the introduction of this book, I'm not a fighter by nature so I love verse 17: ***"You will not have to fight this battle. Take up your positions; stand firm and see the deliverance the Lord will give you…go out to face them tomorrow and the Lord will be with you…" (2 Chronicles 20:17b).*** What great assurance for those in the fight. There is one who fights *for us.* I love how the prophet Isaiah reminds us that the one fighting for his people is Jesus Himself— the suffering servant who is extolled in the servant songs of the prophet: ***"Sing to the LORD a new song, his praise from the ends of the earth…The LORD will march out like a mighty man, like a warrior he will stir up his zeal; with a shout he will raise the battle cry and will triumph over his enemies" (Isaiah 42:10a, 13).***

Isn't it amazing to have one who fights for us? When I was a young boy, my oldest sister would occasionally step in to fight my battle against a neighborhood bully where we lived. One of those fights stands out in my memory. The bully had threatened he was going to beat me up the next day. My sister got wind of this and waited in the bushes (unbeknownst to me) for him to show aggression (which he did) before she stepped out and clobbered him. I've never seen a young woman her age punch a guy in the face and I think it came as a surprise to the kid who was bullying me, too. From that day on, I always felt safe whenever she was around knowing that no one dared touch me or else they would have to deal with my sister! She had my back. God has our back, too.

How does this work? Notice that the prophet tells the King and the people, ***"Take your positions; stand firm and see the deliverance the Lord will give you…" (v.17).*** *"Taking your positions"* is another way of saying, *trust God to do his part if you report for duty.* So often we suddenly stop doing important things when we are under spiritual attack. We stop praying. We stop reading our Bibles. We stop going to church. Spiritual warfare often causes many of us to stop doing what we know is needed.

Survivor of the Holocaust, Corrie ten Boom, was known to have said, "When a Christian shuns fellowship with other Christians, the devil smiles. When he stops studying the Bible, the devil laughs. When he stops praying, the devil shouts for joy." Whenever this happens, it's revealing that we have stopped trusting God to do His part. At times, the fear of our enemy or the fight itself causes us to leave our positions—or to just give up. When this happens, some have a hard time finding their way back. Maybe that's you.

In King Jehoshaphat's story, we discover the importance of standing at our post. That's our part. When I was growing up, a popular statement to a person needing to get busy with his job was, "Just don't stand there, DO SOMETHING." The reverse is true in King Jehoshaphat's story: "Don't just do something, STAND THERE." This simple act applies to so many aspects of becoming more proficient in fighting the good fight. It's so important for us to focus on what God calls us to do—the most important of which is to take our stand—to be unmovable. Good parents stay at their post even when their teenager is giving them trouble or telling them to go away. Their involvement in their son's life isn't based on his wishes for their involvement. Staying "present" when our kids want nothing to do with us isn't easy, but it's one of the ways we show our love to them. In a similar way, this is often when God steps in and does his best work.

When I was just out of high school, I was rebelling toward how my parents viewed a gal I was dating. I felt we were in love and my parents strongly urged me to think a little more about what I was doing. They knew my penchant for romanticism might lead me to rushing into a relationship too quickly which I would eventually regret. In my stupidity, I was considering making a deeper commitment to her regardless of what they had to say about it. We had a few big arguments over this and it got messy to the point of not talking to each other about the relationship.

Keep in mind, that during this time I was attending a Christian university and pursuing a career in ministry. Yikes!

I'm sure my parents saw my stiff-necked rebellion and probably came very close to meddling in the situation. They probably felt they needed to do something, but what? They also knew I was coming to the age when not a lot can be said and their best work now would likely be taking the matter to God and staying at their post. I'll never forget one night coming home from a date with my girlfriend after I had dropped her off at her dorm room hoping that my parents would already be in bed so I could just continue nursing my belief that she was the one for me. As I tiptoed into the house, there was my dad, sitting in the kitchen quietly reading his Bible. He hardly greeted me—but his quietness wasn't from any perception of being mean-spirited or angry toward me. In fact, I felt loved when I walked past him and headed to my room. Why did I feel this way? My dad was standing his post, letting God fight this battle.

As I climbed into bed, I couldn't get the picture of my dad reading the Bible out of my head. I couldn't sleep either. I tossed and turned all night. I don't know how it happened, but the next morning when I woke up, I just knew my parents were right about their concern for my relationship with my girlfriend and knew I needed to break things off—which I did soon afterwards. It didn't take me too long afterwards to see what they had seen. Had I ignored their concerns and did what I wanted to do, I think I would have had deep regrets. In turn, I saved this gal from making a dreadful mistake, too. I thank God for the way he delivered me (and them) in that situation.

My parents stood at their post by remaining in prayer and giving me space even when they were against what I was doing. They did their part, allowing God to do His. I tried to practice this principle with my own kids when they were going through seasons of rebellion with me or my wife or God. While we didn't always see immediate change or victories for us or them, through continual prayer and loving them regardless of their choices, I can attest to God's beautiful and timely manner in maturing them into the persons they are today. We are all still a "work in progress."

Sometimes married couples in crisis want to meet with me because they can't afford a professional counselor (or they don't want to spend the money). I usually find out that the issues are far too complicated for me to solve through meeting with them once or twice. I'm reminded to stand at my post and watch what God will do. I soon discover there are a lot of variables and obstacles, but many times right there in the moment, I feel the pleasure of the Father leading a couple back toward wanting to work on things. They leave our meeting with hope. I stand at my post, but God shows up and does the heavy lifting.

As a chaplain in a local fire department, I'm often sent to situations where there has been an unexpected death. Nothing is more emotionally difficult than knowing I am on my way to a house to meet parents who have just lost their six-month old to SIDS; or I'm in route to an uncontrollable and emotional mother whose teenage son took his life in his bedroom before she arrived home from work. As I drive toward these kinds of situations, I pray, "Lord, I'm staying at my post—the rest is up to you." I often drive back home a few hours later seeing how God did remarkable things and made his presence known; how his mercy and tenderness was apparent even in the darkest moment of someone's life.

Maybe your circumstances right now are nudging you to go offline; to "check out" for a while from those who need you most. Take the message from King Jehoshaphat and decide to take your position and let God take His. Give God a chance to do what He does best; you might just be surprised at what God can do. We'll see later in the book, staying at our post will build our confidence for future skirmishes, too.

Praise must be given its rightful place at the start of the matter

I see a little humor here in the story of King Jehoshaphat. After the consultation with the messenger he ***"...appointed men to sing to the LORD and to praise him for the splendor of his holiness as they went out at the head of the army, saying, "Give thanks to the LORD, for his love endures forever" (2 Chronicles 20:21).*** Let me point out that if praise doesn't lead the way when we face trails and spiritual conflicts, there's going to be issues all the way along that will twist us up and keep us off track. At the core of praise is trust; the belief that God is working out His plan for our lives. This is why we must praise God first—right as the conflict ensues. Praise is a statement of trust. We're saying to God, "I know your purposes will stand and that in your perfect time, you will deliver me, so I will worship you now!" God wants this response from us because without faith, it's impossible to please Him (Hebrews 11:2).

Our trust should be deep enough to also produce joy in our lives. The Apostle James exhorted, ***"Consider it pure joy, my brothers, whenever you face trails of many kinds..." (James 1:2).*** Like the armies of Jehoshaphat, we can set out to do battle with the enemy giving thanks to the LORD because his love endures forever. Look what happens as Jehoshaphat's army shows up for battle singing praise to God: ***"As they began to sing and praise, the LORD set ambushes against the men of Ammon and Moab..." (2 Chronicles 20:22).*** God sets the ambushes against Jehoshaphat's enemies. We can trust God to do this for us, too.

Praise to God expresses a willingness to accept difficulties and hardships

We won't spend much time on this since we considered Job at length in the previous chapter. Our topic is the power of praise when encountering spiritual warfare, and Job's story illustrates this. When Job learns of his tragic and incomprehensible losses, he models something that is extraordinary and relevant to the subject of this chapter—he *worships* God. The text says, **"At this, Job got up and tore his robe and shaved his head. Then he fell to the ground in worship and said, 'Naked I came from my mother's womb, and naked I will depart. The LORD gave and the LORD has taken away; may the name of the Lord be praised'"** (Job 1:20-21).

This is the power of worshipful praise to God. Whether it is musical or not, it's an expression of accepting those *things we are powerless to change in our lives—no matter how severe or consequential they are.* We all have things in our lives we wish had turned out differently. Perhaps there are things in our lives that we wish had never happened at all. Life is full of disappointments and even regrets. Ever since the fall of humanity, we've lived in a broken world—a brokenness that God set in motion to restore from that very moment. Praising God through worship is an expression of one's willingness to move forward, regardless, and even with trust and joy in our hearts and on our lips. To keep trusting and waiting, even in the darkest moments, knowing that God will meet us there.

When I'm choosing to praise God when life feels hard to me (I feel so wimpy at times), I feel God's presence, giving me the assurance I need as if I can hear Him say, "Trust me." In that very moment, I feel I've wandered into a sacred space where God has been waiting to meet me.

When my mom entered glory in 2000, I was with my kids back in Minnesota. She was in a hospital on the Peninsula near the home where I grew up when she finished her fight. The physical distance between me and her when she entered glory somehow reduced the emotional response when getting the news of her passing. I remember my sister, whom I was visiting at the time, waking me up in the middle of the night to tell me she had died. In some ways, it was a relief to hear, as she had suffered a massive stroke the week before and had become less responsive each day. God showed mercy and took her home.

Six years later, I remember getting a call from a neighbor who lived across the street from my dad telling me that she was concerned because a fire engine and a police car had been in front of his house for a while. Judy had to make several calls to track down my phone number and wanted me to know what was happening. Even Judy didn't know what I knew in that very moment. My experience working with the fire department informed me that my dad had also entered glory since a police car was called to a medical scene. After a brief embrace and tearful prayer together with my wife, I got into my car and drove to my dad's house about thirty minutes away. My heart was filled with a range of emotions as I drove across the San Mateo Bridge that Tuesday afternoon in April. My dad and I were so close. I loved him dearly. The impact of losing him felt overwhelming. Losing one's parent, especially when it is the last physical parent one has is very unsettling. But in that moment, I felt the Spirit invite me into worship. As I drove across the bridge alone in my car, I cried out in praise to God for the blessing of my dad and late mom— their love and care for me and my siblings. I felt overwhelmed by the goodness of God.

When I arrived at his house, some neighbors had gathered waiting for me. They already knew he had died and I'm sure they wanted to comfort me, but I was already comforted with an immeasurable comfort from God Himself.

Praise to God somehow subdues the power and influence of Satanic forces

It appears from at least one story in the Old Testament that evil spirits cannot tolerate praise directed toward God. Offering praise to God may be the most effective way to dispel malevolent influences in our lives. I see this in the account of King Saul's torment by an evil spirit that is only subdued when young David comes into the king's chambers with his harp playing music for Saul.

If you know the story, it's curious how it is possible that God would send an evil spirit to torment Saul. From an Old Testament perspective, we need to remember that even Satan and his demons are under the sovereign rule of God; they only function within the bounds of God's rule, no more and no less. Saul's disobedience to God had invited the evil spirits that God sent in judgment against him and eventually, the fall of his kingdom. Saul begins spiraling down in a murderous plot against David, probably psychologically and mentally seduced by these evil spirits in the first place.

This subjection of evil spirits to God is seen in the gospels when demons beg Jesus not to cast them into the Abyss (a kind of spiritual prison for demons) but instead, into a herd of swine (Mark 5:12). Evil spirits are always subject to God. The historian who wrote 1 Samuel records that *"an evil spirit from the Lord tormented him" (1 Samuel 16:14).* David provided music that soothed Saul's troubled heart. It makes sense that if David's music was an expression of his worship to God, then it could soothe the heart of a wild and wicked man who had lost his spiritual bearings. If this was true during the time of the Old Covenant, how much more under the New Covenant might we expect praise to play a part in soothing one's soul and sending evil influences away! Note how the writer describes what took place: *"Whenever the spirit from God came upon Saul, David would take his harp and play. Then relief would come to Saul; he would feel better, and the evil spirit would leave him" (1 Samuel 16:23).*

I'm not suggesting that music alone, or even praise music to God is always the simple answer for sending evil spirits away. There's something here that merits consideration.

Praise to God often allows a breakthrough in our faith journey

I love the story of Joshua taking the city of Jericho. God tells him to march around the city for seven straight days carrying the ark and sounding the trumpet (all an expression of worship). Then on the seventh day, Joshua was to march around it seven times and after the seventh time give a shout and the wall of the city would collapse (Joshua 6:20). I see a picture here of breakthrough power that comes through musical worship and the shout of praise.

Acts 16 also tells the story of when Paul and Silas were in jail and at midnight as they are praying and singing praises to God (Acts 16:25), suddenly, a great earthquake happens and the jail doors fly open and Paul and Silas' chains fall off! I see a metaphor for breaking out of things that hold us as prisoners. Addictions, behavior patterns, the bondage of unforgiveness, in fact, any chains holding us back from what God wants in our lives, can break as we choose to give our praise to God.

In both Biblical stories, there's a clear connection between the people's praise and the breakthrough that follows. If you are in a place where you find yourself up against a wall needing a breakthrough, why not begin to praise God with full abandon and watch what He might do in your life! Not long ago, I found myself fuming over some things that were getting me down. I felt hemmed in, emotionally trapped and fearful. My flesh wanted me do something about it, but I knew that if I listened to my flesh, I'd regret my actions and probably make things worse. I heard the Spirit whisper, "Take a bike ride and worship God."

So, I got up, put on my cycling clothes and hit the road. I put a playlist of some of my favorite praise music and as I road along a country road near my house listening to the lyrics of contemporary music artist, Lauren Daigle, I felt God giving me breakthrough. I heard so clearly God's spirit speaking to me with these expressions: "Why are you so worried? Don't you think I can take care of what you are worried about? Trust me, you know my love for you will be enough." "There's no way to fix this on your own, you need me—and in my time, I will heal and make what you are stressing about something beautiful in your own story." Sometimes the lyrics of songs sung by a talented Christian artist feels like God is speaking directly to me. When I got back to my home about an hour later, I felt completely relieved and at peace. All fear and concern was gone. My chains were broken and I was free!

Praise serves as a prelude for what's coming for all those who belong to Jesus Christ

One can't read through the book of Revelation without being moved by what the saints in heaven will be doing for eternity. There we read that praise-filled worship is going to be a huge part of what we'll be doing in heaven. I sometimes tease, that as a pastor, I'm out of a job when I get to heaven, but our worship pastor is going to be busy!

I'm sure none of us can fathom all of what heaven will be like, but we are inspired by the words of the Apostle John who saw a glimpse of heaven and recorded these words, *"Then I heard the voice of many angels, numbering thousands and thousands, and ten thousand times ten thousand. They encircled the throne and the living creatures and the elders. In a loud voice they sang: 'Worthy is the Lamb, who was slain, to receive power and wealth and wisdom and strength and honor and glory and praise!' Then I heard every creature in heaven and earth and under the earth and on the sea, and all that is in them, singing: 'To Him who sits on the throne and to the Lamb be praise and honor and glory and power, forever and ever!' The four living creatures said, 'Amen,' and the elders fell down and worshiped" (Revelation 5:11-14).*

It appears that we'll be doing some singing in heaven! When I am enthralled with the glory of God during one of our worship services where the music is so beautiful, I feel I've gotten a little glimpse of heaven itself. It makes me yearn for that moment when we will all be standing alongside of angels and fellow saints worshipping God with our voices and song. The crescendo of history and the culmination of the ages is recorded in Scripture as a symphony of praise and adoration of the one true God!

Hallelujah! What better way to close the canon of Scripture than with a reminder of the spiritual war that has waged for millennia has come to an end and God will sit victoriously on this throne.

This is a good place to close this chapter and let me invite you right now, before moving on, to engage in some real heart-felt praise to God!

CHAPTER 6: THE POWER OF PRAISE
DISCUSSION QUESTIONS

1. Why is it important to be reminded of God's character when we are under spiritual attack? How does a posture of worship—even musical worship—help you personally focus on God's character when under spiritual attack? What other ways do you remind yourself of God's character when you feel attacked spiritually?

2. This chapter mentioned a few ways to fuel our faith when we are under spiritual attack. Which way is particularly important for the season of testing you are currently in?

3. When Job undergoes tragic loss, he chooses to worship God. When have you witnessed or experienced a similar response to a tragic loss?

4. Why do you suppose worship subdues Satanic forces whenever God's people choose to engage in it? How have you found this true in your life?

5. How does worship help us have breakthrough when we feel stuck or when obstacles are in our path? How do you see this principle in Paul and Silas' experience in jail? (See Acts 16:25-30)

6. How does the thought of worshipping God in heaven connect with you today? What aspects of worship are likely to be different there than they are here?

CHAPTER 7

WEAR THE ARMOR
The Believer's Protection Against Spiritual Attack

It is the fiercest of all battles. Casualties lie everywhere. The sophistication of the enemy is without rival. Of whom do I refer? Insurgents in a politically unstable or hostile land? A ruthless dictator ravaging an oppressed people? Al Qaeda's malefic brainchild of terror? None of these even come close to the peril with which Christ-followers are confronted daily—even moment by moment. And what makes this battle so perilous is that it isn't detectable in the physical realm. It is completely invisible, waged in the realm of the unfamiliar, and for this reason many consider it unreal.

Nearing the close of his letter to the Ephesian believers, Paul wants to be sure believers are reminded of the spiritual battle that is being waged against them—and more, what can be done about it.

We often wrongly identify the nature of our real struggle as believers. We are tempted to assume it is found in things like dealing with an unruly employee, a difficult neighbor, an uncaring boss, a rebellious teenager or some personal problem we've had little success overcoming. Without discounting the seriousness of these struggles, the true enemy of our souls is the devil, and the battle he wages against us takes place in the spiritual realm (Ephesians 6:12).

When we witness conflicts and hassles in the physical realm, these are signs that there is likely a disturbance going on in the spiritual dimension. Because of the nature of our adversary and the battle pitched against us, we sometimes respond inappropriately. We may become either too casual or overconfident, assuming we are invincible and Satan's schemes too predictable. Or we become overwhelmed and fearful, assuming we are doomed. Neither of these perspectives help us take our stand against the attack.

The best way to handle our spiritual enemy is to be sure we are wearing the full armor God provides for our protection. Paul's words in Ephesians 6:10-18 convey the importance of wearing the armor God has provided for us in order to stand our ground when under the enemy's attack.

Every believer has a complete suit of spiritual body armor ready to be donned. All we need to do is put it on. Paul's exhortation, *"Put on the full armor of God..." (Ephesians 6:11)* describes how we can be clad from head to foot with all the protection we need as we step into the battlefield each day. The goal of donning this suit of armor is so that when the devil has attempted his worst with our lives, we are able to stand (Ephesians 6:11, 13, 14).

Can you imagine how foolish it would be if a soldier in the US military serving in hostile areas were to forego wearing the protection he's been provided? If the enemy knows a soldier is unprotected, the attack is far more aggressive. Believers sometimes wonder why it feels like the enemy has zeroed in on them when, in the midst of their struggles, it becomes obvious they have not chosen to wear spiritual protection. It won't take the minions in Satan's evil system long to figure out which of us are vulnerable.

I remember years ago reading a news article about the protection many police departments were offering at that time to officers who wanted to wear bullet-proof vests. A certain officer in one city had been shot at point-blank range; because he was not wearing his vest, he died at the scene. The article revealed that vests were optional and officers had to purchase them. This particular officer had considered the option but for whatever reason felt he wouldn't ever be in a situation where he needed it, and that decision cost him his life. Soon after that incident, the department allocated funds to make wearing protective vests while on-duty mandatory. Since that time, virtually every other department has followed suit. Officers are aware that it would be foolish to go on duty without wearing the vest.

Believers ought to view wearing their protection mandatory as well. After all, their protection has already been purchased through Christ's shed blood on the cross. All we need to do is be sure we are wearing it each day. Without doing so, it will only be a matter of time before we are confronted with the unexpected and suffer harm. Am I suggesting one's salvation hangs in the balance, or that the great spiritual battle in which we are now engaged in will be lost? Absolutely not.

God didn't provide us armor in order to preserve our salvation, as if it were possible to be taken away, nor did he give us armor to ensure our ultimate spiritual victory. Both salvation and ultimate spiritual victory are already guaranteed through Christ's life, sacrificial death and resurrection. But along the way to the finish line, our enemy the Devil will set ambushes and skirmishes designed to discourage us and make us feel defeated. The "evil day" is any day where Satan's influences and strategies intersect with our lives. I've had a few days recently when I knew Satan had me in his sights. I know it won't be long until I'm there again, and so will you. Let's be sure that no matter what, we are wearing the armor. Don't be home—or leave home—without it.

Earlier in my ministry, I would run into people who knew me as a youth and before we would get too far in our conversation, I'd be asked, "Larry, are you still into that "Jesus thing?" I would chuckle when telling them, "I am—and so much so that I became a pastor!" From there, the conversation would get more exciting! Behind their question is the assumption that my "religious" experience might have faded since they knew me as a teenager. This assumption is understandable, considering how many people appear to have religious experiences that fade over time.

We all know those who appeared to be followers of Christ at one time or another, but later in life showed little interest in spiritual things.

The Belt of Truth

As Paul considered the invisible, yet very real spiritual battle in which all believers are engaged, he provided inspiration on how to protect themselves. Perhaps as he glanced at the Roman soldier whose assignment was to guard his prison cell, he envisioned the protective spiritual armor that, like that of the soldier, protected him as well. The spiritual analogy between what Paul saw as the soldier's protection and the spiritual armor God provides for every believer must have seemed remarkable to him, so he wrote about it.

Central to the Roman soldier's armor was his belt. Paul considered the believer's spiritual armor also harnessed by a belt, calling it the "belt of truth." For the Roman soldier the belt was the central harness to which the breastplate, sheath and undergarments were secured, offering the quickness of mobility necessary when engaged in hand-to-hand combat. Soldiers only fastened their belts when they were being inspected by an officer, or were on duty or in battle. Paul considered it essential that a believer's protection required wearing and fastening a similar kind of belt, one that keeps everything together as he or she faced an unseen but very real enemy.

The belt of truth is important for our protection. First, the word "truth" (Gr., *aletheia*) can emphasize the content of truth—what a person believes. Certainly believing the right things is great protection for anyone engaged in spiritual battle. But perhaps more importantly, this word can be used in the sense of sincerity (i.e., truthfulness) in our walk with Christ. Without integrity, we run the risk of losing the battle when facing temptation or opposition. In other words, if a believer is not fully committed in his heart to following Jesus in all areas of his life, he becomes especially vulnerable to Satan's attack. A half-hearted

126

engagement in spiritual warfare is always a prescription for spiritual disaster.

Many believers experience repeated defeat in their lives simply because they have difficulty pledging themselves to a high-level commitment to follow Jesus. A less than sincere approach to one's Christian walk leads to all kinds of problems. The point Paul is making isn't to judge the appearance of half-hearted faith, but to urge a clear, no-holds-barred commitment to pursuing a life where truth is one's passion from both a content and attitudinal perspective.

If we are wearing the belt of truth, our commitment to Christ won't be marred by hypocrisy or pretension. What people see in us will be the way we really are. When we fall down in our Christian walk, we won't pretend it didn't happen, instead we will repent and admit to others and to God our sins. When we live as Christ desires, we will be quick to point ourselves and others to God's grace and faithfulness; we won't try to "put on" our Christian faces if our hearts and lives need readjusting. Ours will be a life marked by honesty and integrity. Wearing the belt of truth is choosing to walk with integrity and singleness of purpose. Like the Proverb reminds us, ***"The integrity of the upright guides them, but the unfaithful are destroyed by their duplicity" (Proverbs 11:3).***

It is refreshing to be around believers who are wearing the belt of truth. Their honesty is both compelling and contagious. They don't model perfection—only progress. They want their walk to match their talk. When seekers spend time with believers who fasten the belt of truth, it isn't long before they too are considering the claims of Christ. A life lived for the truth is what pierces the darkness and exposes lost people to the light of Christ. It is the truth that sets a person free (John 8:12). We are reminded as drivers to be sure we are buckled up. Let's be sure we live our lives buckled up, too—with the belt of truth. It could save us when we are under the attack of the enemy.

The Breastplate of Righteousness

If you've ever been hit hard in the chest, you know how much it hurts. I remember a couple of years ago going to a driving range to practice hitting golf balls. I was settling in after hitting several balls reasonably straight and long when I decided to tee one up and really give it a rip. I swung hard, feeling the club face make solid contact with the ball. Unfortunately, the ball left the tee so low that it ricocheted off a railroad tie four feet in front of me and returned to hit me squarely in the middle of my rib cage as I was finishing my swing. The thud and sting from the ball hitting my chest, nearly dropped me to my knees. The pain was excruciating. The only thing that kept me standing upright was my pride, fearing that someone who knew me had witnessed my brilliant shot. I quickly left my basket of balls and went home to lick my wounds.

Soldiers who went into battle during the rule of the Roman empire knew that their bodies were most vulnerable in the chest area, and that without proper protection they would surely suffer defeat in the midst of combat. The Romans had devised a chest of armor—the breastplate—which was worn to protect the soldier's torso, safeguarding his heart, stomach and bowels. If a sword or knife of the enemy were to even slightly penetrate this area it would leave the soldier in such a weakened or bloody state that he could no longer fight or resist attack, sealing his doom.

As Paul considered the importance of this piece of Roman body armor, his thoughts turned toward the believer's need for protection when engaged in the spiritual battle. The enemy loves to hit us where it hurts and there are few areas more vulnerable than our heart. For Paul, the heart represented more than a pump to move blood throughout the body. When considering the "heart" he envisioned the center of one's emotions and convictions. The heart is also the place where our appetites for life are cultivated and satiated. When the believer's emotions, convictions and appetites are being protected, standing his or her ground in the battle is guaranteed.

What specifically protects our hearts? Paul tells us that it is the breastplate of righteousness (Gr., *dikaiosyne*) which, in its context, stands for one's uprightness of character. Some have wrongly assumed that the righteousness of which Paul speaks refers to that which Christ imputes to us when we become saved—that we are protected through Christ's perfect life. This is true (see 1 Corinthians 1:30; 2 Corinthians 5:21), but only to an extent. If our protection is solely the righteousness of Christ that we received at salvation, then the believer would have no need to "put it on" (v. 13). Because the believer in Christ is already clothed with Christ's righteousness, Paul clearly envisioned something more.

Paul is referring to our protection against spiritual attack that results when choosing to live morally upright lives. To the degree we strive to develop our character (made possible only through the imputed righteousness of Christ) we are protecting ourselves from satanic attack. Our convictions, emotions and appetites are kept in line with God's plan for our lives. We find the connection between guarding (protecting) one's heart and the choices which contribute to building character in many Scripture passages. Proverbs 4:23-27 provides exceptionally clear teaching:

> *"Above all else, guard your heart, for it is the wellspring of life. Put away perversity from your mouth; keep corrupt talk far from your lips. Let your eyes look straight ahead, fix your gaze directly before you. Make level paths for your feet and take only ways that are firm. Do not swerve to the right or the left; keep your foot from evil."*

Our heart is protected when we are careful not to use perverse or corrupt words and to make sure we are not letting our eyes look upon things we have no business watching. We are protected when we refrain from walking in places that are spiritually unhealthy for us. Our protection comes when we wear the breastplate of righteousness—choosing to walk upright before the Lord and others, then when Satan comes after us and finds we are protected through Christ's righteousness, he has no power over us. But if we are not choosing to walk uprightly, we set ourselves up for defeat.

As you go out into your day or look back over the one you've finished, see if there is or has been an intentional desire on your part to deepen your character by pursuing godliness in your life. If this is so, you can be thankful the breastplate of righteousness is in place. Let the enemy slug away—you are protected!

Feet Shod with the Gospel of Peace

One of my favorite memories from my youth is playing the game of mud football with my friends. I remember how much fun it was to run with the ball in the pouring rain while the opposition tried to tackle me. My wiry frame and considerable speed were helpful in those moments. But more, the fact that I knew where I was running made it easier for me to evade tacklers and work my way toward good yardage after catching a pass or intercepting one. Watching people slip and slide as I quickly changed direction was part of the joy of this lingering memory.

I was shore fishing in the Pacific Ocean this past summer while on vacation with my family. While standing on some rocks about five feet above the water, I attempted to cast out past some kelp beds where I was "sure" to catch "the big one!" As I wheeled around after sending the bait and line toward my desired target, my momentum caused me to lose my footing. I came down squarely on my tailbone which then catapulted me toward the ledge that I was standing over when making the cast. As I was sailing head-first off the ledge into shallow water with lots of sharp rocks, I remember thinking I'd made a big mistake. As providence would have it, my head entered the water at the same time a big wave surged

130

underneath me. The wave's motion and thrust somehow cushioned my fall. My forehead hit a rock, but it was only bruised. My only injuries were a nasty cut on my forefinger, a bruised head and a very sore tailbone. As I limped my way back to where we were staying, I thanked God for his provision in protecting me, but I also couldn't help but think what might have happened had I been higher on the rock or in a different location. Losing my footing could have been very costly.

Roman soldiers didn't ever want to be in a situation where their feet might lose traction. Hand-to-hand combat required that a soldier stand his ground, thereby keeping his balance through the proper use of his center of gravity. Without firm footing, he was doomed to defeat (no pun intended). Roman soldiers knew the importance of having their feet shod with the proper boots so that they could march long distances and fight in the fiercest of battles without falling down. Historians often attribute the military success of Alexander the Great to his infantry being well shod and thus being able to cover long distances over treacherous terrain. When it comes to fighting our spiritual battles we can't afford to fall short of our goal or lose our footing.

As Paul continues to describe the separate pieces of protection that comprise the "whole armor of God" provided for every believer, he points out the importance of one's feet being "fitted with the readiness that comes from the gospel of peace." Though difficult to translate from the original language, most agree that this phrase conveys the idea of how knowing one is at peace with the gospel fits him for standing firm in the battle. In other words, a believer's confidence in his salvation gives him a stability that keeps his feet from coming out from under him in a vulnerable moment.

Many believers suffer a great deal of difficulty in their Christian walk simply because they are never totally sure about whether or not they belong to Jesus Christ. Instead of living with assurance and confidence, they live in doubt and confusion. They find it difficult to share their faith, serve in their church or attempt great things for God. After all, it is hard to do any of these things if one has a lingering doubt he belongs to Jesus. Perhaps you know people like this—or maybe you are that person.

If you are unsure about your faith, there is a vulnerability you are facing that shouldn't be overlooked. As the enemy of our soul, Satan sets up an elaborate scheme that systematically works against the believer who is doubtful about his salvation. A lack of spiritual confidence is one of the most obvious factors that cause a believer to fall. I've seen believers give up fighting against temptation, addiction and compulsions because somewhere along the journey they lost their assurance—or perhaps never possessed it in the first place.

Fitting our feet with the gospel of peace is being sure of our own salvation. It means understanding grace. It means owning the conviction that it is Christ's work at the cross—not our own work that saves us. It means knowing that we are justified by faith. When these principles are operative in our lives, our feet are given firm footing and we are not likely to go down easily—or at all. The battle we face in the spiritual dimension requires that we hold our ground and not slip and fall. Make sure as you go about your day, you've got your (spiritual) boots on!

The Shield of Faith

At one of our community outreaches, a few high school students put on an exhibition of true bravery and skill. With full knowledge of a firing squad equipped with fully automatic paintball guns, and wearing only special eye protection and helmet, they ran back and forth amidst a flurry of paintball rounds with the intensity of what soldiers in real battle may encounter when engaging the enemy. What made them willing (besides their absolute lunacy) was that each one was given a shield that could be used to deflect the shots being fired at them. At various moments during the exhibition, their bravery was heightened as certain female shooters stepped forward in the line of willing participants. Needless to say, these young boys who were being fired at by the crowd suffered many bruises.

In ancient times, using a shield properly often meant the difference between life and death. When a piece of body armor wasn't enough to parry the blow of a giant broad sword, a shield could deaden the otherwise lethal strike. Arrows dipped in pitch, lit on fire and shot into enemy lines also produced perilous results. But a shield used correctly would even arrest and extinguish these flaming missiles keeping the soldier alive.

Believers are sometimes outsmarted or they fall into a vulnerable position when engaging the enemy. In moments like these, they must realize there is a provision made that encompasses more than what has been described thus far in Ephesians 6:10-15. Paul makes this clear when stating, ***"In addition to all this, take up the shield of faith..." (v. 16).*** The original phrase *(Gr., epi pasin)* could mean, "to cover all the rest." There are times when extra coverage is good. The shield of faith provides that kind of coverage.

The Roman soldier's shield (Gr., *thyreon*) was usually made of at least two layers of wood glued together and covered with animal hide. It was bound with an iron edging which made it sturdy and large enough for the soldier to find cover when crouching low to the ground. If needed, his entire body could be protected from assault in this way. Some battle formations lined soldiers side-by-side using their shields as an impenetrable wall of protection. Roman historians cite examples of war heroes returning from battle with hundreds of darts and arrows sticking into their shields.

In a similar fashion, a believer's shield of faith (Gr., *pistis*) protects him from the arrows that Satan shoots at him. We are not told what the arrows represent; they may represent doubt, disappointment or discouragement; they may represent condemnation or accusation by others or even from within ourselves. Satan has many ways of trying to knock a believer out of being effective—though he knows he can't knock him out of the battle completely. But whatever these arrows represent, it is clear the protection of the shield does more than just form a wall between us and our enemy's attack. It extinguishes the attacker's arsenal.

When we are in a situation where we are taking some serious hits, we need to choose to believe God. When we make this choice, our shield is up, and it will work every time. Sometimes I hear the enemy whisper his cruel and abusive accusations at me: "Your life doesn't matter, what real good are you doing?" "You aren't one of God's children, look at what you do sometimes—or what you think about!" "Your kids are going to be mine, I'm going to destroy them." These whispers may sound alarming, but I'm sure you've heard similar ones too. Satan is a liar and the father of lies. Choosing to believe God is like raising our shield so that the flaming arrows Satan shoots are extinguished on impact. They don't penetrate our lives like they would if we doubted God or didn't know His promises or assurances.

I've met people in counseling sessions whose shields were down so often that the enemy could just level up on them any time and shoot away. They constantly live in doubt and discouragement. They have allowed the Devil to shoot them with his fiery arrows. Even as believers, they know very little of God's power. They always want to talk about their problems but never seem to find the solution. When I repeatedly speak to people about the same thing, I realize what is going on—their shield of faith is down.

How does one get his shield back in position to parry the blows of the enemy? It is actually very easy. We must immerse ourselves in God's Word knowing that *"faith comes by hearing the message, and the message is heard through the word of Christ" (Romans 10:17)*. When a believer saturates himself in God's Word, and begins to apply it daily, the shield of protection rises to its proper place.

If you find yourself in a place where you feel Satan has you on the ropes, it's time to quit trying and start trusting. Only as you trust Christ for whatever concerns you, will His protection from Satanic attack be assured. As you go out into your day, make your decision now to believe God. Have faith. Trust Him. There is really no better way.

The Helmet of Salvation

In my senior year of high school, I had a friend who was killed in a motorcycle accident. It was a known fact that what made his condition fatal was the head trauma he sustained due to not wearing a helmet. Ironically, his accident occurred on his way to retrieve his helmet from a shop where it was being painted. I remember his parents weeping at his graveside, lamenting their tragic loss, knowing all the while how different the outcome may have been had their son been wearing a helmet.

Many believers suffer huge losses when waging war in the spiritual realm simply because they don't wear the helmet of salvation. When Paul exhorted the Ephesian believers to "take the helmet of salvation" as one of the final pieces of armor that must be worn when engaging the enemy, it is clear from the context that he wasn't referring to salvation itself. Paul isn't suggesting that the armor we wear when in battle is salvation alone. If that were the case, there would be no need for the believer to take it and put it on (see Ephesians 6:13), for he would already be wearing it.

As the Roman soldier suited up for battle, he would dress himself in tunic, belt, breastplate, sandals and shield—before an attendant or armor-bearer would finally hand him, as the full complement of his outfit, his helmet and sword. The helmet of salvation is the believer's protection against the mental and psychological bludgeoning that occurs when fighting our enemy. Our spiritual enemy loves to mess with our minds. He loves to tell us that we won't survive the battle. He works hard to make us give up before his eminent defeat is recognized. He wants to "psyche us out." For many believers, his strategy works.

But for the believer who wears the helmet of salvation, his hope keeps him going—no matter the odds or how fierce the battle. This hope, as

135

the essence of what we need when facing our enemy, is mentioned in Paul's first letter to the Thessalonians: ***"But since we belong to the day, let us be self-controlled, putting on faith and love as a breastplate, and the hope of salvation as a helmet. For God did not appoint us to suffer wrath but to receive salvation through our Lord Jesus Christ" (1 Thessalonians 5:8-9).*** Our eternal hope through Jesus Christ protects us from the many ways Satan attempts to mess with our minds— or "psyche us out."

The Sword of the Spirit

Finally, Paul refers to one more piece of armor—the only offensive component mentioned in the list: *the sword of the Spirit (v.17b).* To avoid any uncertainty as to the nature of this piece of armor, Paul adds, *"...which is the word of God."* Of the many kinds of swords used by Roman soldiers, the one Paul selected as the instrument we must master for protecting ourselves and advancing against our enemy was the *"machaira."* The *machaira* sword was a short, two-edged blade that was used especially in hand-to-hand combat. Unlike the larger swords that could be swung in wild abandon during a battle, the *machaira* needed to be wielded with precision for it to be effective.

It is without question that God's Word becomes both our most helpful protection and our most strategic weapon when facing our enemy. Jesus used the very words of God to deflect the insidious temptations Satan pitched at Him in the wilderness (see Matthew 4:1-11; Luke 4:1-13), leaving us a vivid example of how knowing Scripture can protect us from temptation.

The proper use of Scripture can also mightily advance the gospel. Speaking through the prophet Isaiah, God assured his covenant people, ***"As the rain and the snow come down from heaven, and do not return to it without watering the earth and making it bud and flourish, so that it yields seed for the sower and bread for the eater,*** *so is my word that goes out from my mouth: It will not return to me empty, but will accomplish what I desire and achieve the purpose for which I sent it" (Isaiah 55:11).* This is why Paul could assert the Word's power and effectiveness as an offensive weapon for doing kingdom work when writing: *"All Scripture is God-breathed and is useful for teaching, rebuking, correcting and training in righteousness, so that the man of God may be thoroughly equipped for every good work" (2 Timothy 3:16).*

As the believer wears each piece of armor, he protects himself from virtually all the ways Satan will try to knock him down. He becomes a soldier in the Lord's army, protecting himself while at the same time becoming dangerously powerful to advance the precious charge he's been given: to spread the glorious gospel of Jesus Christ until He returns!

The Holy Spirit graciously extends to you each piece of armor to be worn for our protection. Now it is time for you to be sure to wear the spiritual armor as you head out to the front lines. As we understand and apply the provision of God's armor available to us, we'll discover greater strength and more frequent victories when the enemy comes around. Don't you think it's time he be shown what you are capable of because you are wearing your armor? Let's not do anything until we're suited up and ready for action.

CHAPTER 7: WEAR THE ARMOR
DISCUSSION QUESTIONS

1. What are some of the common spiritual consequences you have observed with believers who neglect to wear the full armor of God?

2. Why would Paul select the image of a Roman soldier to teach us about developing a good defensive stand against the attacks of the enemy? How does this image inform us of our role in spiritual warfare as followers of Christ? (See 2 Timothy 2:3-4)

3. The armor of God helps a believer to stand his ground while under attack. How well do you do at standing your ground against the enemy's attacks? Where is he most likely to knock you off balance?

4. What piece of spiritual armor do you find easiest to wear and what piece is most difficult for you to wear? Why?

5. Share some of the practical ways each piece of armor listed in Ephesians 6 assists the believer when under attack from the enemy.

CHAPTER 8

CHOOSE YOUR WEAPONS
Our Weapons Are Not of This World

In the last chapter, we looked at the protective armor that God graciously gives all believers to stand firm against the enemy's attack. Now we'll consider two very strategic weapons God has given us to fight in the battle. In athletic contests, we might hear a coach tell his team that the best defense is a good offense or vice versa. For coaches who see a weakness on one side of their team, it's their way of telling them they can make up for it by doing better on the other.

Some teams are purposefully formed around a philosophy that leans heavily on defensive skills and tactics. Other teams are more focused on offensive strategies; but there's no way around it—you can't be a winning team without being good at both. Injuries or matchups might dictate your immediate focus, but in the long run, you can't go very far without being strong defensively and offensively.

It's also true that winning our spiritual battles requires being defensively strong (wearing the armor) and being skilled at offense, too, even if at times, we lean on one more than the other. The Apostle Paul zeroes in on the need of having a good offense when engaging the enemy when writing to the Corinthians: ***"For though we live in the world, we do not wage war as the world does. The weapons we fight with are not the weapons of the world. On the contrary, they have divine power to demolish strongholds" (2 Corinthians 10:3-4).*** Paul's view of waging war in the spiritual realm isn't the same as waging war in the physical realm. Our weapons, according to him, are not of this world, they are spiritual weapons designed to do battle in the arena that isn't merely physical. When addressing the Ephesian believers, he reminds them (and us) that, *"...our struggle is not against flesh and blood, but against the rulers, against the authorities, against the powers of this dark world and against the spiritual forces of evil in the heavenly realms" (Ephesians 6:12).*

In contrast to the Ephesians text that exhorts us to wear God's armor for protection, the 2 Corinthians text suggests that there is offensive *weaponry* available for us. We must wear the armor to protect ourselves, but we also need to be "armed" offensively for battle. Note the plural, "...the *weapons* we fight with..." These weapons, according to Paul, *[have] divine power, able to demolish strongholds of the enemy (2 Corinthians 10:4).*

At the beginning of this book, I suggested that it is difficult to be completely dogmatic about the exact meaning of phrases that deal with the spiritual battle in which we are engaged. This is true for several reasons, not the least of which is that Scripture itself doesn't always answer all our questions about the details of the battle being waged in the spiritual realm. One example of this is right here in 2 Corinthians, where we really don't know what these offensive weapons are. Paul doesn't name them. We only know that whatever they are, they have power to demolish strongholds of the enemy.

I have often wondered why Paul is more detailed about the pieces of protective armor than he is about the weapons we have for demolishing the enemy's strongholds. Back to our coaching analogy, maybe Paul believed the Ephesian believers needed to strengthen their defense and the Corinthian believers needed a stronger offense when engaging in spiritual warfare. Perhaps Paul considered the believer's offensive weapons somewhat obvious to his readers and therefore didn't need to elaborate. Considering these as possibilities, I'd like to suggest what Paul might have had in mind for offensive weaponry when engaging in spiritual warfare.

The work of Satan in this evil world creates chaos and destruction in the spirit realm. But God has given his children weapons no less powerful or effective when applied to the battles into which the enemy lures us. While there may be other offensive weapons available to us, I'd like to suggest two very strategic weapons that are a must; and likely the very weapons Paul assumed were obvious to his readers that can indeed exact heavy damage on Satanic outposts and strongholds. These strategic weapons, I believe, are *Scripture* and *prayer*.

The weapon of Scripture

There is no question that when Paul wrote of weapons that *"demolish strongholds"* he likely envisioned Scripture as one of the most obvious weapons in our spiritual arsenal. Before I continue here, it's important to clarify that when speaking of Scripture as a weapon, I'm not suggesting we use it to bludgeon those who resist or oppose our message. Too many Christ-followers have a reputation of beating people over the head with the Bible to the point that they lose their audience. This can happen even in relationships that share a common faith in Jesus Christ. A dear brother in faith recently lamented that his wife complained that he was being a "Bible-thumper" when it came to his method of trying to lead her deeper in faith. Ouch. To be honest, I remember times when unwittingly, I've done the same thing. It's easy to do this without realizing the damage we do in building bridges for the gospel among skeptics and unbelievers.

Scripture is a powerful weapon, but it must not be used simply to try and win an argument or put someone in their place. Sometimes we use God's Word as a means of pressing others into the mold we envision is best for them without having the right motive or attitude—and our method backfires. This is NOT what I mean when referring to Scripture being an offensive weapon in our arsenal to take down strongholds. I'm

141

referring to something powerfully winsome and effective in our efforts to advance God's work.

Remember how the Apostle Paul, in his letter to the Ephesians concluded that amazing list of protective armor given to every believer? He writes, **"Take...the sword of the Spirit, which is the word of God" (Ephesians 6:17).** Unlike most of the other pieces of protective armor Paul lists in Ephesians 6, the sword of the Spirit, in Paul's thinking, would clearly have been seen as an offensive weapon, too.

It cannot be overstated that the *"sword of the Spirit"* which Paul identifies as the *word of God* is our chief weapon to demolish the strongholds of the enemy. Satan's deceptions are everywhere, and through them, he deceives many—even Christ-followers. The Greek word we translate into our English word, "sword" in Ephesians 6:17 is μαχαιρα (Machaira), which depicts something more like a *dagger* or *stiletto*. In Roman times, the Machaira sword was used only in close combat and therefore had to be used with precision to overcome the enemy. Its size made it difficult to be used primarily in a defensive manner. Thus, we learn that Scripture is a precise offensive weapon that can wield lethal force against the enemy's tactics and schemes. Its implication is that a careful and thoughtful use of Scripture is critical when engaging in spiritual battles offensively. The enemy uses deception and lies to outwit or gain an advantage over us when we are not knowledgeable in God's Word. But when using the truth of Scripture to deflect the lies and deceptions of the enemy, we gain ground in the battle waging in the spiritual realm.

As a background to 2 Corinthians, we discover there were false apostles who had come to the city of Corinth under the guise of Christian faith and they had begun to preach a *different* gospel—and a Jesus that was someone other than whom Paul had known and preached to them. Paul writes, **"For if someone comes to you and preaches a Jesus other than the Jesus we preached, or if you receive a different spirit from**

142

the one you received, or a different gospel from the one you accepted, you put up with it easily enough" (2 Corinthians 10:4). The Corinthian believers were being deceived by false teaching about Jesus Christ and the Apostle Paul was concerned that they didn't seem the least bit bothered by this. They needed to wield the Machaira sword, the precise and powerful weapon of truth that could have revealed and terminated false views of Jesus or the gospel, but they were not doing so.

Today there are numerous false gospels and false teachers who present a "different" message from orthodox Christianity. Sometimes we are exposed to these false gospels when well-dressed people show up at our doorstep with a message that may even sound close to what we believe, but is far from the truth of the gospel of Jesus Christ. We should be wary of such messengers and be ready whenever they come around to testify of our relationship with God through faith in Jesus Christ without apology—and use Scripture as a weapon to offset the enemy's tactics.

Often, false teaching comes through the nonchalant views of professing believers that present a "works righteousness" required for belonging to Christ. The gospel requires a vigilant watch on anyone who distorts the simple and beautiful message of the gospel—that lost sinners are saved purely by their faith in Jesus Christ apart from any work of their own. When false messages and teachers are embraced, they become *strongholds* of the enemy deeply embedded in our culture and world. The best way to bring down these strongholds is by teaching the truth of Scripture and living accordingly.

There's no end to the sheer number of books, philosophies, beliefs and even churches that have forsaken the historical and orthodox faith which we possess in the gospel of Jesus Christ. This concerned the Apostle greatly, moving him to write about these deceivers later in this same letter, *"For such men are false apostles, deceitful workmen, masquerading as apostles of Christ. And no wonder, for Satan himself masquerades as an angle of light. It is not surprising, then,*

143

if his servants masquerade as servants of righteousness. Their end will be what their actions deserve" (2 Corinthians 11:13-15). Paul could see, as should we, that the enemy will be vanquished one day. In the meantime, however, we must fight—and to fight, we need the weapon of Scripture in our hearts and lived out in our daily routine.

Let me also point out here why Paul was so insistent about exposing these false apostles and their message. His concern wasn't only for the preservation of orthodoxy, but also because of these deceiving messengers, true followers of Christ might lose their sincere and pure devotion to Christ: *"But I am afraid that just as Eve was deceived by the serpent's cunning, your minds may somehow be led astray from your sincere and pure devotion to Christ" (2 Corinthians 11:3).* For Paul, and for us, the danger of false teaching is being led astray from our *pure devotion* to Christ. If we belong to Jesus, we can never lose our *salvation*, but according to Paul, we can be led away from our *devotion* to him. How many people do you know once claimed to know Christ but whose devotion to Him has now waned? This was one of Paul's greatest fears among his converts and it causes fear in me, too, as one who desires every believer in Jesus to be passionately devoted to Him and centered on *truth*.

Paul was insistent about this very thing when addressing the elders of the church at Ephesus: *"Keep watch over yourselves and all the flock of which the Holy Spirit has made you overseers" (Acts 20:28).* Paul gets more specific as he continues, *"Be shepherds of the church of God, which he bought with his own blood. I know that after I leave, savage wolves will come in among you and will not spare the flock. Even from your own number men will arise and distort the truth in order to draw away disciples after them. So be on your guard" (Acts 20:28b-31a)!* I have a feeling that if Paul were writing today to the church where I pastor, his warning wouldn't be any different. These changes happen very subtly. I am saddened by the great educational institutions in our country that were founded on Christian orthodoxy and today don't hold to the essential doctrines of Christian faith. The problem Paul saw as possibly coming to the church at Ephesus is the same problem that we see happening all around us in educational systems and even churches— and it's happening in individuals, too.

In his short letter we identify as 2 John, the Apostle John acknowledges his joy in knowing followers of Jesus are standing firm in the truth: *"To the chosen lady and her children, whom I love in the truth—and not I only, but also all who know the truth—because of the truth, which lives in us and will be with us forever...It has given me great joy to find some of your children walking in the truth, just as the Father commanded us..." (2 John 1-2, 4).* In this short section, the Apostle John mentions truth no less than four times! Scripture is only a viable weapon against the enemy's strongholds when it is viewed as absolute truth. Short of this, the enemy has a clear advantage of protecting his territory.

The weapon of Scripture—God's Word—is a weapon we must choose to use in the good fight that we are called to engage in daily. While it is true that the Word of God is being maligned and rejected by those who fall prey to the enemy's tactics, there are timely and powerful Scriptures that are particularly helpful and encouraging when considering the importance of holding fast to the Word of God as a primary offensive weapon in our spiritual battles. The writer of Hebrews states, *"For the word of God is living and active. Sharper than any double-edged sword, it penetrates even to dividing soul and spirit, joints and marrow; it judges the thoughts and attitudes of the heart" (Hebrews 4:12).* Notice here, the imagery of the battle we are in as God's Word is described as a "double-edged" sword proving its potency in fighting against the enemy.

The Prophet Isaiah also reminds us of Scripture's potency: *"The grass withers and the flowers fall, but the word of our God stands forever" (Isaiah 40:8).* This means that Scriptures' power never recedes.

Its power is consistent always. In his prophecy, Isaiah views Scripture as God's emissary that faithfully carries out its objective without failure: *"As the rain and the snow come down from heaven, and do not return to it without watering the earth and making it bud and flourish, so that it yields seed for the sower and bread for the eater, so is my word that goes out from my mouth: It will not return to me empty, but will accomplish what I desire and achieve the purpose for which I sent it"* (Isaiah 55:10-11).

One of the most powerful New Testament Scriptures that affirm God's Word is always effectual comes from the writings of the Apostle Paul where he tells his young disciple Timothy, *"All Scripture is God-breathed and is useful for teaching, rebuking, correcting and training in righteousness, so that the man (or woman) of God may be thoroughly equipped for every good work"* (2 Timothy 3:16-17).

I marvel at the many times people approach me after a sermon I've given and express how God spoke to them directly about a problem, temptation, burden or crisis they happened to be in—and how God's Word brought them immediate clarity about what they needed to trust and act upon. That's because of God's promise nestled in the words of Paul to Timothy—God's Word will do its job if we present it accurately and hold to it unswervingly.

We see from these Scriptures that a weapon we *need* to use when engaging in spiritual warfare is Scripture. To use it properly, we need to know Scripture well because Satan knows it too, though he distorts it for his advantage. When we use Scripture properly in our spiritual battles, we too, can pull down the strongholds of the enemy!

The weapon of prayer

As we've already read, the pieces of spiritual armor that Paul mentions in Ephesians 6 are not entirely defensive. Some of them can be used offensively as well. The sword of the Spirit, which we've just examined can be used offensively and so can prayer. Most commentators separate the protective armor from what follows in the Ephesians 6 text—but we learn that Paul's final exhortation concerning what God provides to do battle with the enemy is prayer: ***"And pray in the Spirit on all occasions with all kinds of prayers and requests. With this in mind, be alert and always keep on praying for all the saints" (Ephesians 6:18).*** The Apostle Paul views prayer as that which ensures complete victory as we fight our spiritual battles and so he includes it with his description of the armor we are to wear when going into battle.

Fighting and winning in the spiritual realm demands a prayer strategy. Our desire to make everything in our lives bow in submission to the authority of Jesus Christ mandates this. There are many distractions and diversions that come at us as we pursue a life of total surrender to Jesus. Our hectic schedules, personal concerns, work obligations, unexpected trials and other normal life occurrences continually contribute to the potential of straying off course in our walk with Jesus. The believer's body armor is more than enough to protect him from the adversarial situations that can blur his focus on the big picture, but even more, the power and efficacy of prayer rounds out the full complement of the believer's protection and gives him the staying power needed for keeping him upright in battle. It also gives him the power to advance and take territory of the enemy.

Paul's strategic placement of this idea nearing the close of his letter to the Ephesians makes this clear. We see this in each phrase Paul uses in his exhortation. ***"And pray in the Spirit on all occasions..." (Ephesians 6:18).*** Once the believer has thoroughly understood and applied the spiritual protection afforded him, he must also pray. Wearing the armor without engaging in prayer cannot ensure full protection, nor can it help us bring down spiritual strongholds of the enemy. Prayer plays an essential role in the fight.

The opening phrase in this exhortation alerts the reader of two important insights. First, Paul exhorts his reader to, *"pray in the Spirit."* The phrase *"in the Spirit"* is more literally *"in the realm of Spirit,"* which underlines the need for a believer's prayer life to be prompted and guided by the Holy Spirit Himself. The phrase that follows underscores this truth: *"...on all occasions"* (Gr., *en panti kairo*), which points to the need of praying for a specific opportunity more than merely praying at a specific moment in time. This is understood with Paul's use of the Greek word, "kairos" which describes seizing opportunity rather than merely filling up our time with something. It is being keenly aware of how potent our prayers can be when realizing how God moves through His Spirit in response to our prayers.

The action Paul seeks to enlist is that of having a watchful eye for those things in our lives which demand immediate attention through prayer. There are probably many things we face daily that, if we are attentive, will lead us to pray. If, however, we are inattentive to the realm of the Spirit's work or prompting, we are likely to pass up such opportunities. We often miss opportunities for impacting our present situations simply because we are not aware of where the Spirit is at work and so we are not compelled to pray. If there's something I've learned about prayer, God cannot answer if we don't pray. I hear believers sometimes complain about unanswered prayer, but I think the far greater problem for most believers is prayerlessness.

I was getting ready for bed one night when I received a text from a young man I had donated a vehicle to a couple of years ago. Teddy was a graduate of "Teen Challenge," a ministry begun in the late 1950s by David Wilkerson who was prompted by God to reach out to gang members of New York City. Over the years, untold numbers of people of all ages have found salvation in Christ and freedom from addiction to substances and a life of violence.

148

When Teddy first came to our home and picked up our vehicle, he couldn't have been more thankful. He looked at our Toyota Corolla with 200,000 miles on it as if it were a Lincoln Continental. Before he drove off, we prayed together asking God to keep it running and service his needs as he followed Jesus' plans for his life. We kept in touch a few times since then as Teddy shared about things God was doing in his life. The text he sent that evening, however, had a desperate tone: *"Please pray, the car you gave me two years ago was just stolen from in front of my house!"* I quickly responded to him saying I would pray. My wife and I took hands and brought this simple request, *"Lord, you know Teddy needs a car to get to work. He's doing so well. Please see that the car is returned in one piece so he can keep his job."* Only thirty minutes later, Teddy sent another text: *"A miracle happened! My car was recovered already and it's back at my house! Thank you for praying!"*

I wish I could say that all my prayers were answered that quickly! For most of us including me, there's usually a lot more time between a request and God's answer. That's because God always works with a much bigger picture in mind. We should never worry when our prayers are not immediately answered. We can trust God is working out his plans for us. But I couldn't help rejoice in how God does, at times, love to answer our requests very quickly. And Teddy, along with my wife and I were blessed to be included in this kind provision of God answering our prayers.

But it isn't just becoming more aware of opportunities to pray that inspires the Apostle's instruction. He continues, **"...with all kinds of prayers and requests..." (Ephesians 6:18).** As we move through our day, our prayers can take on various forms, described in the two Greek words Paul uses: *proseuche* (prayers)—a general term for prayer—and *deesis* (requests)—the term that zeroes in on specific supplication. As a believer moves through the day, every avenue of these two categories should be implemented.

Ask yourself how often through any given day you are drawn to pray for someone or something. If prayer occurs often and in various circumstances throughout your day, you will be utilizing both general prayer and specific supplication. "Thank you, Lord, for this day." "Please give me patience with my boss at work." "I need boldness to share the gospel with my neighbor." "I feel tempted Lord. Help me!" "I praise You for helping my child today." "I'm afraid, Lord; please give me courage." These are mere fragments of the longer and more detailed conversations we have with God when we utilize prayer as we ought to. Even short prayers like these offer evidence that we are giving attention to the realm of the Spirit.

Finally, Paul wants us to understand our role in helping others through our prayers. ***"With this in mind, be alert and always keep on praying for all the saints" (Ephesians 6:18).*** Our prayers impact the spiritual health of others. Our investment in prayer can produce rich dividends in the lives of those for whom we pray. Overcoming temptation, being encouraged, waiting on God, and experiencing peace or a physical touch are just a few ways our prayers can impact someone's life. Are there those you know whose situation might improve through your commitment to pray for them? The answer, of course, is yes. Having this awareness requires staying alert and persevering.

I keep a prayer journal. It's loaded with people's names and situations for which they have asked for prayer. It also includes people on my heart with a specific prayer agenda I have for them. I pray specifically for all members of my family and the needs I recognize in their lives every day. I've got spiritual kids, too. I pray for them very specifically. I pray for the staff at my church and fellow pastors I know in the community. I pray for people in my life who have yet to confess Jesus as their Savior. I pray for people who need healing. There are other categories that include names of people who need specific prayer. Every day, as much as I am able, I bring all those people to God in prayer. Without most of them even knowing it, their faces and circumstances are impressed on my heart and brought to the throne of grace each day. Whether sitting quietly before the day begins, or driving, or doing a workout at the gym, these are opportunities to lift people up in prayer. While it is a compulsion of mine, it isn't a burden. I love working my way through my prayer journal each day knowing that even if I can't see what God is doing with my specific prayers, I believe my prayers are doing something. God promises me that they are.

The importance of praying this way should not be underestimated. There are few joys as rich in the Christian life than experiencing answered prayer for one's self or for others. Keeping our focus when under attack of the enemy and helping others to do so, will require being saturated with prayer. What's your prayer saturation-level today?

There is a passage in Mark's gospel about the link between spiritual warfare and prayer. There was a man in the crowd one day, whose son was possessed by an evil spirit and wreaking havoc in his son's life by causing him physical harm. The man came to Jesus pleading with him to do something about this, explaining, *"I asked your disciples to drive out the spirit, but they could not" (Mark 9:18b).* When Jesus asked that the boy be brought to him, the demons manifested a vicious attack on the boy, throwing his body to the ground and thrashing it around, even causing him to foam at the mouth (Mark 9:20). After a brief inquiry from Jesus about the boy's background, the man petitions, *"If you can do anything, take pity on us and help us" (Mark 9:22).* I love Jesus' response: *"'If I can? Everything is possible for him who believes'" (Mark 9:23).* The father's response is so familiar to any of us who believe but have a history of experiences that tell us otherwise: *"I do believe; help me overcome my unbelief" (Mark 9:24)!* Jesus identified the evil spirit as the cause of the boy being deaf and mute and called it out of him, leaving the boy looking dead before Jesus picks him up by his hand, standing him up on his own two feet. What a miracle!

After the crowd went away and Jesus was alone with his disciples, they asked him, ***"Why couldn't we drive it out?"*** Jesus replied, ***"This kind can come out only by prayer" (Mark 9:29).*** That ought to at least suggest that sometimes when taking on the forces of evil, prayer is the *only* weapon that will work. Some manuscripts of this account include "fasting" with prayer which would indicate a longer season of focus and spiritual attention for the battle and going after the enemy's stronghold. Combining fasting with prayer is often a potent weapon in breaking the enemy's stronghold.

How often do we really take time to do battle with the enemy through prayer *alone*? Why is prayer, for many of us, a last-ditch effort? Why have prayer meetings waned in their importance in many churches and with believers? We think we are too busy to pray, or perhaps too sophisticated to pray. Maybe we are too selfish to pray, too proud to pray, too distracted to pray. As a result, many strongholds of doubt, unbelief and evil exist in our personal lives and ministry environments. Might this be the very reason for the struggle we are facing now?

Let's look at a wonderful promise for the believer found in Psalm 91:11. As you read this, ask yourself where this shows up in the gospel narratives: ***"For he will command his angels concerning you to guard you in all your ways" (Psalm 91:11).*** This reference is cited by Satan when tempting Jesus in the wilderness (Matthew 4 and Luke 4). Somehow Satan thought he could leverage this point to cause Jesus to do something very foolish by putting His father to a test to prove his love for him. Jesus doesn't buy it, nor should we. We should trust God, but not presume that without an intentional dependence on Him, everything will just work out.

What other connection can we draw from this passage? We might consider a passage in the book of Daniel where Daniel prays concerning the pronounced judgment on Israel seen in the vision he received from the angel Gabriel. Daniel knew that Israel's captivity would last seventy years and at the time of this vision, he realized this seventy-year span of time was nearly over. What is going to happen next?

Daniel sought the Lord in *prayer*. While praying, Gabriel, the one who had brought the vision, comes to Daniel in swift flight and says: ***"Daniel, I have now come to give you insight and understanding. As soon as you began to pray, an answer was given, which I have come to tell you, for you are highly esteemed"*** **(Daniel 9:21-23).** Amazing! God dispatches an angel to minister to Daniel's request the moment he begins praying. Who wouldn't want to have that assurance when praying? God wanted Daniel to know that He heard his prayers. Let's not forget that God tells us the same thing in the Apostle John's first epistle, ***"This is the confidence we have in approaching God: that if we ask anything according to his will, he hears us. And if we know that he hears us—whatever we ask—we know that we have what we asked of him"*** **(1 John 5:14-15).** In this sense, we have the same assurance that Daniel received from the angel when bringing our requests to God—he hears us—and if he hears us, we know He will answer.

If that isn't fascinating and encouraging I don't know what is! But there is something even *more* fascinating as we go back to the story of Daniel, and it's found in the very next chapter of his prophecy. It's now two years later and Daniel has received another vision, this one about a great war that was coming—the war of all wars sometime in the distant future of Israel. It was so terrifying to Daniel that when the revelation was given to him, he mourned for three weeks; he ate no choice food, had no meat, no wine touched his lips and he used no bathing and hygiene lotions until the three weeks passed (Daniel 10:2-3). Then, beginning in Daniel 10:4 we read of a vision that Daniel has with another angelic visitor, likely Gabriel again, who refers to another guardian angel, Michael, serving in the heavenly realms. This angel has many characteristics of a theophany, a pre-incarnate view of Christ. I know all of this seems a little difficult to comprehend, but stay with me.

Daniel 9:12 reads, *"Do not be afraid, Daniel, since the first day that you set your mind to gain understanding and to humble yourself before your God, your words were heard, and I have come in response to them."* Now look at what comes next, *"But the prince of the Persian kingdom resisted me twenty-one days. Then Michael, one of the chief princes, came to help me, because I was detained there with the king of Persia. Now I have come to explain to you what will happen to your people in the future, for the vision concerns a time yet to come" (Daniel 10:12-14).* Yikes, this is crazy stuff! Most Bible scholars believe that the "king of Persia" is a demonic spirit that held authority in a geographic area which was trying to hinder the unfolding of God's plan. I wonder sometimes if when we pray, it launches a battle in the heavenly realms between angels and demons. There was a battle going on in the heavenly realms to which Daniel is given insight to remind us that there is a battle waging in the heavenly realms in our lives, too, just like Paul taught in Ephesians 6:10ff.

All of this speaks of the New Testament witness found in Hebrews 1:14: *"Are not all angels ministering spirits sent to serve those who will inherit salvation" (Hebrews 1:14)?* When we pray we engage at a level of spiritual warfare that we don't fully comprehend. When we pray we are advancing the purposes of God and dispatching heavenly messengers to carry out God's bidding on earth. When we pray, we literally set in motion, "your will be done on earth as it is in heaven" (Matthew 6:10). When we pray, we are pulling down fortresses that oppose the purposes of God. When we pray, we dispense of doubt and we put to flight evil messengers. When we pray, we can trust, whether we see or not, the hand of God is moving! Prayer is an offensive weapon in our arsenal against evil.

The exhortation for believers to pray about all things always is all throughout Scripture. As an overall exhortation, I like how the Apostle

Peter frames this: *"The end of all things is near. Therefore, be clear minded and self-controlled so that you can pray" (1 Peter 4:7).*

We know that Scripture is an amazing weapon. We also know that prayer is an amazing weapon where we move the hand of God in accordance with His will. As I close this chapter, let me offer another weapon that you perhaps haven't considered that breaks strongholds of the enemy. That weapon is *you*.

The weapon of a surrendered life

As a short addendum to what we've learned about our offensive weapons, consider your very life as a weapon God can use to break the strongholds of the enemy. This weapon should not be overlooked. Being committed to truth in the word of God is a great weapon; being committed to pray for the will of God is a great weapon; and being committed to a life surrendered to the ways of God is where it all comes together.

Jesus said, *"If anyone would come after me, he must deny himself and take up his cross daily and follow me." (Luke 9:23).* Jesus invites us into a life of full surrender. This is known as a life of discipleship. This is the life of being a Christ-follower. For when we are dead to ourselves and alive to Christ, we are a weapon that pulls down the enemy's strongholds.

Why? Because surrendered lives *obey* God and when we obey, we put the enemy to flight. Surrendered lives *believe* God and when we believe, we put the enemy to flight. Surrendered lives *forgive* others and when forgiveness is given, we put the enemy to flight. Surrendered lives *love* as Christ loved and this puts the enemy to flight. Surrendered lives do good to others; deeds of kindness and compassion, which puts the enemy to flight. In short, when we manifest the life of Christ in any situation, we put the enemy to flight!

See yourself as a weapon to do war against the enemy. Paul wrote about laboring and struggling with all of Christ's energy which so powerfully worked within him (Colossians 1:29). He asserted that there was power behind the scope of his comprehension to do the work of God (Ephesians 3:20). Paul wrote of running the race as to win (1 Corinthians 9). In the tone of rebuke, the chronicler of the Old Testament wrote against the wicked king Asa, *"For the eyes of the Lord range throughout the earth to strengthen those whose hearts are fully committed to him" (2 Chronicles 16:9).* This is a powerful reminder to each of us. We are an unstoppable force against the enemy when we surrender our lives to God.

When we become committed to the word of God, the will of God and the ways of God in our lives, the enemy of our souls hates it, leaving him no other option other than to retreat. This is what the Apostle James points out, *"Submit yourselves, then, to God. Resist the devil, and he will flee from you. Come near to God and he will come near to you" (James 4:7-8a).* For many of us, the biggest reason we are not a weapon in the hand of God to put the enemy to flight is simply because we are not fully surrendered to Jesus. You can be a Christian and not be surrendered to Christ—did you know that? Passive or active rebellion to Jesus and neglect of His purposes in our lives will only make us weak and anemic followers. To be honest, I think our enemy smiles whenever believers avoid surrendering to God's word, will and ways. This is because we pose little or no threat to his schemes and activities when we are this way.

Love, kindness, compassion, justice, obedience, forgiveness, praise, acceptance, perseverance and a host of other weapons of righteousness are forged in the life of anyone fully surrendered to Jesus Christ. John wrote, *"Whoever claims to live in him must walk as Jesus did"* *(1 John 2:6).* We can't really use the weapons of Scripture and prayer if we're not sincerely surrendered to Jesus.

Many of us are allowing the enemy territory and strength simply because of our obstinate refusal to obey God. Perhaps we are harboring a lack of forgiveness, or we are demonstrating pride. Maybe we are using harsh and abusive words toward people far from God, or we are allowing any kind of sin in our own lives to go unchecked. Then we wonder why the enemy has such control and isn't fleeing from us.

If you are wanting to put the enemy to flight and pull down some of his strongholds, then choose the weapons of Scripture and prayer and surrender your life fully to Jesus Christ. For the weapons we fight with are not as the world's and they have knock-down power in the spiritual realm.

CHAPTER 8: CHOOSE YOUR WEAPONS DISCUSSION QUESTIONS

1. Why is truth a watershed issue in today's culture? Where is the attack on truth most evident to you?

2. What, in your opinion, has caused the most erosion to the belief that the Bible is truth and can therefore be depended on for our understanding of God and how to live in a manner pleasing to Him?

3. Why are many believers unsure that the Bible is the one true source of truth?

4. Why is the resource of prayer underutilized by many believers as a spiritual weapon when engaging with the enemy? How is this resource used in your own life at the present time? How has your prayer life grown recently?

5. If prayer is what taps into spiritual power when facing the enemy, what distractions do you feel Satan's system might create in order to keep a believer from praying more often and more effectively?

6. Why is a life surrendered to God such a powerful weapon against the enemy? What are other kinds of supplementary weapons that come along with a life that is truly surrendered to God?

7. How does it make you feel to know that angels are "ministering spirits sent to serve those who will inherit salvation?" (See Hebrews 1:14)

8. James 4:7 exhorts, "Resist the devil and he will flee from you." How does resistance to the devil look in practical ways?

CHAPTER 9

RUNNING TO BATTLE
Building Confidence for the Fight

Let's face it. Not all of us feel good about fighting, about contests, about going to war, in any realm whatsoever. I can relate to those of you who feel this way. I said in the introduction of this book and have reiterated it throughout, by nature, I'm not much of a fighter. I'm timid and often fearful and when I see trouble coming, I usually do all I can to avoid it. My memories of those difficult years growing up and dealing with the neighborhood bully are not happy ones. I remember being teased, pushed around and intimidated by various individuals who crossed my path as a young boy growing into adolescence. Being skinny and wearing glasses were usually the focus of my tormentors. And I've already admitted that at one point in my childhood, it was my older sister who bailed me out of a fair amount of hazing.

In my junior and senior high years, I had a few experiences where I had to choose whether to fight or to back down. I was one of those kids who usually backed down. This may sound spiritual, since Jesus taught us to turn the other cheek, but the truth is simply that I didn't ever want to fight. My confidence in those situations was extremely low.

Not so with my good friend, Peter. Peter loved to fight and he could fight like few people I have ever known. He didn't start fights, he ended them. He wasn't a bully. He didn't go into his day looking for a fight, but if Peter saw someone being picked on or bullied, he had no problem sticking up for the victim, which usually meant taking on the assailant(s) himself. There were more than a few occasions in high school when my friendship with Peter kept me safe and put *him* in the principal's office. It was good to be friends with Peter but I always felt a little jealous that I didn't have the confidence that he had when trouble came knocking. Peter could keep his cool and try to disarm the situation but if he needed to, he wasn't afraid of the fight. Peter's approach to trouble is what we must learn as we face our spiritual battles.

When I encounter spiritual warfare, I'm learning to be more like my friend, Peter. Instead of running for cover or hiding someplace out of the enemy's view, I'm learning to stand my ground and fight. I'm learning to engage. I'm learning to enter in. I'm learning to be more confident when facing my spiritual battles. Would you like more confidence when facing your spiritual battles? If so, I've got some encouraging things to share with you.

It's time to learn how to grow in confidence when facing and engaging in the spiritual battles that come our way. I'm sure there is more to be said about building confidence when engaging in our spiritual battles, but I believe if we apply the simple principles I'll lay out here, we will start experiencing a little more confidence in the spiritual battles that come our way. Let me offer you four simple things you can start applying to your life today that will bolster your confidence.

Show up

Paul invites his young protégé in faith, Timothy to **"fight the good fight of the faith" (1 Timothy 6:12).** Paul likens this image of spiritual warfare as being a *fight*; and here he even calls it a **"good fight."** In the original Greek, the phrase is, *agonizou ton kalon agona*, which, translated very literally could read, *"agonize the good agony"* or, *"war the good warfare."*

The Greek verb *"ago"* first became associated with an athletic contest and later became associated more universally with the idea of *"contending with adversaries."* This was the image that Paul had in mind when he thought of our spiritual battles. They were not unlike the contest one might have with an athletic opponent in the sports arena or a soldier on the battlefield.

160

The first place when spiritual conflicts arise is to engage, or to *enter in.* Don't be a defector—you must face the opposition.

What kind of contest would it be if you went to watch a professional football game and your team's opponent didn't even show up? Obviously, there would be no contest. If this were the case, there can be no real *victory* because there is no real *engagement.* Paul is inviting young Timothy, and by extension, each of us not to be afraid of our opponent but rather to take the fight *head-on.* When the fight comes to us, we must fight.

If you are familiar with Paul's letters, you know he's already used this phrase with Timothy earlier in his letter to him. ***"Timothy, my son, I give you this instruction in keeping with the prophecies once made about you, so that by following them you may fight the good fight, holding on to faith and a good conscience" (1 Timothy 1:18-19).*** The Apostle is encouraging Timothy to show up—to not be afraid of the fight he is entering daily.

You might also remember that when Paul was nearing the end of his life, he wrote, ***"I have fought the good fight, I have finished the race, I have kept the faith" (2 Timothy 4:7).*** Paul learned confidence when engaging in spiritual battles to the degree he could refer to them as "the good fight." I think Paul's confidence in the fight allowed him to see his conflicts in the spiritual realm as beneficial and could thus name the fight, "good."

When the battle comes, and it will, we must show up. We must engage. We can't afford to bail. When you feel the enemy trying to get you to avoid the conflict, show up anyway. When you know that your input and your presence will make a difference, show up. When it comes to building confidence for our spiritual battles, a big part of it is simply showing up. We saw this previously in the situation with King Jehoshaphat and the prophet Jahaziel who spoke these words to him: ***"Listen King Jehoshaphat and all who live in Judah and Jerusalem! This is what the LORD says to you: 'Do not be afraid or discouraged because of*** *this vast army. For the battle is not yours, but God's. Tomorrow march down against them. They will be climbing up by the Pass of Ziz, and you will find them at the end of the gorge in the Desert of Jeruel. You will not have to fight this battle. Take up your positions; stand firm and see the deliverance the LORD will give you, O Judah and Jerusalem. Do not be afraid; do not be discouraged. Go out to face them tomorrow, and the LORD will be with you"* (2 Chronicles 20:15-17).

I love this! Just take your positions and see what God is going to do! Apparently, a big part of the battle is just learning to show up to see how God is going to work. If God is the one who ultimately fights for us and it is His battle more than ours, then why don't we just show up to see what he will do? God wants us to show up so we can witness his power at work.

I should be quick to confess here that for most of my career as a pastor, I've battled with the issue of fear. I'm often afraid when facing difficult situations or when I'm not sure what to do. But one thing that has helped me counter my fear is simply *showing up*. I've gone to meetings where there were really important issues to discuss or a confrontation to be made, or a person who is upset and wants to accuse or be angry about something. As reluctant as I might feel for showing up for something of this nature, I hear the whisper of God's Spirit saying, "I've got this. Just show up and I'll give you the words to say." I can't count the number of times as I was driving home from one of those real difficult situations, it was clear to me that God had done something special. In that moment, I realized that my showing up wasn't what made God work. Showing up allowed me to see God work—that's why we need to show up. It's not for us to fight as much as it is for us to see how God fights in extremely difficult situations. The battle belongs to the Lord, remember?

Not long ago, I met with a married couple who were deep in conflict. The husband claimed to have fallen out of love with his wife and that he didn't see much sense in continuing their relationship. They both recently started attending our church and were new to faith. Knowing a little of their background, I didn't feel at all confident in my ability to turn them around. I showed up—and so did God. After an hour or so discussing their issues, I offered to pray for them. The husband would later admit that it was in that moment that he felt the Spirit of God begin to arrest his heart. At this time, and apart from his wife's knowledge, he was having an affair. The Spirit of God intervened and over the course of several weeks, he began experiencing deep conviction about what he was doing. The power of transformation was at work as he eventually came to the place of confessing and renouncing this illicit relationship. The power of the Spirit was also at work in his wife's heart, allowing her to forgive him and begin a process of reconciliation. It all started with a meeting where God wanted to do something, but I would have missed it had I not shown up.

This is the first way to build confidence in our spiritual battles. Show up. I've been showing up to these kinds of things for a long time and by God's grace, I'll keep showing up. I want to invite you to keep showing up, too.

I think that the enemy loves to take us out of the fight. He'd much rather we didn't show up when he's trying to knock someone out of the fight. His system will intimidate, threaten, accuse, scorn, blame, and attack us so viciously that we are likely to be tempted to turn and run. If that is you, it's time to turn around and give notice to our enemy that the days of running away are over. It's time to start showing up to things where God is wanting to reveal His power and to prove that the battle you face is one He has chosen to fight for you.

This can happen in your home, at work or at church; the battleground can be anywhere. Do you know how many couples divorce because it seems like the easy way out of their conflict? Or how many become absentee parents because it is the easy way out of dealing with a difficult kid? Or how many quit their jobs because of how difficult things might seem? I think of those who change churches, or worse, just drop out of church altogether simply because things have become difficult. If we want to build confidence for the battle, we need to show up to worship. Show up to pray for someone. Show up to serve. Show up to care. Showing up is a huge part of building our confidence. Keep showing up! Fight the good fight!

Grow Up

In addition to showing up for the battle, it's important that every believer gets on track with growing up in his or her faith. Our spiritual growth is a huge confidence builder when dealing with spiritual attack. Nothing grows our faith stronger and faster than understanding and trusting God's character. There are no two ways about it; to understand and trust God's character demands that He becomes the primary object of our *delight* and our *devotion*. Peter echoes the psalmist when he writes, *"Like newborn babies, crave pure spiritual milk, so that by it you may grow up in your salvation, now that you have tasted that the Lord is good" (1 Peter 2:3).* Peter borrows this sentiment from Psalm 34: *"Taste and see that the Lord is good; blessed is the [person] who takes refuge in Him" (Psalm 34:8).*

Peter's exhortation is all about our spiritual growth. Growth is dependent on understanding and applying God's character in our lives. God wants us to grow in our faith so that we will trust Him when we are thrown into the fire of testing. That's why trusting God's character is huge for building our confidence for the battles that are before us.

In the context of the believer's spiritual battles being waged against evil spirits that have gone out into the world carrying a false gospel and proclaiming a false Christ, the Apostle John writes, *"You dear children, are from God and have overcome them, because the one who is in you is greater than the one who is in the world" (1 John 4:4).* The

Apostle John is saying if you belong to Christ, you are from God and have *overcome* all of the evil messengers of Satan. He says this not because his readers were any greater than the messengers of Satan. He says this because *God* is greater than these evil messengers—and God lives in us! If he lives in us, we know that He contends with spiritual beings who set out to attempt harm against His work and His children. Who is this God who dwells in us? He is the Lord Almighty! Are you growing in your knowledge and trust in Him?

There's a great example in the Old Testament of how understanding God's character and trusting Him produces incredible confidence in the face of spiritual assault. When a few of Israel's finest young men had been exiled to Babylon and conscripted into the king's service, their names were changed to strip them of their former identity as followers of Jehovah. When faced with the ultimatum to bow in worship to the king's image of gold or be thrown into a blazing furnace, they refused, knowing the trustworthy character of their God—Jehovah. Their explanation to the king proves their understanding of God's character and their trust in Him: ***"If we are thrown into the blazing furnace, the God we serve is able to save us from it, and he will rescue us from your hand, O king. But even if he does not, we want you to know, O king, that we will not serve your gods or worship the image of gold you have set up"*** *(Daniel 3:17-18).*

Trusting God gives us bold confidence in the face of our spiritual enemies. It also resigns us to whatever fate God allows for His glory. I can only imagine the somber reality these young men faced as they were tied up and thrown into the blazing furnace! But even more, it's fun to imagine the sudden and inexplicable turn of events when the king sees the three young men, along with a mysterious fourth person walking amidst the flames without being burned. Immediately, the king is transformed and converted to acknowledge the Most High God! I'm sure the demonic host who hoped to rid the world of God's chosen servants were wringing their hands in disgust and torment as God's glory was revealed that day!

Knowing and trusting God's character keeps us stable when the world we are living in is crumbling around us. The world of our careers, personal relationships, family and our finances are all places that can come tumbling down. When we really know and trust God's character, we are steady as can be—no matter what the outcome. We can say with confidence that, *"If God is for us, who can be against us" (Romans 8:31)?* To the question of what can separate us from the love of God we know with confidence that death can't and life can't. Angels can't. Demons can't. Things in the present can't. Things in the future can't. No power, no height, no depth, nor anything else in all creation will be able to separate us from the love of God that is in Christ Jesus our Lord (Romans 8:31-39)!

When facing terrible odds, knowing and trusting God's character led the Apostle Paul to write, *"But we have this treasure in jars of clay to show that this all-surpassing power is from God and not from us. We are hard pressed on every side, but not crushed; perplexed, but not in despair; persecuted, but not abandoned; struck down, but not destroyed" (2 Corinthians 4:7-9).*

Growing spiritually also helps us to stay steadfast no matter what the enemy throws at us. We read Paul's words to the Corinthians, *"No temptation has seized you except what is common to man. And God is faithful; he will not let you be tempted beyond what you can bear. But when you are tempted, he will also provide a way out so that you can stand up under it" (1 Corinthians 10:13).*

We grow up when we understand and trust God's character in our lives. The Apostle Peter exhorts his readers, *"But grow in the grace and knowledge of our Lord and Savior Jesus Christ" (2 Peter 3:18).* Paul writes to the Ephesians, *"Instead, speaking the truth in love, we will*

in all things grow up into him who is the Head, that is, Christ"
(Ephesians 4:15).

I've observed over the years that immature believers are most vulnerable to the enemy's attacks. Without understanding God's character, young or spiritually immature believers are tempted to take matters in their own hands and quickly get themselves into a mess. Good churches work hard at discipling their members to know God so that when faced with temptation or another kind of spiritual attack, they can stand firm.

The fine arts pastor at our church demonstrates the kind of maturity needed to be steadfast when Satan attacks. Over the course of a year, our church presents three theatrical outreaches which are often the target of the enemy who loves to create any number of setbacks and challenges knowing that many will be exposed to the gospel. When the gospel goes out to twelve thousand people in a Broadway-scale theatrical program, complete with a full orchestra, over one hundred cast members and hundreds of volunteers, one can imagine the many ways Satan tries to disrupt and derail what's going on.

But Kevin often stops at crucial moments amidst the preparations or even at the pre-performance prayer time to remind everyone participating that God is faithful and Satan can't gain any ground if we trust God. His pre-performance talks to the cast and orchestra sound like a commander sending his troops into battle and fueling their hearts for sure victory over the enemy! It's inspirational to sit with the cast and hear him exhort everyone to trust God for what He alone can do.

I want to encourage you to take stock right now in your knowledge and trust in God's character if you feel you are under spiritual attack. If your knowledge and trust in God is deficient or is waning, then I want to encourage you to commit to growing again in your relationship with God by reading, studying and applying God's Word and taking time to seek the heart of God through prayer. It's important to show up. It's important to grow up. There's something else we need to bolster our confidence in engaging with the enemy.

Listen Up

There is an incredible link between our *past victories* and our *present challenges*, in that the former brings confidence to the latter. It's amazing what happens when we get a few wins under our belt when we face our enemy. When we see God do His thing, suddenly we feel less intimidated the next time we feel the deceitful accusations of the enemy. But the question is, will we remember what He has done when we need to?

We need to listen up if we are going to recall the things in our *past* that will help us in the *present*. A great example of this is found in the story of David and his battle with Goliath, the Philistine giant. I'm going to assume that you know this story but if you don't, read the account in I Samuel 17. It is one of the most amazing and encouraging stories of how we are to fight our spiritual battles. David is a young man (a teenager) who goes out on the front lines of battle with food for his three older brothers. When he comes to the front lines of the battle, he hears Goliath doing his routine rant on the people of God, defying their army and the God they serve. David can't believe the Israelite army is putting up with this nonsense and starts asking those near him, *"Who is this uncircumcised Philistine that he should defy the armies of the living God…what will be done for the man who kills him" (1 Samuel 17:26)?*

The news about David and what he said on the front lines was reported to King Saul and the next thing David knew, he was standing in front of King Saul. David's opening line to King Saul is amazing considering his age and position: *"Let no one lose heart on account of this Philistine; your servant will go and fight him" (1 Samuel 17:32).* Saul objects to David's offer, telling him he's only a boy and that Goliath has been a fighting man from his youth (1 Samuel 17:33). But David is listening to the Spirit and He is reminding him of things from his past that will have direct impact on what's going on in the present. David recalls how God delivered him from the lion and the bear without him receiving so much as even a scratch. Listen to his closing argument to the King: *"The Lord who delivered me from the paw of the lion and the paw of the bear will deliver me from the hand of this Philistine"* *(1 Samuel 17:37).* Remembering how God has worked in our past gives us *confidence* toward the battles we face today. This was true for David and it is also true for us.

As I reflect over the many issues, conflicts and challenges I've faced in my life, I can't think of a single time where God didn't reveal his strength, wisdom, provision or redemption at some point throughout each of them. Don't get me wrong, sometimes my understanding of what God was doing didn't come until much later, and even when things didn't come together the way I envisioned them doing so, God made it plain to merely trust Him because He knows what He's doing. Having this kind of background at my disposal, if I just stop and think for a moment when entering a present dilemma, my heart is comforted and I gain courage to face it. Our memory is the means which activates our faith.

As the children of Israel were preparing to enter the Promised Land, God instructed them to choose twelve men from among the people, one from each tribe, and each one was to take up twelve stones from the middle of the Jordan river where the priests stood with the Ark of God as the Lord held back the waters for them to pass. What was the purpose for doing this? Joshua tells the people, *"These stones are to be a memorial to the people of Israel forever"* *(Joshua 4:7).*

As the rocks were picked up and taken across the river and the priests and all the people passed through the river on dry ground, Joshua further explained the purpose of the memorial stones.

> *"In the future when your descendants ask their fathers, 'What do these stones mean?' tell them, 'Israel crossed the Jordan on dry ground.' For the LORD your God dried up*

the Jordan before you until you had crossed over. The LORD your God did to the Jordan just what he had done to the Red Sea when he dried it up before us until we had crossed over. He did this so that all the peoples of the earth might know that the hand of the LORD is powerful and so that you might always fear the LORD your God" (Joshua 4:21-24).

I love the clarity behind this simple act: so that the *generations to follow* would know that the hand of the Lord is powerful and so that they might fear the Lord their God. Do you know what sets us apart from the foolish and ungodly people who join in Satan's grand design? It often comes down to simply remembering what our God has done for us. This generates and perpetuates our *fear of the Lord*. This is not a cowering fear, but a *reverential* fear.

Not long ago, I was speaking to someone who professed to be a Christian but his brand of Christianity had no room for the fear of God. He adamantly objected to my assertion that the Lord deserved our reverential fear. He said confidently, *"That's negative and the god I serve is all around me and in me and in everything else. The god I serve tells me that the fear of God that you say is important is unnecessary and only a trap for gullible and weak people."*

As he was speaking, I felt the Spirit whisper the truth of one of my favorite Psalms: **"An oracle is within my heart concerning the sinfulness of the wicked: There is no fear of God before his eyes"** *(Psalm 36:1).* The wisdom literature of the Old Testament repeats the importance of having a reverential fear of God and the benefits that come with it, **"The fear of the Lord is the beginning of wisdom, and knowledge of the Holy One is understanding" (Proverbs 9:10).** And, **"The fear of the Lord adds length to life, but the years of the wicked are cut short" (Proverbs 10:27).** Finally, **"The fear of the Lord is a** *fountain of life, turning a man from the snares of death" (Proverbs 14:27).*

When we show up and trust God's provision our confidence grows in the fight. When we grow up through gaining a better understanding of God's character and trust what God alone can do, we experience greater confidence in the battle. When we listen up by recalling the way God has worked in our past and the importance of maintaining a godly reverence for Him, our confidence is bolstered when engaging our spiritual battles. There's another way to increase our confidence when going to battle.

Speak Up

There is something about testifying about what God has done in our lives that builds our confidence for the battle. A major overcoming agent in the battle that wages against the enemy is our testimony, our story of God's power and leading in our own lives. The enemy LOVES to silence our stories; to keep us quiet about the things we have seen God do. When was the last time we testified to others about what God has been doing in our lives? When we testify to our family, friends and even those who oppose us, we put the enemy to flight. He hates this!

There are so many places in Scripture, but one that will help us see its importance and relevance to the spiritual fight we are in daily is found in Revelation 12:11 where we read of a scene in what I believe is still in the future. Satan and his angels are hurled to earth to inflict all the wrath and fury possible, knowing their time is short (this is during the great and terrible tribulation period). Voices come from heaven and declare that *"...the accuser of our brothers, who accuses them before our God day and night, has been hurled down. They overcame him by the blood of the Lamb and by the word of their testimony" (Revelation 12:10-11a).* The blood of Jesus and our testimony has invincible power over our enemy. Don't forget this. Satan would love it if you did!

Speak up about God's goodness. Speak up about what God has done for you. Speak up and tell your friends and your neighbors and the people you meet at the gym that you serve a God who is faithful, powerful and wonderful. Whenever we do, we put the enemy to flight.

When I read the Psalms, this is what I see David doing in so many instances, especially when he is experiences conflict after which God's hand of deliverance is sought. He declares the power and victory that God will have over his enemies. Psalm 18 is a great example of what we find throughout the Psalms. David begins, *"I love you, O LORD, my strength. The Lord is my rock, my fortress and my deliverer; my God is my rock, in whom I take refuge. He is my shield and the horn of my salvation, my stronghold. I call to the LORD, who is worthy of praise, and I am saved from my enemies" (Psalm 18:1-3).* Notice that for David, it was speaking God's praise that brought salvation from his enemies. This is true for us, too.

Sometimes when I'm praising God in worship, I am reminded of this passage and realize that as I praise God, He is at work subduing the schemes that the enemy is attempting in my life. I wonder if believers recognize the power of declaring God's praise as a counter to the enemy's tactics in their lives. In Psalm 18, David is testifying of God's saving power, of God's deliverance from all his enemies. I love this. It's truly amazing. The power of testimony. The power of our stories.

I don't think any of us fully understand just how powerful our personal testimonies are for building our own confidence or encouraging confidence in others. When someone says, "I was down for the count. I was on the ropes but my heart turned to the Lord and I called to Him and He heard me and saved me!" When people testify by sharing details of how God delivered them, it is so inspirational and connects with people on so many levels. Satan's system of evil and wickedness loses traction in people's lives who hear what God is doing. The cool thing about walking with Jesus is that there should be new chapters from the story of our lives all the time. Do you have any new material? What has God done lately in your life? Where has he rescued you? Where have you seen His deliverance? Speak up about it and your confidence will soar. The confidence of others will grow as well. Guaranteed! As I was considering this in my own life, I received a text from a friend for whom I pray often. I had sent her a text earlier in the day expressing that God had laid her on my heart with a specific burden to pray for her. Her text explained that the timing of my text couldn't have been better. She had just had a very difficult encounter with a family member who doesn't know Christ and she felt her sister had been extremely unkind to her and misunderstood something that had taken place between them. She said in the moment my text arrived, she felt loved by God and not to worry about her sister— but to love her and bless her regardless. That's the hand of God at work!

At a recent men's ministry event, the story of one of our older saints touched the lives of younger believers who were there. Both young and old felt the power of God's Spirit, using someone's story to bring hope and encouragement through the difficult seasons of life. I was reminded at that meeting of what the Psalmist declares, *"One generation will commend your works to another; they will tell of your mighty acts" (Psalm 145:4).*

Building our confidence toward engaging the enemy isn't that complicated. All we really need to do is to show up, grow up, listen up and speak up of what God is doing in our lives. I'm wondering as you are reading this now, if the Spirit of God might encourage you to aim at even one of these principles and experience the beauty and joy of increased confidence toward engaging the enemy. If so, you might find yourself running toward and not away from the conflict that is most troubling you today.

CHAPTER 9: RUNNING TO BATTLE
DISCUSSION QUESTIONS

1. Why do some believers lack confidence when engaging in spiritual warfare? Identify the common fears associated with "fighting with the devil." How confident are you when you know a spiritual battle is imminent?

2. Why is the knowledge of, and belief in God's character so critical to gaining deeper confidence when in spiritual warfare? What aspect of God's character is particularly helpful for you when engaging the enemy?

3. When the Scripture talks about "the battle belonging to the Lord," what does this mean specifically to you? What part must we play if in fact, the battle "belongs" to the Lord?

4. Share a few experiences when you personally witnessed God's power in delivering you from a difficult situation. What are a few things you remember most leading up to the moment when God revealed Himself and brought the needed deliverance?

5. Read through a portion of the story of David and Goliath recorded in 1 Samuel 17:41-51. What stands out to you about David's attitude toward Goliath? How did God reveal Himself in that situation?

6. How do you remind yourself of special moments in the past when you witnessed God do something extraordinary in your life or ministry? Do you have anything akin to Joshua's memorial stones (Joshua 4:21-24)?

7. Who needs to hear about something God has done for you lately? When will you tell them?

CHAPTER 10

DESTROYING SATAN'S WORK
Depending on Christ's Finished Work

Sometimes when we look around, it appears that Satan is winning in this spiritual war in which we are engaged. Crimes against humanity, brutal and senseless atrocities, the escalation of hate, war, famine, disease, racism, and a host of discouraging realities give evidence of a world void of the love and care of God. Many people, including some Christ-followers conclude that if there is a spiritual being known as Satan, he's far from conceding defeat and in fact, looks to be headed for victory.

There's a different reality that we've been considering throughout this book. It's this reality that we must now look at more closely so that our perspective on this troubled world remains true to Scripture's claims. American writer and radio broadcaster, Paul Harvey was known for "The Rest of the Story" segments that consisted of stories presented daily on ABC Networks with key elements and details of a story concealed until the end. Each segment would conclude with the famous tag line, "And now you know the *rest* of the story." I can still hear Paul Harvey's voice inflection on the word, "rest" in that tagline to underscore that the listener needed all the information to make real sense of what in the beginning of the story seemed obvious—but incomplete.

In a similar way, the story unfolding around us and its conclusion seems obvious to the uninformed: Satan has this world under his control. There are details, however, that when inserted into the context of what we see in our world, dramatically changes the outcome of the bigger story arc of history. And it is that detail we turn our attention to in this chapter.

The overlooked and neglected detail in the story arc of history is that God's Son, Jesus Christ was sent to our world to specifically and utterly destroy the devil's work. There is no greater truth than knowing Jesus was successful, triumphing over His enemies, including most importantly, the devil and his purposes and plans. The Apostle John makes this clear in his first epistle, *"The reason the Son of God appeared was to destroy the devil's work" (1 John 3:8b).* This is one of the most exciting and triumphant statements we find anywhere in the Bible concerning our true hope in *spiritual warfare.*

Therefore, unpacking the truth behind 1 John 3:8a is of utmost importance for all who follow Jesus. The Apostle John tells us the reason and the purpose for Jesus' coming was specifically to destroy the devil's work! We find recorded in the book of Genesis that war was declared and Messiah's victory assured in this epic contest between Satan and Jesus Christ. God pronounces emphatically, *"He will crush your head and you will strike his heel..." (Genesis 3:15).* The enemy's doom was set at the beginning of humanity's downfall. And throughout the generations ever since that dreadful day when brokenness entered our world, we've been waiting for what's been promised. According to John in his epistle, what was promised has come to pass. Jesus successfully waged war and was victorious over our enemy. In fact, the text of 1 John 3:8 also helps us see that Jesus' incarnation is a direct assault on all that the enemy stands for and has promoted throughout the world since his fall. Here we are reminded of who our real champion is—Jesus Christ our Lord!

The life and death mission of our Lord Jesus was to deliver a death blow to Satan. You and I have the honor and privilege of living under the reality of Christ's victory over Satan today and every day! It is this truth that is the "rest of the story," offering every believer hope in a world still broken under what appears to be the unstoppable destruction of our enemy.

In the next few pages, I'd like us to consider exactly what is the devil's work that Jesus came to destroy. And having identified the work Jesus came to destroy, show how his life and sacrificial death does, in fact, destroy it completely. The devil's work, though extensive in many ways, finds traction through at least three primary strategies, all of which were given a death blow through the person and work of Jesus Christ.

The devil's work minimizes the certainty and sentence of sin

When we go back to the very beginning of humanity, we begin to understand the fundamentals of the devil's work. In his first appearance with Adam and Eve, he attempts to minimize the certainty and sentence of sin. His first words to Eve were, **"Did God really say, 'You must not eat from any tree in the garden'" (Genesis 3:1b)?** Notice that the devil's strategy centers on *doubting* whether God really ever said Eve shouldn't eat from that tree. God had made perfectly clear to Adam and Eve, the extent of their freedom in the garden—and his instructions were designed for their good: **"You are free to eat from any tree in the garden; but you must not eat from the tree of the knowledge of good and evil, for when you eat of it, you will surely die" (Genesis 2:16-17).**

Eve counters the devil's strategy by stating that God did not prohibit them from eating of *any* of the trees *except* the tree in the middle of the garden, the tree of knowledge of good and evil. The devil, however, counters her response by categorically denying God's sentence of judgment if they ate from it: **"You will not surely die" (Genesis 3:4).** This has been the devil's method from the beginning of humanity's existence in the garden. He strives to minimize the certainty of what sin is and the consequences of giving in to it.

One of the ways that the devil promotes this minimization of sin's certainty and the consequences of giving in to it is by suggesting we justify our actions through comparison with others. It's easy to minimize in our own minds both the reality of sin and its consequences when we look around and find others whom we consider greater sinners than ourselves, especially if those who seem to be sinning more are doing well in their lives. In the gospel record, Jesus confronts the self-righteous religious people who were experts in comparison which allowed them to have an elevated view of themselves. He warns, *"You have heard it said, 'Do not murder' ...but I tell you that anyone who is angry with his brother will be subject to judgment" (Matthew 5:21-22).* The self-righteous Pharisees thought they were better than anyone guilty of murder because they had avoided taking someone's life, but they couldn't see that anger was equally as condemning since the act of murder starts with anger in the heart. The Pharisees were no less guilty than murderers and they couldn't see this. They couldn't see it because Satan desires to cause people to minimize their sinfulness and the consequences that follow. Let's not forget that the Sermon on the Mount found in Matthew 5-7 denounces many other heart issues that are as serious as the actions they produce.

We see this also in the account of the woman who was caught in the act of adultery (John 8). You remember that this woman was caught in the very act of adultery and brought to Jesus as a test to see how Jesus would respond. The account begs the question of how a woman caught in adultery didn't implicate the man who was with her. It quickly becomes obvious that there's something amiss going on here, but the unfair treatment of the woman notwithstanding, let's consider why all this was going on to begin with.

The Pharisees want to know if Jesus would adhere to Mosaic law and have the woman stoned for her offense, or would he show mercy on her, thus showing that He was not aligned with the law of Moses? It was a veritable "Catch-22." As always, Jesus masterfully approaches the issue by putting these men to a test as well. He simply says, *"If any of you is without sin, let him be the first to throw a stone at her" (John 8:7).*

178

The narrative tells us that *"those who heard began to go away one at a time, the older ones first, until only Jesus was left with the woman" (Matthew 5:9).* Then Jesus pronounces his offer of forgiveness without condemning her. He exhorts her to leave her life of sin. Though not found in the text, I always envision that after this incident, Jesus went and found the man who was part of this charade and lovingly spoke truth and conviction into his life, too.

These evil men could easily have stoned this woman because in their minds she was a greater sinner than themselves. I've learned that our human nature is so good at detecting the sin in others but very weak at detecting it in ourselves. Raising kids offers lots of evidence about this. One sibling will cry out toward the other, "Look at what he did! He should be punished!" Never do our kids come to us and say, "I did this terrible thing and I should be punished." We make good judges but we're not very good at offering mercy. Remember the story Jesus told of the Pharisee who stood up and prayed about himself: *"God, I thank you that I am not like other men—robbers, evildoers, adulterers—or even like this tax collector. But the tax collector stood at a distance. He would not even look up to heaven, but beat his breast and said, 'God, have mercy on me, a sinner.' 'I tell you that this man, rather than the other, went home justified before God'" (Luke 18:11-14).*

I point out these stories and references in the gospels because it was the missional intention of Jesus Christ to come to destroy the system that the devil has created that minimizes the certainty and sentence of sin. But the devil is still hard at work in our world plying his trade to all he can deceive.

One of the ways we see his tactics at work in our world is by removing even the word "sin" from our speech. The word "sin" isn't a popular word. There is pressure in our culture to avoid calling anyone a "sinner" since the image it sends, we are told, is negative and hurtful. In our culture, "tolerance" is the greatest of all virtues and to call something sinful is often viewed as the worse kind of hate. At this point, those who value tolerance become completely intolerant and yet never see the duplicity of their thought process. This is also part of the devil's work.

Believers even at times substitute the word "sin" for words like "mistake" or "slip-up" or "blunder." The word sin has Biblical synonyms: iniquity, immorality, depravity, debauchery, evil, and transgression. But these words are not very popular in our culture and using them invites criticism. When we soften the reality of our evil intentions or waywardness, we play into the devil's age-old strategy of minimizing both the certainty and the sentence of sin. God doesn't need to forgive our mistakes; we are human and humans make mistakes. We might call someone by the wrong name. We might forget someone's birthday. We might pay a bill with the wrong amount of money. These, and a host of other simple slip-ups can be corrected, but we can't correct or overturn our sins alone. If we sin, we have become slaves to sin (John 8:34). Paul wrote, *"We know that the law is spiritual; but I am unspiritual, sold as a slave to sin" (Romans 7:14).* Our sin problem has only one remedy—the precious blood of Jesus Christ.

In the book of Romans, which is the clearest treatise on the true nature of our sinful state and the gospel of Jesus Christ, Paul clearly states, *"...for all have sinned and fall short of the glory of God" (Romans 3:23).* If you are familiar with Paul's letter to the Romans, you know that this statement falls on the heels of several Old Testament quotations affirming that there are none who are righteous, none who seek God. As sinners, we are helplessly lost and separated from a righteous and holy God. Apart from His intervening grace and mercy, all of us would be eternally lost and bound for hell due to our sin. In a culture that elevates fairness, we must be reminded that it would be totally fair for God to cast all of humanity into hell for eternity since we are all sinners. But God's love refuses to do what's merely fair—so he sends his perfect Son to pay our penalty for sin and open the door of salvation. Paul reminds us of this when writing to the Ephesians: *"You were dead in your transgressions and sins, in which you used to live when you followed the ways of this world...like the rest, we were by nature objects of wrath. But because of His great love for us, God, who is rich in mercy, made us alive with Christ even when we were dead in our transgressions—it is by grace you have been saved..."* (Ephesians 2:1-5; v.8a).

Somehow, the essential point of our sinfulness prompting our recognition of our need for a Savior is becoming less mainstream in the presentation of the gospel these days. If people don't consider themselves sinners, then there is really no point in them looking for a Savior. Yet, one of the roles of the Holy Spirit is to convict the world of *"...guilt in regard to sin, because men do not believe in [Jesus]..." (John 16:8-9).* Do you understand that according to Jesus, the greatest manifestation of sin is unbelief? Most people only view various deeds as sin, and they are blind to the reality that the true sin that God is concerned about most in someone's life is their refusal to trust Him for the salvation He graciously invites them to experience. To be honest, I think one is arrogant and self-absorbed to deny he is a sinner. But at the forefront of this reality is knowing that the proof that one is a sinner lies in the fact of his/her refusal to believe Jesus to the point of following Him.

While people might admit that they sometimes do things they shouldn't, most fall short in admitting they are sinners simply because they don't believe in and follow Jesus. To believe in Jesus is to openly acknowledge we are sinners and need a Savior. The Apostle John writes, *"But you know that he [Jesus] appeared so that he might take away our sins. And in him is no sin" (1 John 3:5).* John clearly points out, *"If we claim to be without sin, we deceive ourselves and the truth is not in us...if we claim we have not sinned, we make him out to be a liar and his word has no place in our lives" (1 John 1:8,10).*

Jesus destroys the devil's work by becoming our sin offering

The good news of the gospel is that Jesus gives Himself as a ransom for our sins. When we proclaim this truth and as we *"walk in the light as He is in the light, we have fellowship with one another, and the blood of Jesus, his Son, purifies us from all sin"* (1 John 1:7).

While the devil has been busy minimizing the certainty and sentence of sin, Jesus set out from heaven to destroy his work by giving Himself as our sin-sacrifice. We, who have received victory over the devil's work by claiming Jesus as the true and only acceptable sacrifice that paid for all our sins, cherish the privilege of declaring this truth with our lives and our words so others may escape the death-grip of our adversary and become truly free. It's exciting to partner with Jesus every day in this beautiful sweet communion of destroying the devil's work through proclaiming the gospel.

The devil's work distorts the reality and finality of death

The Bible teaches that death is both real and final and that the condition of our soul at the time of our death is what determines our eternal state. This isn't meant as a scare tactic, it's the truth. If someone dies without ever trusting in Jesus Christ to provide forgiveness and power to live for God, that person will enter eternity separated forever from God and true fulfillment and reward. God created humanity for himself—to exist in beautiful and intimate relationship forever. When sin entered humanity through the disobedience of the first Adam, that relationship was broken and requires reconciliation.

I just pointed out that we're all sinners (Romans 3:23). To be clear about what it means that we are sinners, let me emphasize that we sin because we are sinners. You'll probably need to read that sentence again. Most people miss this truth when contemplating the reason for our sinfulness. There are those who distort what the Bible says about our sin nature, suggesting that the reason we are sinners is because we sin. The

182

argument follows that if we can just avoid any specific sin, we can escape the sentence of being "sinners." But this isn't true. We sin *because* we are sinners. It's our nature to sin. We are born with a "sin" condition.

Every parent has the memory of their first child being born. In the minutes that follow that miracle of new life, a proud mom and dad cherish the beauty and loveliness of such a small and helpless baby being held in their arms. This child, they often surmise is *perfect*. While the special reality of bearing one's offspring never goes away, the once naïve belief that your child is perfect begins to fade about the time they reach two years of age. As cute and loving as a little child may be, there's no mistaking the fact that embedded in every child is selfishness, stubbornness and a host of more insidious realities that will likely come out as the child grows. None of these attributes are taught to the child, they come from within. It's unmistakably a part of their very nature. Anyone who rejects the Bible's teaching on the embedded sinfulness of human beings starting at birth, simply hasn't had or spent much time around children. The Apostle Paul makes this abundantly clear in Romans 5: ***"For just as through the disobedience of the one man the many were made sinners, so also through the obedience of the one man [Jesus], the many will be made righteous" (Romans 5:19).***

Because we are all sinners, the reality and finality of death must be understood and embraced: ***"For the wages of sin is death…" (Romans 6:23a).*** I've been around many people when death has occurred and I've found that most people are very confused about the true implications of a sinner's passing if that person had never trusted God's provision for forgiveness and new life. Most people assume that their loved one has simply gone to a "better place"—their problems are over, they are no longer suffering, they are finally enjoying all the things they had hoped for in this life. But this isn't true if the one who dies had never embraced God's gracious invitation found in the gospel. This is where the devil's work becomes apparent. Clearly, most people, no matter what their religious background, have a distorted view of what happens after death.

I've known many people who are terrified of death. They are held in the bondage of their fear of death and it pushes them to all kinds of diversions, doing all they can to promote their safety and sustainability. They try to stay in control of every little thing in their life to divert any possibility of death coming upon them prematurely. Others try to beat the odds of death by being physically fit or doing all sorts of nutrition enhancements. The goal becomes staying young so one never grows old and dies. As ridiculous as this may sound, I sincerely believe many people push death so far out of their minds they have convinced themselves it will never happen to them. I've heard of people who travel to places where the moonlight or the sunlight imparts a kind of life-enhancing element that increases longevity and pushes back the reality of death. Don't get me wrong, I'm not suggesting we not take care of our physical bodies and do what we can to stay healthy to live long and fulfilling lives, I'm simply pointing out that for many people, the thought of death is very distant indeed.

A few years ago, when both Steve Jobs (founder of Apple) and Al Davis (owner of the Oakland Raiders) died just days apart, there was talk about how people never thought these guys would die. Speaking of Al Davis, former coach and sports broadcaster, John Madden said, "I just never thought he'd die." Really? I doubt John Madden really feels this way, but it does point to how we tend to live our lives without coming to terms with the reality or the finality of death, because the devil's work is to promote a naïve and ignorant view of death.

The other way that the devil works to distort the reality and finality of death is by reducing the traumatic nature of death. Those who buy into this aspect of his work, assume a posture that sees death as a part of life— no big deal. This is part of the devil's work, to desensitize our thinking about death and not fear what we should fear if we don't have a relationship with Jesus Christ when the day of our death arrives. Speaking of Al Davis, the Oakland Raiders played the Sunday following his death and the team pulled out a dramatic win against the Houston Texans. That day, the Raiders' coach extolled his team in a post-game interview saying this remarkable win was attributed to Al Davis, "…this was Al Davis with his hands on the ball! He was looking down on us and helping us win." Really? I wondered, did the Raiders' coach really believe Al Davis intervened from some other world to give his team the advantage? I am inclined to believe the Raider's coach did believe that Mr. Davis intervened. People who misunderstand the reality and finality of death say and believe all kinds of interesting things about death. Some believe that when people die, they become guardian angels. Some believe the deceased becomes a sort of spirit guide to them for the rest of their lives. When people believe these kinds of things about death, they are simply creating their own reality which is nothing more than an illusion. This is part of the devil's work. He distorts the reality and finality of death.

The Bible declares that *"it is appointed to die once and then to face judgment" (Hebrews 9:27).* If a person is outside of having a relationship with Jesus Christ, should they look forward to death? If death means certain judgment between a holy God and an unholy human being, that would not be something someone unprepared should be looking forward to. Death comes to all of us but arrogance and pride causes lost sinners to set aside any need for preparation and simply look forward to going to some better kind of existence. Unbelievers are not aware that the reason they have a belief in the afterlife is because God put it there in the first place. The wisdom literature of the Old Testament reminds us of this truth: *"He has set eternity in the hearts of men; yet they cannot fathom what God has done from beginning to end" (Ecclesiastes 3:11).* While the God-given awareness of life after the grave is imbedded in our hearts, we are clueless to the reality of what awaits apart from what God's Word reveals. If we neglect God's truth, we make up our own.

We either pretend that death will never come to us or we accept it without understanding the terrible consequence of dying without trusting in Jesus Christ. Another strategy of the devil regarding the distortion of the certainty and finality of death is promoting the idea that when someone dies, they just cease to exist. No more existence. Lights out. Game over. No conscious awareness of anything after we breathe our last breath. Paul addressed this idea and goes further in his argument for the resurrection of those who die when writing, ***"If the dead are not raised, 'Let us eat and drink, for tomorrow we die" (1 Corinthians 15:32).*** With this mentality, we just live it up today because tomorrow, if we die, it will be over. Many people are living this way and don't really know why. They are living proof of the devil's work that distorts the reality and finality of death.

Let's not forget that something else that is closely related to the devil's distortion of death's reality is the sheer number of people who die every year due to the murderous actions of others. Satan loves death— especially if he can promote those willing to act on their hatred or unstable emotional impulses to take the lives of others. Every time I read of a murder or active shooter scenario, I am led to Jesus' description of the devil, ***"The thief comes to steal, kill and destroy" (John 10:10a).*** The devil loves to kill. Jesus even called him a ***"murderer from the beginning" (John 8:44).*** Why should we be surprised by the inexplicable and bizarre murder cases we read about in the daily news? Let's not forget the many lives that have been lost under the evil intent of despots who rule and reign is marked by murdering those who pose a perceived threat to their agenda—and the devil absolutely loves all of this. People dying outside of belonging to Christ reflects his continued rebellion to the plans of God and wanting others to experience the same fate awaiting him.

Jesus destroys the devil's work by tasting death for us and conquering it through his resurrection

The writer of Hebrews points out that Jesus *"...suffered death, so that by the grace of God he might taste death for everyone" (Hebrews 2:9).* He continues, *"Since the children have flesh and blood, he too shared in their humanity so that by his death he might destroy him who holds the power of death—that is, the devil—and free those who all their lives were held in slavery by their fear of death" (Hebrews 2:14-15).*

The devil ensnares lost sinners through their fear of death. This may seem counter to what we've just covered in describing his specific work of distorting one's view of death or its certainty. It's also true however, that one of the devil's distortions about death includes an inordinate fear of it. Clearly, without knowing Jesus and believing that he's gone before us, the portal of death feels overwhelming and foreboding. I've been present with people in their final conscious moments who do not share in the confidence that comes from belonging to Jesus. Often, their countenance is filled with fear and anxiety, and rightfully so. On the other hand, being in the presence of God's people as they near that mysterious threshold, there's an entirely different atmosphere; there's a palpable peace, even a joy for what lies ahead.

So thoroughly has Jesus' death and resurrection destroyed the devil's work, believers revel in what awaits them. Ruth was a beautiful ninety-nine-year-old woman who became a Christ-follower when she was eighty-six. Ruth had never experienced any real health issues in her ninety-nine years, but suddenly cancer took over and in a few short weeks, she left this world and entered the joy of her Savior, Jesus. When hearing Ruth had taken ill, I was away on vacation. I hoped to be home in time to give her my love and blessing for being such a wonderful encouragement to me and our church. God gave me the opportunity to see Ruth three times before she entered glory. Each time I visited, she had the most beautiful

187

smile on her face. All she could talk about was finally being with Jesus and how she couldn't wait to be there with him. In the presence of her family, she shared her burden for each one to know and follow Jesus. Her faith kept her heart full of anticipation for how God would work in her family. It was so clear that when we prayed, she was already sensing the presence of Jesus even though her body was still lingering. She finally passed in total peace and with that smile on her face all of us had come to love.

Jesus destroys the devil's work by conquering death and granting lost sinners eternal life through faith alone. In the gospel of John, Jesus addresses this very thing: ***"The thief comes only to steal and kill and destroy; I have come that they may have life, and have it to the full"*** ***(John 10:10).*** For Ruth and millions like her, approaching death's door brought a beautiful anticipation for what is ahead for those who belong to Jesus. I stress that this is a far cry from the kind of wishful thinking and blind faith people outside of God's family sometimes feign in view of their approaching death. Christ's destruction of the devil's work is so complete and true, it defies explanation, yet it's more real than anything a person can imagine. Because Jesus has already made a way for us, through his death and resurrection, all we need to do is come to Him in faith and receive the life He alone offers.

The devil's work conceals the gospel and glory of Christ

The devil's work goes far beyond minimizing the certainty and sentence of sin and the reality and finality of death. He also works at concealing both the gospel and the glory of Christ. His aim is always to keep the gospel from being heard and the glory of Jesus Christ from being seen. He hates the gracious and saving work of Jesus Christ. When successful, his methods keep people from being transformed by Jesus' limitless love.

We read this in Paul's letter to the Corinthians, *"The god of this age has blinded the minds of unbelievers, so that they cannot see the light of the gospel of the glory of Christ, who is the image of God" (2 Corinthians 4:4).* It may be news to some of us that the devil works to blind people from seeing their need for Jesus. For those of you who already know this to be true, have you ever wondered *how* he does this? How does the devil blind the minds of unbelievers? The devil does this through a host of methods including, but not limited to, materialism, hedonism and even religion. Most people go through life so focused on what's immediately next for them, they rarely stop to wonder if any of their pursuits will provide the meaning they hope to achieve in life.

I met John shortly after I become the pastor of the church where I serve. John had worldly wealth, a beautiful family, good health, close friendships and anyone looking at his life from any distance, he appeared to have it all. One day I asked John to have coffee in hopes I would discover that underneath all his success, he'd admit to something missing in his life—and then I would present intentionally that what was missing was a relationship with God. As we sipped our coffee, he admitted that his time in church was more about appeasing his wife than about his own hunger or need for God. Knowing the gospel cuts through all excuses and reservations for the one who doesn't see his need, I gently asked permission to share with him how he could experience forgiveness of sins and a new life through following Jesus. He shrugged his shoulders and said, "Sure." John listened attentively and even gave tacit approval to many of the things I shared with him. After I'd done my best to share about his need to know Christ, John remained confident that while some of his family needed God, he was doing just fine on his own. *Thanks, but no thanks.* Perhaps his education, career and worldly success were barriers to him seeing his true need for the gospel. The devil is behind every person's false assessment of being okay in life apart from calling out for God to be gracious in forgiving sin and imparting new life.

189

It's a work of grace whenever a person comes to see his need for Christ; whether the person is a professional woman at the top of her career or a distinguished scholar contributing to the body of knowledge, a white collar, blue collar or no collar person—all are equally needy for the gospel. When God begins to draw someone and open their eyes, they come to Jesus without reservation.

Ryan was a guy who grew up in the church but his thirst for money, success and relationships sent him on a search that led him far from the God he had been introduced to as a child. But his love for basketball brought him back to church at our early morning pick-up games. For nearly two years, Ryan seemed cold and indifferent to any invitation I would give him to come check out Sunday morning worship services. There were times I asked what he was looking forward to in hopes it would lead into spiritual discussions. Most times, it was clear he wasn't interested. In fact, one time Ryan explained that he was considering becoming a Buddhist. I cringed inwardly and cried out to God for Ryan to see Jesus.

Then the day arrived. Without me knowing the background, Ryan later told me that one morning as he woke up and looked at the woman sleeping next to him who was his live-in partner, he suddenly felt a deep foreboding of having missed God's plan for his life. Later that week, he was playing basketball in our church gym when the ball went out of bounds and came to a stop near the feet of a beautiful young woman who happened to be in town visiting her mom. As she handed the ball back to Ryan, he asked what she was doing there and she said that she was going to attend a young adults meeting that night. God used this young woman to help open Ryan's eyes to suddenly see that the pang of his heart earlier that week was leading him to check out the young adult ministry in our church. I know what you are thinking, perhaps Ryan was just interested in getting into a new relationship? If you didn't know what happened next, you might be right. Ryan did attend that young adults meeting and the spark ignited into a flame. I'll never forget the morning that Ryan asked me for books to help him grow as a new believer. I invited him to a Bible study I was leading and he's been growing strong in his relationship with God. Ryan and Aiden eventually married. The whole story is a miracle.

Hearing Ryan talk now about his conversion is one of the most encouraging things ever. He's so passionate to serve God and be a godly man and husband. His life is completely changed. Ryan's story reminds all of us that no matter how far or disinterested a person may seem to be toward Jesus and His gospel, God is able to break through and bring life to the one who needs it.

The devil works hard to send messengers who distort the truth of the gospel by declaring salvation or a relationship with God *apart* from the person and work of Jesus Christ. The message of "doing it on your own" is everywhere and people buy it hook, line and sinker. Most people have a very firm belief that they've figured out how to be right with God—be good enough or be better than the next guy and you've got it made. His distortions are found everywhere.

The Apostle John warns of this in his epistle:

"Dear friends, do not believe every spirit, but test the spirits to see whether they are from God, because many false prophets have gone out into the world. This is how you can recognize the Spirit of God: Every spirit that acknowledges that Jesus Christ has come in the flesh is from God, but every spirit that does not acknowledge Jesus is not from God. This is the spirit of the antichrist, which you have heard is coming and even now is already in the world" (1 John 4:1-4).

The gospel can be distorted only slightly and people can still miss the point. I've spoken to people who never heard in the church where they grew up, that one must believe in Jesus Christ to be saved. Somehow, for many it is about staying in the lane of religious ritual, being moral or even just being a nice person, that really matters. Perhaps this has been your experience, if so, it's time to step out of distortion and into the light of clarity. Believe Jesus died for you and arose from the grave to give you the power to live a new life.

Paul wrote concerning this to the Galatians, *"I am astonished that you are so quickly deserting the one who called you by the grace of Christ and are turning to a different gospel—which is really no gospel at all. Evidently some people are throwing you into confusion and are trying to pervert the gospel of Christ..."* *(Galatians 1:6-7).* The Galatians had been persuaded into a gospel that was not what they had learned from Paul. It was a gospel that included one's need to work for salvation. It was Jesus plus some kind of work in order to be saved. This is heresy and must be rejected.

Paul rebuked those at Corinth for being so gullible and accepting of counterfeit teachings: *"For if someone comes to you and preaches a Jesus other than the Jesus we preached, or if you receive a different spirit from the one you received, or a different gospel from the one you accepted, you put up with it easily enough..."* *(2 Corinthians 11:4).* Those who peddle these distorted messages are described later in the chapter, *"For such men are false apostles, deceitful workmen, masquerading as apostles of Christ. And no wonder, for Satan himself masquerades as an angle of light. It is not surprising, then, if his servants masquerade as servants of righteousness. Their end will be what their actions deserve"* *(2 Corinthians 11:13-15).* Notice in the context of spiritual warfare, Satan masquerades as an angel of light and so do his servants. It's easy to be misled.

How many false christs are out there? Plenty. There is the christ of the cults, of spiritualists, of new agers, of humanists, of ritualists that all hold some view of Christ that is *less* than who he actually is. Who is the true Christ? According to Scripture, he is God incarnate (John 1:1,14), Lord of and over all (Colossians 1:18). He is the Alpha and Omega

192

(Revelation 1:8), the first and the last (Revelation 1:17), the beginning and the end (Revelation 22:13). Paul writes, *"He is the image of the invisible God, the firstborn over all creation. For by him all things were created: things in heaven and on earth, visible and invisible, whether thrones or powers or rulers or authorities; all things were created by him and for him. He is before all things, and in him all things hold together. And he is the head of the body, the church; he is the beginning and the firstborn from among the dead, so that in everything he might have the supremacy" (Colossians 1:15-18).* There is no one more powerful and capable to deal with the devil than Jesus.

Jesus destroys the devil's work by revealing himself to those he came to save

While the devil is busy concealing both the gospel and the glory of Christ, Jesus is busy revealing himself to those he came to save. His revealing work is fascinating and miraculous. For some, Jesus is revealed in very inexplicable ways. For others, he reveals Himself in very simple ways. Jesus revealed himself to me as a young boy. From my earliest memories, I recall having no doubts about the existence of God and my need for Jesus to forgive my sins and give me eternal life. As an elementary school aged boy, I remember memorizing Scriptures while attending the Baptist Church's Sunday School classes where my parents were members and we attended as a family on Sundays. There was one Sunday that, as a third-grader, I felt the personal tug of Jesus, knocking at the door of my heart. Since I believed in God and trusted what I had been told about the Father's Son, Jesus, I easily opened my heart and believed in Him. I would soon begin to understand it was the Spirit, the third member of the triune Godhead who had led me to truth and allowed me to hear Jesus' personal invitation to be saved. I was baptized as a young boy but my conversion seemed more like an easy but necessary next step in my walk with God. In the years that followed, my faith became more mature and I grew into a better understanding of what it meant to follow Jesus. God revealed Himself to me as he does to so many others—very simply without anything overtly miraculous, though let's not forget that all conversions are miraculous since they involve bringing a dead person back to life (Colossians 2:13).

God may also reveal himself to others in more extraordinary ways. Recently I watched a short documentary on the life of Pistol Pete Maravich, who was known for his dazzling skills on the basketball court. Pete's revolutionary contribution to the sport of basketball is unprecedented. He changed the game for both players and spectators. Pete had an obsession with playing basketball that started at seven years of age. His father intentionally lured him into playing the sport believing he would one day become a legendary player in the game.

It is believed that Pete's obsession with the game of basketball was in some ways, a reaction to the emptiness he found in his life in virtually every other area. His father, a coach and former player, dreamed of one day coaching his son at the collegiate level. He had his own obsession with the game. This obsession grew even more when his dream came true and he became the head coach for LSU, working a deal to bring his son Pete to attend the University and play for him. Pete's collegiate career broke more individual records on the court than any previous player in the history of the game. He would later describe his life as becoming a living basketball with no other life but to play and win games.

Pete's mom had become so depressed for having no relationship with her husband or her son. She suffered depression, became an alcoholic and eventually took her own life. Tragedy and sadness seemed to travel alongside of Pete Maravich's basketball career. Without going into more detail about the illustrious career Pete would have even as a pro basketball player, I found the documentary so interesting as it pointed out that after Peter retired from basketball due to an injury, God showed up and literally spoke life into his soul late one night, waking him from his sleep. Virtually out of nowhere, God made himself known to Pete and miraculously saved Him. The final eight years of his life was devoted to sharing the life-saving message of the gospel of Jesus Christ to as many people as he could. During this time, his father, Press, also came to trust in Christ before he succumbed to cancer in 1987.

Pete was scheduled to do an interview on a Christian radio station one day in early January of 1988. People who worked for the organization where he was going to be interviewed invited him to play some pick-up basketball the morning of the radio interview. As one who loves to play the game of basketball and sometimes fantasizes about playing a pick-up game with Golden State Warriors, Steph Curry, I can't imagine those guys getting to play a pick-up game with the legendary Pistol Pete Maravich! It was that morning, however, after playing basketball with some new friends at a church gym that Pete suffered a massive and fatal heart attack.

The late James Dobson, founder and radio voice for Focus on the Family was on the court that morning playing with Pete and later testified to his shocked listeners that Pete had died in his arms. Pete was only forty years old. But before he left this world to enter the next, the most amazing and miraculous thing had happened—God has revealed Himself to him, through the person and work of His Son, Jesus Christ. For roughly thirty years, the devil had concealed the gospel and glory of Christ from Pete Maravich, but then Jesus Christ destroyed the devil's work when He revealed Himself to Pete. This is, and will always be the greatest miracle of all when Christ is revealed and someone responds in belief.

If you have yet to believe in Jesus, then the devil's work is still being done in your life because his work is to conceal the glory and gospel of Jesus Christ so that people won't believe in Him and be saved. Yet, I declare to you that Jesus Christ lived a perfect life and died a brutal death so that by trusting in Him you can have new life. Jesus is the only way, the only truth and the one true life to which no one comes to the Father without trusting Him alone. Have you come to Him? If you haven't yet done so, now is the time. Listen to the great Apostle Paul as he reminds the Corinthians of this truth: *"I tell you now is the time of God's favor, now is the day of salvation" (2 Corinthians 6:2).*

If you hear the voice of the Spirit of God inviting you to come, to believe that Jesus died for you and arose from the grave to forgive you and give you eternal life as well as a new power to live right now, then come to him *today.* Coming to Him means simply to believe in Him. If you do, you destroy the devil's work in your life and through testifying of this miracle from God in your life to others, you also will be destroying the devil's work. Isn't it about time?

CHAPTER 10: DESTROYING SATAN'S WORK
DISCUSSION QUESTIONS

1. In what ways do you see the issue of "sin" being marginalized in our culture today? How is sin being marginalized within the body of Christ and among believers? Why is this a sign of the devil's work? How did Jesus counter this reality with His own mission?

2. Jesus made a huge point about sin being more a matter of the heart than simply an act or behavior (See Matthew 5:21-47). Why does it feel "safer" to define sin by specific actions rather than issues related to the heart?

3. In what ways do people try to avoid the reality of death? If the Bible teaches that death is the consequence of sin, how come people fail to see this connection? In what ways do you see the devil's system working to distort this reality among the unsaved?

4. How does Paul's argument for the resurrection in 1 Corinthians 15:32 relate to the way people think and live today?

5. How have you seen the devil's work in concealing the gospel and the glory found in Jesus Christ? What are some of the ways the devil suppresses the truth of the gospel and the person and work of Jesus Christ?

6. In view of the devil's methods, in what ways can a believer align himself to the mission of Jesus Christ in destroying the devil's work? Where do you need stronger alignment to Christ's mission in your own life?

CHAPTER 11

BE STRONG IN THE LORD
Maintaining Daily Strength for the Battle

Throughout this book, I've aimed at providing a Biblical perspective for our fight against the powers of darkness. Being more confident to engage in spiritual warfare is important, but so is realizing the fight is far from over. We won't be finished fighting the good fight until Jesus returns or we go to be with Him. Our spiritual battles will continue to be waged in the heavenly realm as long as we are alive. The evidence is the ongoing battle as seen in our daily encounters with temptation, evil, pain, suffering and a world seemingly bent on destruction. Some days, we feel strong while other days, we feel weak; but fight we must, all the way to the end.

I like how the Apostle Paul recognizes this in his last New Testament letter, written just prior to what most Bible scholars believe was the end of his life. He addressed his young protégé, Timothy: *"For I am already being poured out like a drink offering, and the time has come for my departure. I have fought the good fight, I have finished the race, I have kept the faith. Now there is in store for me the crown of righteousness, which the Lord, the righteous Judge, will award to me on that day—and not only me, but also to all who have longed for his appearing" (2 Timothy 4:6-8).* What a tremendous perspective on fighting all the way to the end. Paul had the finish line in view with full confidence that he had kept the faith. He anticipated receiving his eternal reward.

As we examine our lives, a good question to ask ourselves is whether we are determined to keep fighting with our faith in tact, all the way to the end? Most people don't intentionally set out to toss their faith aside, but the slow drift toward nominal Christian living is real and obvious in many believers—robbing them of the rewards God wanted to give them. If we aren't intentionally fighting to the end, then the inevitable spiritual drift that follows will certainly disqualify us of our reward. Christ-followers too often focus only on the assurance that their salvation is secure. They forget, however, that while their salvation is secure, their future reward is determined by faithfulness all the way to the end. The Apostle Paul reminds us that when our works are tested by fire at the judgment seat of Christ, if those works are burned up, we will "suffer loss" even though we are still saved (1 Corinthians 3:15).

I've been around believers who remain engaged in the battle and those who, at some point in their past seem to have given up. There's nothing more encouraging than to see people fight the good fight with a loving and obedient passion all the way to the end of their lives. Conversely, there's perhaps nothing more disappointing than to see people who've obviously dropped out of their commitment to serve Jesus and are no longer engaged as they once were. My good friend and colleague Mark has been a passionate Christ-follower engaged in the good fight since the time of his conversion in his early 20s. He's not been perfect, but I've never known a season in his life marked by anything other than a clear passion to pursue God's will while standing firm against the schemes of the devil. I can think of several others in my life that have modeled this kind of commitment and spiritual fortitude—brothers and sisters whose lives compel me to keep fighting the spiritual battles that come. Their inspiration in my life is immeasurable.

I can also think of those, who for various reasons, have lost their passion and the fire that once burned hot for God. Their once white-hot passion has cooled down to a smoldering ember. For these, perhaps the pace of life, crushing demands, adverse circumstances or even the spiritual battle itself just wore them down, eventually producing a joyless, lifeless existence. All of what was once powerful and vigorous in their walk with God is now clearly diminished.

A while ago, a dear friend I knew when I was in my teens showed up at one of our church's gospel theatrical outreaches. He told me that he and his family wanted to visit so many times but they had never gotten around to it. We hadn't seen each other in over 40 years! Bill was incredibly involved in the youth ministry I attended as a high schooler. He had such a vibrant and committed walk with God. He and I loved being a part of the leadership team and involved in everything going on in that ministry.

Our paths separated as he went off to college and I began my initial career pursuit of becoming a firefighter. Now that we had reconnected there in the lobby of our church after such a long separation from each other, I was eager to hear about his life. It was clear that his life now was mostly directed toward raising his family and running his business. As we shared these moments together, he made no mention of his love for God or His desire to serve in ministry as once was true of him. He had a beautiful wife and two college-aged kids, a successful career in the tech industry and enjoyed his time off at the cabin they had built in a quaint little mountain community near Lake Tahoe. Life was great, or at least he made it sound that way.

Time didn't allow for us to connect more deeply about how our lives seemed so differently focused, but as we exchanged stories of what life was like for both of us now, it became apparent that somewhere along the way, Bill had stopped engaging in the spiritual battle. He was clearly on the sidelines and sadly, didn't seem to know—or maybe he didn't care. Over the years, I've met so many people like Bill; people who, at one point in their lives, had been so engaged in the spiritual battle only to have ended up on the sidelines later on.

It is for people like Bill, and a realization that all of us, including myself, are vulnerable to losing our spiritual fervor, that I write this chapter. I am convinced that a high percentage of Christ-followers view their once passionate walk with Christ as having lost its fervor due to becoming some kind of victim. Someone carried out a destructive plan that damaged their lives, or personal choices turned into habits that became uncontrollable, or life just dealt a set of circumstances that were too much to overcome. If you are feeling this way as a believer, I've got good news for you. *You are an overcomer.* Paul writes to the Romans, ***"...we are more than conquerors through Him who loved us" (Romans 8:37).*** Do you consider yourself more than a conqueror? You should! Because that's who you are if you belong to Jesus!

Be strong in the Lord

The only way to remain in the mindset of an overcomer and not see yourself as a victim, is to maintain daily strength for the battle. In short, we need to learn what it means to be strong in the Lord—every day. Do you know what it means to be strong in the Lord? Three times in the New Testament and more than thirty times in the Old Testament, that phrase is used in the context of spiritual challenges or tests of faith. It's a great phrase to repeat to ourselves for remaining present in the fight. I hope we will learn to remind ourselves more often to be strong in the Lord whenever we are facing a spiritual challenge or crisis. If we do this, acting upon what it means, we reduce the chances of being sidelined in our faith and overcome by the enemy.

The Apostle Paul writes about this as he begins his great treatise on wearing our spiritual armor: ***"Finally, be strong in the Lord and in his mighty power" (Ephesians 6:10a).*** Understanding and obeying what this means, ensures our present and continuous engagement in the battle. Let me offer four simple ways to do this.

Make a decision

Some believers refuse to own any kind of responsibility to *respond* when in the midst of spiritual warfare. I'm not suggesting that it is our response *alone* that secures our victory, I simply want to convey that when facing the spiritual battles that will come, we must do our part. Our part, according to the Apostle Paul when facing our spiritual battles, is to be strong in the Lord and in His mighty power.

Notice a couple of things Paul reveals to us in Ephesians 6:10a. First, there is a point of finality to his exhortation to us. He writes, "Finally..." meaning, *"What remains after everything I've instructed you Ephesian believers, is to be strong in the Lord."* In this letter, Paul has already written extensively and insightfully about the strength and power that the Lord provides for His people. In Ephesians 1, we read that it was Paul's prayer that they would somehow see and embrace this power the Lord graciously provides: **"I pray that the eyes of your heart may be enlightened in order that you may know the hope to which he has called you, the riches of his glorious inheritance in the saints, and his incomparably great power for us who believe" (Ephesians 1:18-19a).** Stop right here. Do you see this *"incomparably great power for us who believe?"* It is not a human-centered power, rather, **"That power is like the working of his mighty strength, which he exerted in Christ when he raised him from the dead and seated him at his right hand in the heavenly realms, far above all rule and authority, power and dominion" (Ephesians 1:19b-21a).** Now, that's what I call power!

A little later in the letter, Paul reminds the Ephesians what God's power enables believers to do: **"Now to Him who is able to do immeasurably more than all we ask or imagine, according to his power that is at work within us..." (Ephesians 3:20).** This has always been one of my favorite Scriptures. To know that we have a power within us that is able to do immeasurably more than all we ask or imagine, sounds too good to be true, yet, we know it's completely true because it's here in

God's trustworthy word! These truths were foundational to Paul's exhortation, *"Finally...be strong in the Lord" (Ephesians 6:10a).*

Everything we do begins with a decision. And no decision is more important than when we are confronted with a spiritual attack, we decide to be strong in the Lord and His mighty power. Another way of looking at this is having a positive orientation toward the battle. Some people understand this the wrong way and are more like the little boy getting ready to go out and play in his little league baseball game who says to his mom, "We are going to lose today!" Wanting to bolster his confidence a little, she replied, "Son, you need to be more positive." After thinking about it a minute, he then responded back to her, "You're right mom, I'm positive we are going to lose!" That is how some of us are when it comes to our spiritual battles. We assume our defeat from the start. We are positive that the outcome won't be good.

When I began working as a youth pastor at a Baptist church in San Jose in the late 1970s, I recruited a young married couple to help me in my ministry. Lee and Glenna were amazing. One thing that made them so amazing was Lee's confidence that no matter what, he could trust God to get him through.

Lee was in his thirties when we first met, but was convinced God had called him to become a dentist and to set up a network of dental offices throughout the United States. He had no solid income and only an undergraduate degree with no medical background. In preparation for funding dental school, he bought and sold used cars while never missing a youth event or retreat sponsored by our church. As much as I loved Lee and wanted to support his dream, it seemed a little out of reach.

Along the way toward his career goals, he had many setbacks. I would often ask him what he thought when things didn't seem to be working out for him. There wasn't even one time when Lee responded to his present challenges without fully believing that God would come through and make a way as long as he kept strong in the Lord. Lee's strength in the Lord at crucial moments meant stepping out in faith. In the years that followed, Lee not only was accepted into dental school and finished with honors, he also opened a practice that eventually went nationwide with dental offices throughout the Midwest. In God's providence, Lee died unexpectedly due to an illness, but not before seeing his dream realized. I'll never forget the strength and vision of this young man who followed his dream giving God the credit all the way along.

It's amazing how this theme of the Lord's strength and its availability is prevalent throughout the Bible. Let me cite just a few that are familiar to most of us: *"I love you, O LORD, my strength...It is God who arms me with strength and makes my way perfect...You armed me with strength for battle; you made my adversaries bow at my feet" (Psalm 18:1, 32, 39).* One of my all-time favorite Scriptures is, *"God is our refuge and strength; an ever present help in trouble" (Psalm 46:1).* Here's another: *"O my Strength, I watch for you; you, O God, are my fortress" (Psalm 59:9).* And, *"The LORD is my strength and my song; he has become my salvation" (Psalm 118:14).* The prophet Isaiah writes, *"Surely God is my Salvation; I will trust and not be afraid. The LORD, the LORD, is my strength and my song; he has become my salvation" (Isaiah 12:2).* The prophet Habakkuk adds to these beautiful reminders: *"The Sovereign LORD is my strength; he makes my feet like the feet of a deer, he enables me to go on the heights" (Habakkuk 3:19).*

In the Middle East, where the writers of Scripture lived and served God, there is a rugged wild goat known as an ibex that lives in the steepest and most mountainous terrain of this region in the world. Ibex are known for their sure-footed ability on nearly vertical rocky terrain allowing them to escape predators and move quickly to water from the safe haven of altitude. Every time I read Habakkuk's promise of the Lord's strength making his feet like the feet of a deer, I'm sure he had an ibex in mind.

And then I realize this is true for me, too. I can scale the heights when the enemy is in pursuit because the LORD is my strength.

Early in my ministry, I had the opportunity to do some mountain climbing in Yosemite with some friends who were experienced climbers. Our ascent that early spring day, they assured me, would be perfect for a beginner. When we walked up to where we would begin the climb, my confidence was shaken by the sheer angle of the initial ascent. "You're taking me up there?" I thought to myself. One of my friends scurried up the rock escarpment carrying a rope and climbing gear while my other experienced climbing friend gave me some tips about how to climb. After about twenty minutes, an uncoiled rope dropped near where we were standing and a distant voice came from my friend up top telling me to start climbing when I was ready. My other friend quickly got me into my climbing harness, attached me to the rope and told me to basically pretend the rope wasn't there. "Just climb without depending on the rope unless of course you fall, then it will catch you." he said. Very reassuring I must say! I found it hard to concentrate on everything he was saying since the fear of climbing up that rock face was suddenly real—and terrifying. Two things he said stood out to me: "You will need to climb, but you can do it, and if you get stuck or slip from the rock, don't worry, the rope will save you." With that, he patted me on the shoulder and said, "Up you go!"

I started to climb. I got to a place where I couldn't see my friend at the top, nor my other friend at the bottom. I was working hard to focus on where to place my hands and feet—it was getting steeper with each step. I could feel my feet starting to slip on the granite. My hands were sweaty. At one point, I remember glancing down to see where I had come from in case I needed to retrace my steps and descend. In that moment, I experienced a sort of mental panic over the fear of falling even though I knew I was fastened to the rope. I literally had to force my mind to overturn the anxiety that was starting to take over. "Trust the rope and keep climbing," I said to myself as I took another step upward. I should also admit that in addition to my fear of falling, I feared being teased by my friends had I frozen there on the rock requiring one or both of them to rescue me. Confession is good for the soul.

Deciding to trust the rope and move forward was essential to overcoming the mental battle I was fighting. It was also helpful to stop looking down. The same is true when we face our spiritual battles. We must decide to trust God and keep moving forward. We also need to stop looking at anything that instills fear and damages our forward momentum. This is, I believe, what Paul was referring to when he commanded the Ephesians to "be strong in the Lord." By God's grace, I was able to make it to the top of the 100-foot "beginner's climb." While I didn't pursue climbing as a hobby, I have always appreciated the amazing faith and confidence of climbers to trust their gear and move steady forward with relative safety.

It is amazing there are so many things we look to for our strength in times of challenge and difficulty. Some people decide their strength comes through their financial reserves. Others find strength in their relationship connections. Sometimes people look inwardly for the ability to reason or intellectually find their way out of trouble as a means of strength. People find refuge in securing a better environment, or the right job with the right income. We look to all kinds of things and all sorts of people for the strength we think we need to carry on. While these things might be helpful and might even be a means at times for God to help us in our spiritual battles, we must never bypass our need to decide first to be strong in the Lord and His strength remembering the promise of Scripture: *"He gives strength to the weary and increases the power of the weak" (Isaiah 40:29).* What a promise to depend on when fatigue or doubts overwhelm us. A decision must first be made to be strong. There's something else that is important, too.

Be in partnership

Deciding to be strong in the Lord isn't a one-sided affair. When we decide to trust God's Word and make the Lord our strength, God comes alongside to give us the strength we need—His strength becomes our strength. The transformative power of God does its work in us and through us, *"...both to will and to work for his good pleasure"* *(Philippians 2:13).*

Sometimes during my workout at the gym, I go to the bench press. I'm not as strong as I used to be (which isn't saying much) and occasionally my enthusiasm makes me feel stronger than I am. On more than one occasion I've gotten stuck on my final rep demanding that someone standing nearby come to my aid. I'll never forget one time when this happened, a muscle-bound guy quickly arrived putting his hands under the bar and he began whispering, *"You got this...it's all you."* The humor of the moment combined with both embarrassment and complete muscle failure made his statement laughable. I can assure you that it was "all him" in that moment as the bar slowly moved to where he could rack the weight. The effort I had behind its movement was barely measurable.

This is similar to the way God's strength works through us. As we call on the Lord's strength, his power works through us despite whatever deficiencies or weakness we might have. In fact, according to Scripture, His power is made perfect in our weakness (2 Corinthians 12:9). The grammatical construction of Ephesians 6:10 also shows the verb, "be strong" in the passive mood, meaning that the strength comes from God, not us. Like at the bench press, it appears that it is our strength being helped by another, when in reality, it's the strength of the other doing the heavy lifting. God always does the heavy lifting.

Jesus spoke of this and the Apostle John dutifully recorded it for us in his gospel: *"Remain in me, and I will remain in you. No branch can bear fruit by itself; it must remain in the vine. Neither can you bear fruit unless you remain in me. I am the vine; you are the branches. If a man remains in me and I in him, he will bear much fruit; apart from me you can do nothing" (John 15:4-5).* Most of us know that the life of Jesus becomes present in us through the Holy Spirit, whom the Father sent, as promised in Joel 2 and Jeremiah 31 and in other places in the Old Testament. These prophetic words are fulfilled in Acts 1 when Jesus told his followers to remain in Jerusalem until they received what the Father had promised (Acts 1:4-5) which was the gift of the Holy Spirit. Even before the Holy Spirit had been sent into believers at Pentecost, and subsequently to all believers ever since, God worked all this out so that we'd have the power needed to fight in the spiritual realm.

His partnership in this warfare guarantees all the power we need for the battle, but we must be careful to remember that the power doesn't originate with us. God is very particular about our need to know who is giving the power and how it is being distributed. He gives us power which comes through the agency of the Spirit in our lives—the power doesn't originate with us. This is beautifully illustrated in Zechariah 4:1-6 where we learn that Zechariah is given a vision to encourage Zerubbabel to finish the rebuilding of the temple and to assure him that the power of the Spirit will make this happen. A lamp stand with seven lights (wicks) are fueled by two olive trees. In the vision, Zerubbabel is to know that instead of bowls containing a limited provision of oil, the olive trees themselves would be the source indicating a constant, unlimited, self-sustaining supply that would never go dry. Zerubbabel's work on the temple and in the lives of the people was to be completed, not by human might or power, but by divine power—a power so constant and sufficient guaranteeing the work will be accomplished as God said it would! We need this reminder, too.

Some of us are distracted by what we think we bring to the table. We become self-reliant, self-sufficient and self-dependent. All of that changes when we understand what it means to *"be strong in the Lord and in his mighty strength" (Ephesians 6:10a)!* We begin to understand that first, a decision is needed and second, that a partnership is expected. We have the power of the Holy Spirit who has regenerated us, anointed us, sealed us and by simply yielding to him daily in our lives, we are empowered to do all He wants us to do.

In Ephesians, the Apostle Paul reminds God's people, *"Do not get drunk on wine, which leads to debauchery. Instead, be filled with the Spirit" (Ephesians 5:18).* The proper image of being "filled" is not of water being poured into a glass, but a hand going into a glove. The filling that Paul refers to relates to "control" rather than quantity. As a hand fills a glove and directs the fingers of the glove as it wishes, so the Holy Spirit fills our lives and directs us however He wishes.

In spiritual warfare we realize our fight is against the world, the flesh and the devil which encompasses all the enemy's domain. When it comes to the flesh, Paul writes in Galatians, *"Live by the Spirit, and you will not gratify the desires of the sinful nature" (Galatians 5:16).* He writes in Ephesians, *"The acts of the sinful nature are obvious: sexual immorality, impurity and debauchery; idolatry and witchcraft; hatred, discord, jealousy, fits of rage, selfish ambition, dissensions, factions and envy; drunkenness, orgies, and the like and those who practice these will not inherit the kingdom of God" (Ephesians 5:19-21).* It's important to realize Paul isn't giving his readers an exhaustive list. He lists the obvious, but for the person who hopes to escape judgment, he includes the little phrase, "and the like" showing that there is no end to the expressions of the flesh.

Contrast Paul's list of the expressions of the flesh with what emerges in the person under the control and power of the Holy Spirit: *"But the fruit of the Spirit is love, joy, peace, patience, kindness, goodness, faithfulness, gentleness and self-control" (Galatians 5:22-23).* This is what partnership looks like. When we are being strong in the Lord we clearly demonstrate the fruit that comes from the Spirit. A decision is needed and a partnership is expected. What else might the phrase "be strong in the Lord" allude to the believer engaged in spiritual warfare?

Don't be surprised at the challenge

Life isn't easy. To live for Christ and fight against forces in the spiritual realm will be an incredibly great challenge. If you assume that following Jesus and remaining in the will of God is easy, I've got news for you—it isn't. Let me be quick to say that along with the challenge, there is great peace and assurance that drives deeper meaning and satisfaction into everything a Christ-follower does. Just because our lives as Christ followers aren't easy, doesn't mean our lives aren't incredibly fulfilling! People who see challenges negatively are easily discouraged at the realization that the spiritual fight can take a toll. This alone is why many create their own reality of what it means to follow Jesus. Part of a false reality is assuming that problems and challenges never come to us from God. Job puts this in a very matter-of-fact fashion when he says, ***"Shall we accept good from God and not trouble" (Job 2:10)?***

Scripture affirms that problems and challenges are actually permitted by God for our good. In 2 Corinthians 12, the Apostle Paul is recounting a vision he experienced; whether it was while in his body or one of those "out of body" experiences, not even Paul actually knew, but it was so amazing and glorious to hear and see things that were inexpressible; things a normal human isn't permitted to talk about. This heavenly vision gave Paul a small glimpse into what Heaven is like. I would love to have had that experience, wouldn't you? Well, maybe not after reading what comes next in the narrative: ***"To keep me from becoming conceited because of these surpassingly great revelations, there was given me a thorn in my flesh, a messenger of Satan, to torment me" (2 Corinthians 12:7).*** Now, I ask you: Do you still want to receive a spectacular vision? Like me, you might not be too sure about that now!

This messenger of Satan—the thorn in Paul's flesh, as Paul referred to it was an extremely difficult, personal and ongoing challenge for Paul. As to what it actually was, the explanations are many: Jewish persecution, carnal temptation, a physical malady like epilepsy, or a problem with his eyesight or even a speech impediment. No one knows for sure what this "thorn" actually was and I think God wanted it this way. This was so challenging that Paul asked the Lord three times for Him to remove it. It's likely that the three times refer more to seasons than simply three separate requests. Whatever Paul meant, one thing is clear, Paul didn't want it in his life.

Notice the subtle detail as to where this challenge originated, *"...there was given me a thorn..."* implying that the one who gave it to him was different than the messenger of Satan. This of course leads us to the seemingly dreadful reality that the origination of the thorn could be traced to God Himself. The challenge we face, no matter how big or small, no matter how frequent or random, is given to us by God. We might be wondering why a loving God would allow experiences and seasons of difficulty in our lives. The student of Scripture will find many reasons why God allows, permits and even sends his children difficult things to deal with in life. He does so to test us, purify us, build our character, humble us, teach us or for an opportunity to witness to others. These are just a few reasons to help provide a rationale for why a loving God allows hard and difficult things to happen to his kids. God permits his children to receive what Satan's messengers might dish out but He does this out of His love for us and because he will use all of these things to shape us into the image of His Son, Jesus. Remember, *"Those whom he foreknew, he predestined to become conformed to the likeness of His Son, so that he might be the firstborn among many brothers" (Romans 8:29).*

My friend Jim was a good business man with a big family and lots of friends. Most importantly, he was a follower of Jesus. He faithfully attended church and served in many capacities. He was an outdoor enthusiast. He enjoyed hunting and fishing and life just couldn't have been better for him. One day, however, Jim went to a doctor complaining of a pain that wouldn't go away. He was diagnosed with stage 4 pancreatic cancer and presented with various treatment options. None seemed very hopeful. I remember Jim sharing this story with me, stating that as the doctor explained his diagnosis to him, he was literally shaking and felt ready to collapse right there in the doctor's office. It was so overwhelming to think that his life could be over so soon.

After the initial shock and the crisis that news like this brings, Jim called on the Lord in prayer and gained new strength. It was as close to an audible voice as Jim had ever experienced in his fifty-plus years of walking with Jesus. In that very moment, Jim felt assured that as terrible as his diagnoses was, God was allowing it for a reason. In the months that followed, Jim's life was completely transformed. He underwent the most drastic cancer surgery and experienced even more challenges during his recovery. Doctors hadn't given him much hope but God sustained him, giving him a strong and vibrant life for nearly three times the length doctors estimated he would live. During all this time, Jim was sharing his story of faith with as many people as would listen to him. Only God knows the number of people Jim led to trust in Jesus Christ in hospital rooms, chemo clinics, our church prayer room and out in the community. He was an effective and powerful evangelist.

I remember once when Jim shared with our congregation about how God was using his illness to advance the gospel. He said, "People sometimes ask me if I wished I had never been diagnosed with cancer. You might think I'm crazy, but my answer is, 'Absolutely not!' Cancer put me right in the place where God could finally show me what life was about. He completely took over and filled me with his power. I've been able to tell hundreds of people about God and his grace for me through His Son, Jesus. I wouldn't change that for anything." When God took

Jim home to glory, everyone in our church knew the impact he had made for the Kingdom. He had fought the good fight and kept the faith, and great was his reward.

Admit your weakness

Here's the strange thing: You can't become strong in the Lord until you can admit just how weak you really are. When the Apostle Paul asked God to take away his thorn, the answer was given to him, *"'My grace is sufficient for you, for my power is made perfect in weakness.' Therefore I will boast all the more gladly about my weaknesses, so that Christ's power may rest on me. That is why, for Christ's sake, I delight in weaknesses, in insults, in hardships, in persecutions, in difficulties. For when I am weak, then I am strong" (2 Corinthians 12:8-10).* Paul is literally saying that when he was weak and called on the Lord, then he was made strong. This is how the power of God is leveraged in our lives—through our weakness.

If we want to be strong in the Lord, we must admit our weaknesses. This is why one of the characteristics of holiness is humility. In our pride, we refuse to humble ourselves and admit our weaknesses, thus limiting the power of God available to us. However, the moment we admit to God, and sometimes to others, that we are weak in ourselves and only through His strength are we made strong, God's power shows up. When God's power shows up, people are transformed. The community of God's people is the one place where God's power should be unleashed in increasing measure through the humility of God's people admitting their weaknesses. In most churches, people are afraid to admit to being weak. A culture is created where it's wrong to be weak and we become judges of each other assuming ourselves as superior. In places like this, God's power is limited.

I'll never forget the Sunday I couldn't finish my sermon due to an overwhelming sense of my weakness as a father, a Christ-follower and a pastor. There have been many times in small groups, among fellow leaders and in one-on-one sessions where I've admitted how weak I am. And I've always desired to show from the pulpit that I am just as needy as the next person when it comes to experiencing God's power and grace.

But on that one Sunday a few years ago, the circumstances of my life and the personal disappointment I was experiencing broke me, in front of our entire church. I remember choking back the tears as I mumbled something about feeling so weak and how I needed God's grace to show me how to lead my family who was experiencing some very difficult issues, before walking off the platform. I remember walking out the back door of the church and heading straight to the parking lot where I got in my car and drove home. I sat in my living room with my wife, weeping as my phone blew up with voice-messages and texts of encouragement and love from so many people. "We love you, Pastor Larry!" "We're praying for you, Pastor Larry!" "Our family is going through a very hard time, too, Pastor Larry. Thank you for being courageous enough to tell us so we can be open, too." Over and over throughout that day, and in the days that followed, God sent people to come alongside of me and my family to love and support me. Somehow, a simple but honest admission of my weakness, broke open the power of God among many in our church family.

In the weeks that followed, I heard many people comment about how the admission of their pastor's weakness and desire for God's power, galvanized their own commitment to follow Jesus and get more connected in our church body. I heard one new attender say at one of our large men's gatherings, "When I heard Pastor Larry admit to being weak and needing God's strength to lead his family well, I looked at my wife and said, 'This is the church for us.' We're tired of going to churches where the pastor seemed to be perfect and no one could have problems." I was choking back tears again, realizing that this is a way God's power is unleashed within his body—through admitted weakness.

The simple summary of this entire book can be summed up in this statement, *"Be strong in the Lord and in the strength of His might" (Ephesians 6:10).* The battle we face is fierce. The weapons that the enemy wields against us are strong, but nothing compares to the power of God. When we are strong in the Lord, nothing can defeat us. God reminds us through the prophet, *"...no weapon forged against you will prevail, and you will refute every tongue that accuses you. This is the heritage of the servants of the LORD, and this is their vindication from me,' declares the LORD" (Isaiah 54:17).*

The fight we engage in today will still be around tomorrow. We must remember simply to never give up, to fight all the way to the finish, using every resource God gives to us, and to be assured of our victory. Then, if God gives us grace to know we are at the end of our lives, we can say with the Apostle Paul, *"I have fought the good fight, I have finished the race, I have kept the faith. Now there is in store for me the crown of righteousness, which the Lord, the righteous Judge, will award to me on that day—and not only to me, but also to all who have longed for his appearing" (2 Timothy 4:7-8).* This is what blesses and glorifies our Lord Jesus. This is what makes the world take notice and this is the good fight and the believer's hope in spiritual warfare. So be strong in the Lord my friend, and stay strong so you may fight the good fight.

CHAPTER 11: BE STRONG IN THE LORD DISCUSSION QUESTIONS

1. What are things we turn to when we feel we need strength? Why is it that often we look to other people or things for strength before looking to Jesus? What are some ways to direct our hearts to Him more readily when we need strength?

2. Why is it crucial for believers in Christ to yield and depend on the indwelling of God's Spirit to experience the strength we need in specific situations? Why do many believers fail to see the powerful and available resource of the Holy Spirit?

3. How does Zechariah's vision of the olive trees and lamp stand point to our need to recognize where our strength comes from? Where does Zechariah 4:6 need to be applied in your life right now?

4. Consider the following passages and comment on how aware you are of your need for the Spirit's work in your life: Ephesians 5:18; Galatians 5:22ff

5. How conscious are you of the fact that God allows and even leads us into circumstances where we are challenged and buffeted by the enemy? Give a few reasons why God would allow this. Tell of an experience when you recognized this to be true in your life. (See James 1:2; 2 Corinthians 4:7-12)

6. Paul indicates that the key to experiencing the strength that God offers is admitting our weakness. How is this counterintuitive to the way we normally think and act? What kinds of attitudes and actions might develop in our lives if we learn to admit being weak?

CHAPTER 12

PUTTING IT ALL TOGETHER
Developing Disciplines for a Victorious Life

My first summer camp experience occurred during the summer following my freshman year in high school. Three-hundred high school kids converged at Sugar Pine Conference Grounds near the southern entrance to Yosemite National Park. We were in for an incredible week of vigorous physical competition and high-octane messages aimed at introducing all of us to the purposes of God in our lives. The moment I stepped off the church bus, I felt something special was in store for all of us.

Those who programmed the week did a great job engaging high school kids who thrive on competitive games and sports in the midst of the spiritual emphasis that each day brought to the campers. Everyone was placed on a team and the team I was on had a fair amount of athletic kids. We did pretty well in the sporting events throughout the week. At the first night's chapel service, we all heard about the big mountain run that would require sending one person from every team to compete in this epic downhill race. Everyone on my team felt I was the best candidate to run the race since I was thin and wiry and looked the part. The race would be a six-mile trek down the mountain, cross country style, with the last leg of the race about one mile on a forest road leading into the camp where all the teams would assemble at the finish line.

I really didn't want to run in this race. Though I may have "looked" like a runner, I hated running and had never competed in even one race before that day. Like all kids my age, running for "time" in P.E. was about all the experience I had. I remember my time for running a mile was about seven minutes and change. This was a far cry from being truly competitive—and even worse, finishing the mile at an average pace nearly killed me every time. I hated running.

As the eleven others got in the make-shift shuttle to head up the mountain to the starting line, I remember looking around at what appeared for the most part, to be a group of highly dedicated and disciplined runners. I may have had a similar body type, but it seemed to me they were far more ready to run in a way to get the prize. We lined up on the crest of a mountain after a short series of instructions and directions for how to make our way down and back to the camp. I hadn't listened very closely because I figured I would just follow the ones (everyone) in front of me.

The gun sounded and off we went. My competitive drive sent me running strong for the lead as we headed down the steep terrain. I think I held second place for a good five minutes before I started cramping up and losing my speed. One by one, the other runners made their way past me. When we reached the road leading back into the camp, I think I was in tenth place—and I felt at least grateful I wouldn't finish last. When I finished the race, I learned that one of the runners had sprained his ankle and couldn't finish. With this bit of news, I realized I had in fact finished dead last. Most of my team left the bridge where runners came across at the finish line and only a handful of kids were around by the time I showed up. I got a few "Hey, way to hang in there!" as I came wheezing by. It was a humiliating experience, though part of what made the week so memorable for me.

At times, I reflect over that experience and consider the metaphor the Apostle Paul shares with the Corinthians about how the Christian life is much like a race that we run, and the importance of running in such a way as to get the prize (1 Corinthians 9:24). I've been in seasons of my life when I have not run the race as if to win. Like that day in the mountains outside of Yosemite so many years ago, I've found myself in the humiliating experience of running myself into the ground rather than victoriously aiming at the finish line. Most of us can relate to moments and seasons like this in life.

Some of us will choose not to run in a way to win the race. The Apostle Paul wrote that a game-changer in living for Christ is being committed to strict training like the athletes who compete for a prize. Considering the spiritual contest in which we are engaged, I've found a few simple, but very powerful things that every believer can practice to ensure victory. Running to win doesn't require special expertise or talent but rather, a tenacity to stay committed to some basic disciplines and pursuits in our walk with Christ.

Read and obey Scripture

For some reason, most believers have trouble reading Scripture and obeying what it says. This is, in my opinion, the most important discipline of all, for the one who desires to run the race and win. My recognition of this discipline came early in my walk with Jesus.

The summer before entering middle school, my dad took me on a camping trip. I didn't know it at the time, but he intentionally planned this campout to be my initiation into my teen years as an adolescent. In looking for a good place to camp, we stumbled upon a little mountain stream nestled in the High Sierras called Herring Creek. This place would remain special my entire life, even up to the present day.

The first morning after my dad cooked and served me a delicious breakfast, he pulled out a New Testament and, with some simple instructions, told me to take a walk into the woods, find a quiet place and read the book of Colossians and listen for God's voice while doing so. When I was finished, I was to return to our campsite. I was a believer at the time, but had never been challenged in my faith, nor had I ever really shared my faith with any of my friends. I went to church with my family, but hadn't seen the importance and relevance of walking in an intimate relationship with Jesus Christ. Further, at the time, I don't think I'd ever read the Bible for myself with the aim of listening for God's voice.

I found a good spot where I climbed on top of a large rock where I made my perch and began reading. I'm sure my dad had prayed this would be a significant time for me. As I began reading, I became aware of God's voice speaking through His Word. Suddenly, everything I was reading seemed so personal as if God were speaking right to me. Phrases like, *"...we have not stopped praying for you and asking God to fill you with the knowledge of his will through all spiritual wisdom and understanding" (Colossians 1:9)* seemed to beg the question of my own knowledge and understanding of God's will. I kept reading, *"For he has rescued us from the dominion of darkness and brought us into the kingdom of the Son he loves, in whom we have redemption, the forgiveness of sins" (Colossians 1:13-14).* "Really?" I found myself thinking more deeply about my relationship with Jesus and what He had done for me than at any other time in my past.

I was hearing the voice of God for the first time as an adolescent simply because I was reading God's Word with an open heart asking God to speak to me. At one point in my reading, I remember that little section on family where children are exhorted to obey their parents (Col. 3:20) which also brought a level of relevancy and conviction I'd not experienced before. After I finished reading, I remember sitting on that rock and considering the powerful words I had read, and more, the realization that the God of the universe was speaking through those words directly to me. It was like being born again—again.

When I got back to the campsite, my dad asked me simple questions about what I had read and what I understood God was saying to me. My insights were probably not very profound to him, but I'm sure he was excited to see that I connected with God's voice being the Scripture. The following morning, I followed in a similar exercise, reading the book of

Ephesians. Again, both insight and conviction poured into my soul. I came home from that trip with some amazing memories of spending time with my dad, but most of all, felt connected to God in a way I hadn't up to that time. It was amazing.

That weekend changed my life forever. To this day, I've found the power and relevance of beginning each day and staying connected as much as I'm able throughout the day to God's Word. It is truly the food I need to nourish my soul at the deepest level. When it comes to spiritual warfare, the Bible itself testifies of its critical place in warding off the enemy's attack. I love what David writes in the Psalms, *"I seek you with all my heart; do not let me stray from your commands. I have hidden your word in my heart that I might not sin against you" (Psalm 119:10-11).* While there are so many other places in Scripture where one can turn to see the importance of developing a consistent daily time of reading and reflecting, this one text alone provides the impetus for doing so.

Most believers have never read through the Bible even once. Reading the news, the sports magazine, business periodicals, fiction and non-fiction from popular culture seem to derail our reading of God's Holy Word. I was fortunate to have a father who introduced to me the importance of reading God's Word so I could hear God's voice at an early stage in my walk with Jesus. Thankfully, even if my own father had not done so, I had many pastors and leaders who urged and modeled this essential practice. I can honestly say that without this discipline in my life, I am sure I would have lost many of the spiritual battles that Satan designed for my downfall.

Don't get me wrong, I've had my share of failure which resulted from seasons of undisciplined time in God's Word and worse, not obeying the instruction it made abundantly clear to me. It would be disingenuous of me to pretend that I'm always reading and obeying God's Word, yet this is sincerely my aim as a follower of Christ.

221

When I meet with people who are in some form of spiritual crisis, I ask, "How serious are you with reading and obeying Scripture?" Nearly always the response is, "I know I should read the Bible more." Drilling down into that statement, I usually learn that the person may read God's Word once or twice during the week and whatever is read is quickly forgotten. This might be you. If it is, the discipline of reading and applying God's Word daily can't be overstated. It's critical for being victorious over the enemy.

Many believers also struggle to see the connection between reading Scripture and obeying it. The Bible wasn't meant to be read purely for information. Scripture's intent is transformation and transformation occurs through response and that response is obedience. King David posed the question, *"How can a young man keep his way pure?"* His answer was direct and to the point: *"By living according to your word" (Psalm 119:9).* Living according to God's Word simply means obeying it. The Apostle Paul reminds Timothy of this truth when saying, *"All Scripture is God-breathed and is useful for teaching, rebuking, correcting and training in righteousness, so that the man of God may be thoroughly equipped for every good work" (2 Timothy 3:16-17).* God's Word is useful for actionable responses leading to transformation in the life of every believer.

The last thing that Jesus instructed his Apostles was to make disciples of all nations baptizing them and "teaching them to obey" all he had commanded (Matthew 28:20). Teaching followers of Jesus to obey God's Word is essential for spiritual victory over the enemy. When this isn't one of the primary objectives of disciple-making environments, is it any wonder that the enemy seems to have his way among new and immature believers? But with a realignment to one's intake of God's Word and obedience to it, the believer can experience resiliency against attack and more frequent victories along the way.

Even believers who are not immersing themselves in Scripture daily are likely to know a fair amount of truth already through sermons they've heard, not to mention the resident teacher, the Holy Spirit indwelling them. The bigger issue is not knowing more, but obeying what is clearly known. When we encounter spiritual attack, we must remember that few things put the devil to flight as quickly and thoroughly as a life submitted to God. The Apostle James makes this clear: *"Submit yourselves, then, to God. Resist the devil, and he will flee from you" (James 4:7).* If we are submitted to God and our posture resists whatever the devil might be throwing at us, we can be assured that the devil will have to flee from us. I like the image of the devil actually running away from us. He's running because he knows he can't compete with a heart in love and submitted to Jesus.

Pray without ceasing

For many believers, prayer is an exercise that merely optimizes transactions with God. Like a menu from which we choose things we want or think we need in our lives, our prayers become perfunctory and void of intimacy. In truth, however, prayer is evidence of our submission to God. It's proof we are convinced we have no power, no victory apart from God. It's our built-in dependency meter on how much we trust God over our own efforts and abilities.

When Jesus saw his disciple Peter being buffeted by Satan, he didn't counsel him or offer insights into fighting the battle—He simply prayed for Peter (Luke 22:31-32). If Jesus knew Peter needed his prayers more than his advice or teaching, then perhaps we should take note. Maintaining a prayer focus in our lives at all times is surely a key to a victorious life for ourselves and also for others.

Fundamentally, prayer aligns our hearts to what God desires. While it's exciting to know that God hears our prayers and answers them in his perfect time (John 14:14), it's more exciting to view prayer as a constant tethering of our hearts to the heart of God regardless of how He may answer us. This tethering is the means by which God keeps our attention where it ought to be. This is because our lives tend to move in the direction of our focus. This is why the writer of Hebrews exhorts us to **"fix our eyes on Jesus" (Hebrews 12:2).**

I love the game of golf. I'm not very good, but occasionally, I hit a shot that keeps me coming back. One of the things I learned early in my game was that I will likely hit the ball wherever I'm most focused. If I'm lined up for an approach shot to a green close to a water hazard, my focus will likely determine the ball's flight. If my focus is on the water hazard, well, there's a high probability my ball is going in the drink. If my focus is on the green, I have a better chance of getting the ball there safely. While this isn't always the case when playing golf, it's almost a sure thing in the realm of our spiritual lives. If we're focused on ourselves, our needs, our desires, our... (fill in the blank), then our lives will tend to revolve around—you got it—US! If we're focused on God, then our lives will be pleasantly directed toward all He has for us. Our lives tend to move in the direction of our focus.

Every day as I pray for the people in my prayer journal, I experience the anticipation of how God is going to answer my prayers; but more, I experience the greater effect of sensing the loving presence of my Savior who knows my heart and rejoices that I belong to Him. It may sound odd to admit that the greatest joy in my praying for others isn't in the answers God sends, but in how he uses prayer as a means of moving my heart closer to His.

I think believers don't pray as often as they should because their focus is wrong. Focusing on receiving what we ask for isn't the point of prayer. When the answers don't come as quickly as we'd like, we get discouraged and we stop praying. The right focus, however, is on God Himself, regardless of whether God answers the way we have petitioned Him. When our focus is on God and not on what we might "receive," we become more intimate with Him. There is nothing more beautiful and life giving than to feel the closeness of God. It also permits our greatest protection against losing ground to our enemy when in spiritual warfare.

The enemy loses leverage in our lives as we grow more in love with God each day. When a couple is deeply in love with each other, no rival can disrupt the bond they share. Their relationship finds security in the sheer joy and knowledge that their experience with each other is satisfying at the deepest level. Putting the enemy to flight in our lives happens when we grow into deeper intimacy with God and that intimacy happens through prayer.

This is why the Apostle Paul urged believers to pray without ceasing (1 Thessalonians 5:17). Having a constant focus on God in our lives isn't a perfunctory exercise. It's rooted in love and true intimacy. When you are in love with someone, you think about them constantly. You see them everywhere you go. You feel their presence in every conversation, every experience, every joy and even every sorrow. You simply can't get them out of your thoughts. There's a constant inner dialogue with your lover even without words being shared. This is the beauty of true love. It's what God desires for us—and with us. Religion cannot promise intimacy with God. Only deepening our relationship with God can assure the intimacy we all crave with our Creator and prayer is the conduit that allows this deepening to occur.

Picture someone in love with God in the way a young couple may be in love with each other. Every moment of every day, God comes to mind. In every experience, there's an internal dialogue going on directed toward God: "What would God think of this?" "How would God want me to respond to this?" "I wonder if God would like to share this experience with me?" In short, we become consumed with bringing God into every part of our lives. We simply can't get enough of His presence.

It's not that the enemy won't attack us if we are intimate with God. The enemy is going to attack us over and over and in every kind of circumstance, so our intimacy with God through communing with Him becomes paramount. This is illustrated when Satan comes after Jesus immediately following his public baptism as he takes time to commune with his heavenly Father by fasting and praying for forty days (See Matthew 4 and Luke 4). Were it not for the intimacy that Jesus shared with his Father, the enemy would have had the upper hand. Jesus was victorious over the enemy's attack because Jesus was spending time in unceasing prayer with His Father. If Jesus needed prayer for victorious living, it goes without saying we need it, too.

Build and protect meaningful community

Jim is one of my closest and dearest friends. We met when his kids attended my youth ministry and we found out that we both shared a love for fishing. He told me of a secret fishing hole he'd found a few years before and suggested we go there together. I jumped at the opportunity. We met after work one Thursday afternoon and drove all the way to Redding, CA—about four hours away—to get to this secret "honey hole." As we drove along, we covered great topics like deer hunting, backpacking and other outdoor adventures we'd experienced in our lives. We hit it off. We finally arrived at a parking lot in a desolate area somewhere in Shasta County late that night and crawled into our sleeping bags and went to sleep.

We woke up at dawn, crawled out of our bags and into the crisp mountain air, gathered our fishing gear and hit the trail. We walked only a short distance when we arrived at the stream he had promised would be great fishing. It is a tributary of the McCloud River. What he didn't tell me was that in order to get to this amazing spot, we'd need to cross the river in order to access the exact place he had in mind. It was about 45 degrees on that early spring morning and the stream was snowmelt runoff that fed Lake Shasta.

I'll never forget him telling me it would be best if we stripped down and just carried our clothes and gear over our heads in order to keep everything dry as we crossed. Without wanting to be wimpy about it, I followed his instructions and we both waded into the freezing water buck naked, carrying our socks, boots, pants, shirt and fishing gear over our heads (try not to visualize this scene). The part Jim didn't tell me—and the part he didn't really know himself was that the place where we were crossing was actually deeper than he expected from the last time he was there.

We both completely submerged at the same time as we tried vigorously to keep our clothes dry and our gear from washing down stream. Any passers-by might have thought we were two dolphins in a water-theme park practicing our synchronized movements. Did I mention the water was freezing!? When we finally made it to the other side, our clothes were soaked, we were shivering cold but at least we still had our fishing gear. Of course, these kinds of obstacles mean nothing to those who are accessing a great fishing spot that no one else knows about. When we finally arrived at the fishing hole, we eagerly got our fishing rigs ready and dropped our lines into the deep pool of swirling water. And then we waited. And waited. We fished all morning and caught only a couple of small trout, that if memory serves me right, we ended up tossing back. We laughed so hard all the way home over the unproductive adventure we'd shared that day.

Little did we know that over the 35 years that followed that adventure, Jim and I would share numerous trips together skiing, fishing, backpacking, riding horses, hunting, and riding motorcycles across the Western United States. We shared these experiences at times with members of his family and a few other dear friends, too. The greatest thing about my relationship with Jim wasn't the activities we experienced together, but the friendship and fellowship in Christ we shared throughout.

Jim was a true spiritual mentor in my life. He was like a father, brother and best friend all wrapped into one. Because of this, we shared our spiritual journey together. I walked alongside of him during challenging times he experienced in his family. He walked alongside of me during rough seasons in my life and family. When we spent these special times together, we always had rich discussion around spiritual things. We often read Scripture and spent time praying with and for each other. Jim has been a constant source of spiritual vitality in my life and I thank God for him.

Having Jim in my life has, among other things, provided me with an example to follow. Being a few years older than me, I've looked up to him and learned so much about following Christ, being a good husband and father, and serving the Lord wholeheartedly. I will never stop thanking God for the relationship God allowed me to share with Jim. While we now live about 250 miles apart, we still hope to share more experiences together.

Thankfully, over the years, God has brought many precious friends into my life. Mark and Tom have met with me for breakfast every week for the past twenty-five years during which time we share our lives, needs for prayer, matters of concern and things we are excited about. I often wonder where I would be without these two men in my life. They've laughed and cried with me. They've challenged me, encouraged me and sometimes just listened to me. They remind me of the truth revealed in Proverbs, *"As iron sharpens iron, so one man sharpens another"* *(Proverbs 27:17).* My life is richer for having these men in my life. Even in the difficult times when their counsel seemed hard to receive, the truth of the Proverb comes through: *"Wounds from a friend can be trusted, but an enemy multiplies kisses" (Proverbs 27:6).* Many people only want others to tell them what they want to hear. True friends say things that might hurt but are spoken for our good. Mark and Tom have been true friends and helped me experience community at very deep levels.

Space limitations won't allow me to tell of the many men and women who have impacted me so deeply and whose prayers and support have meant the world to me. Each of these dear brothers and sisters have played a critical role of providing prayer and spiritual support for my life, ministry and family over the years. I am eternally grateful for the spiritual protection and span of care they have given me. I couldn't fight the good fight without them.

The Wisdom literature says, *"Two are better than one, because they have a good return for their work: If one falls down, his friend can help him up. But pity the man who falls and has no one to help him up! Though one may be overpowered, two can defend themselves. A cord of three strands is not quickly broken" (Ecclesiastes 3:9-10, 12).* In the battle that wages in the spiritual realm, few things are as important as having meaningful community; a group of godly people who pray for us and with us.

Had I not had the spiritual support of those who I've shared about briefly here, I would surely have fallen down many more times and wonder if I would have ever gotten back up again. God did not intend for us to go up against an enemy so strong and relentless as our adversary on our own. The importance of God's presence notwithstanding, people are needed to provide meaningful community to help us be victorious.

I meet people who profess to follow Christ, but live in spiritual isolation. They have no meaningful community from which to develop Christ-centered relationships where love and care is mutually shared. These people are often ignorant of the destructive plans the enemy has for them, or they are living in the wake of that destruction already in one form or another. One of the safest and surest ways of securing a hedge of protection over us is to build meaningful community into our lives.

I've gently reminded people over the years that the community that really fosters the kind of spiritual support and protection we are discussing here, is found in the local church, the body of Christ. The New Testament writers viewed this kind of connection as critical and that which should not be forsaken. The writer of the book of Hebrews exhorts his readers, *"Let us not give up meeting together, as some are in the habit of doing, but let us encourage one another—and all the more as you see the Day approaching" (Hebrews 10:25).*

The timelessness of this exhortation goes without saying. Professing believers today are often in the habit of skipping community. This has been a problem since the inception of the church. Chances are, those who struggle most in their battle with the enemy are often isolated from other believers. We were created for community and without it, the enemy is sure to exact a greater toll on our spiritual lives.

Whenever I meet professing believers who seem unconcerned over their lack of true community, I think about those nature documentaries that feature stories about lions who begin to stalk a large herd of water buffalo and know they have no chance of going up against such a giant herd of animals. But everything changes when they give chase and the herd begins to run away causing some to break off and not have the protection they need. It's the animal that gets separated from the herd that is most vulnerable to attack. This is not only true in nature, but it's true in the spiritual realm, too. When we are isolated from the body of Christ, we are vulnerable to the attack of the enemy.

Don't give the devil a foothold

We lose many of the spiritual battles we encounter simply because we unwittingly give the enemy a foothold in some area of our lives. The Apostle Paul uses these exact words when writing to the believers in Ephesus: *"…do not give the devil a foothold" (Ephesians 4:27).* In the context of this exhortation he warns of not letting our anger get the best of us. Some of the Ephesian believers were apparently allowing their anger to simmer rather than pursuing reconciliation and peace among each other. I don't think it's a stretch to assume that any area of moral or ethical compromise can offer leverage to our enemy in some aspect of our lives.

Things that might even begin somewhat innocently can often turn into an area of concern as the enemy begins to stress the boundaries we might normally protect. Brad was a business man who, in a moment of weakness, borrowed some cash from the office where he worked for a personal need, intending to pay it back but he never did. He knew it was wrong and vowed to himself he'd never do it again. His dishonesty went undetected.

A short time later, he found himself in yet another financial bind and once again, succumbed to the temptation of using some of the business money for his own needs. This time, he needed a larger sum of money and while his conscience was telling him not to do it, he stole money from the business anyway. This pattern repeated itself a couple more times until he was caught and convicted. His business was merciful in that they reduced the charges which made him not spend as much time in jail as would have been the case normally. He suffered shame and the difficulty of being trusted in future employment. I remember hearing his emotional confession to me over what he knew all along was wrong. Brad had given the devil a foothold from which to work and it nearly destroyed his life. Thankfully and by the grace of God, Brad is through the toughest part of this season of his life and things are looking up for him.

Rick had a beautiful wife and a dream to live sexually pure in his marriage. But by exposing himself to pornography repeatedly at a young age, he had given the devil a foothold. Being married didn't solve his problem with lust for other women and soon he found himself viewing pornography regularly while hiding it from his wife. Like all destructive habits, they eventually manifest themselves and Rick was no exception.

Thankfully, Rick got into recovery and eventually found deliverance and hope through the forgiveness and power of Jesus Christ. But Rick openly testified to men around him and even his entire church family that giving the devil a foothold started his life on a journey of self-destruction that, had it not been for the grace and mercy of God in his life, would have surely ruined his marriage and himself.

Debbie was a typical high school girl from a solid Christian family, but in her junior year, she became friends with a group of students who introduced her to the party scene. The parties she frequented offered her recreational drugs and alcohol. Out of her fear of rejection, she began participating in taking substances that her friends deemed "harmless" and that which would bring her an amazing "thrill." By her senior year, Debbie's life had become unmanageable; drugs and alcohol had completely taken over. I remember meeting with her a few times between rehab programs that her parents paid for her to attend. She readily admitted to her regret of allowing a few small compromises to eventually become bigger problems that would take over her life. She seemed hopelessly lost with no real desire to change her life and become the person who not long in her past, was free from addiction and full of hope.

Debbie eventually became homeless and over the years, I've lost track of where she is. I can only pray that one day, she woke up to the lies of the enemy and came running back to Jesus. If she did, I know he received her willingly and gave her the strength to become all He intended her to be. As far as I know, her story is still being written though I have no knowledge of any details about her today.

I could go on telling of more stories that illustrate the oft repeated pattern of allowing some small compromise in one's life that gave the devil a foothold. And let me be clear that the names offered in the previous illustrations are made up, though the stories are real. The point I wish to make is this: To be victorious in our spiritual battles, we must be vigilant of never giving the devil territory which he can use to do more harm in our lives. All of us make mistakes. All of us choose at times, to disobey God and do what we think will bring us happiness, but the moment we realize what's going we must confess and repent, turning back to the gracious God we serve.

Confession is merely agreeing with God over what he says is true. When I confess to the sin of greed, I am simply agreeing with God that I desire more than I need. When I confess the sin of lust, I agree with God that my impure thoughts can't be properly legitimized in accordance with His will. Confession without repentance is shallow and limits our transformation. Only as we turn away from our sin and return to God (repentance) can we experience the transformation we need to remain victorious.

Be Humble

Humility isn't something most people pursue. Being humble in our culture is often viewed as weakness and those who view it this way, see it as having a significant downside. The downside is missed opportunities, waiting too long for things needed presently and ultimately not getting what one thinks he needs. But a far greater downside that no person in his right mind would want is that without humility, God opposes us. Yes, it's true that God opposes the proud. Whenever my pride takes over, I set in motion the opposition of God toward me, yet the promising upside of humility, set in contrast with God opposing us, is that He gives grace to the humble (James 4:6).

When it comes to the spiritual battlefield, we need God's grace because the thought of him opposing us is rather untenable. Our pride actually places us in direct opposition to Him, narrowing our chances of having victory over an enemy that knows our weaknesses and how to unravel our confidence in the fight. It's one thing to have the devil against us; it's another to know that as long as we are proud, our God opposes this error in our character.

At the core, humility is having a proper understanding of ourselves which produces confidence in God rather than in ourselves. Whenever we transfer the object of our confidence from God to ourselves, we're in big trouble, especially when we are battling against our enemy. He'd love for us to assume that it's our strength and power that overcomes his schemes and strategies knowing that as soon as this happens, our defeat is guaranteed.

The Apostle Paul revealed our need to put confidence in God and not ourselves when he writes, ***"But we have this treasure in jars of clay to show that this all-surpassing power is from God and not from us" (2 Corinthians 4:7).*** The context of this truth is embedded in the rigorous and unrelenting struggles we face in our lives: ***"We are hard pressed on every side, but not crushed; perplexed, but not in despair; persecuted, but not abandoned; struck down, but not destroyed" (2 Corinthians 4:8-9).*** Even when we are hard pressed, perplexed, persecuted and struck down, the all surpassing power of God is enough to keep us from being crushed, despairing, abandoned and destroyed. The opposite is also true. When our pride causes us to assume that our own power can stand up against life's strongest storms, we are bound to be crushed, despairing, abandoned and even destroyed.

My friend Duane is often a reminder to me of how God gives grace to the humble. Duane is the owner and president of a large company that also has many subsidiary businesses. He is an aircraft enthusiast which led him to become an excellent pilot himself and one who also understands the mechanics of everything on an aircraft and how it is to perform. My estimation of Duane's character couldn't be higher—and humility is one of those traits that is easily recognized in his life.

When I've visited him at his company headquarters, I've observed how he walks among his employees without any sense of being their boss. He is loved and admired by those who work for him because he doesn't make his position his focus; and his knowledge and business acumen never overshadow his gracious spirit towards others. He welcomes strangers into his home, invests personal time in caring for the people of

God through the local church and gives generously of his resources for Kingdom work.

I've known many successful businessmen and women over the years, and Duane is a great example of one who never uses his position to gain some kind of advantage for himself. Like Paul wrote to the Philippians, we must all demonstrate the humility of Christ (Philippians 2:8). People like Duane are a minority in our culture. When there's so much about which he could be prideful, he receives God's grace in abundance proving James' axiom that this is what God does for those who are humble.

Since being humble guarantees God's grace, it's been my desire over my pastoral career to always remember that the all surpassing power is from God and not from us. This alone has led the way for many victories over which the enemy tried to work defeat in my life. I think many Christian leaders have suffered defeat in their lives by the plans of the enemy simply because they assumed they could rise above whatever temptation or trial that came along—on their own strength. King Solomon wrote, ***"Pride goes before destruction, a haughty spirit before a fall" (Proverbs 16:18).***

My longtime ministry mentor used to remind me when hearing of a leader's moral fall: "Larry, the moment you think it will never happen to you, watch out!" I've carried that around in my head since the days that Pastor Jake drilled it into me over three decades ago. I constantly remind myself that greater men and women than I have suffered great defeat due to their false assumption that they were strong enough to take care of matters on their own.

The devil hates it when we come to the end of ourselves and fully yield our lives to Jesus Christ, depending on His sustaining power to protect us from the enemy and to give us victory when temptation and trials come our way. Truly, one of the greatest ways to sustain a steady pattern of spiritual victory is to stay humble, depending on the power of

God that lives within us and not trust our own abilities, reputation, gifting or anything else besides Him to carry us through.

Focus on what to pursue more than on what to avoid

Finally, I think victory is certain if we focus on the things we should pursue rather than the things we should avoid. Our Christian experience depends always on movement in an upward direction. The Apostle Paul reminded the Philippians to *"...press on toward the goal to win the prize for which God has called [us] heavenward in Christ Jesus" (Philippians 3:14).* In the context of Paul's exhortation, we learn that often this will require forgetting what is behind so we can strain toward what is ahead (Philippians 3:13). The things we might need to forget about could be past accomplishments and victories since it does us no good to rest on our laurels. Too often, believers become too enamored with past accomplishments which dull their sense of drive for what God wants to do next in their lives. Sometimes local churches do the same and remain frozen in a time capsule of the "good 'ol days" where great things were done in the name of Jesus. It's okay to celebrate our victories and accomplishments, but let's not stay focused on them. God has new things in store for us.

Other things we might need to forget about are our past defeats. At times, I've stalled out in my faith journey simply because I couldn't get over the failure I experienced personally or in some kind of ministry endeavor that shook my confidence. We all have things in our past that we wish we could do over, make better and see a different result, but that's the thing about focus—if it's too much on our past, we get stuck and movement becomes very slow or even non-existent.

This is the trap the enemy has lured some of us into repeatedly in our lives. It's been my desire to compel all of us to press on, move forward and never stop trusting God for the new thing(s) He wants to do in our lives. To avoid the trap of being stuck with focusing too heavily on something either good or bad in our past, we must pursue what God has for us now.

When writing to his young disciple Timothy, Paul suggested some great things to pursue that destroy the malady of being stuck in our past or focusing too much on things we should avoid. He writes, *"Flee the evil desires of youth, and pursue righteousness, faith, love and peace, along with those who call on the Lord out of a pure heart"* *(2 Timothy 2:22).* Show me someone focused on righteousness, faith, love and peace, and I'll show you someone who isn't being dragged down by either past accomplishments or failures. God knows that we are at our best when we are moving in concert with his desires for our lives toward things that build us up and transform our lives and those around us.

There's nothing more exciting than pursuing the good things God desires to bring us lasting satisfaction in life. Righteousness, faith, love and peace are easily things that do just that! A young man whom I've mentored the past couple of years is (as I write) serving on a mission's team during a week when many of his peers are headed to beaches in southern California to celebrate for a week of carefree fun. Matt's passion for serving Christ has given him the desire to pursue God's priorities for his life—and he's reaping the benefits of making this choice. God is filling him up and giving him a joy and satisfaction that is palpable every time I get a text from him or see him in person.

Another young man I've mentored for several years struggled for a long time with pornography. For many years, his focus was on avoiding this dreaded and destructive behavior and while he experienced a modicum of victory from time to time, it seemed to repeat often which led him to feeling defeated. Then one day, his focus shifted from avoiding pornography to pursuing righteousness. This was a game changer in his life which has led him to a deeper and more satisfying walk with Christ ever since. By God's grace, he no longer feels the pull of the addictive cycle of pornography. God has set him free because his focus is now on righteousness, faith, love and peace. He's a changed man. The challenges may feel even deeper now for him, but that's because the enemy has lost a significant battle in his life and now new strategies are being foisted against him.

I joined him for coffee a while back to catch up on what was going on in our lives. As I approached the table at the coffee shop where he had been waiting for me to arrive, I loved seeing his Bible opened and a notebook filled with notes with things God was teaching him about pursuing righteousness in his life. In a follow up text to me, he said, "There are a thousand fires all around and I'm trying to survive. I'm listening for the voice of my creator and I'm being sustained. The Lord is doing something powerful. I know I've not arrived but he is keeping me. And His timing is what is most important." I'm so proud of this young man and his pursuit of what's good and right in his life and how this is transforming him every day—and it can transform you, too.

The point of this book hasn't been to make us experts in casting out demons, nor has it been to make us merely more knowledgeable of spiritual warfare. The real point has been to compel each of us toward a life that honors God; to pursue Jesus Christ with greater abandon and to find more joy and freedom knowing we are victorious in Christ!

If you feel just a bit more excited about the promises and resources God has given you to fight the enemy and you are willing to engage him because of it, then my work is done. So let's stay in the fight. It's the good fight and we've already heard the victor's song:

"Hallelujah! For our Lord God Almighty reigns. Let us rejoice and be glad and give him glory! For the wedding of the Lamb has come, and his bride has made herself ready."

Revelation 19:6-7

"Now have come the salvation and the power and the kingdom of our God, and the authority of his Christ. For the accuser of our brothers, who accuses them before our God day and night, has been hurled down. They overcame him by the blood of the lamb and by the word of their testimony; they did not love their lives so much as to shrink from death."

Revelation 12:10-11

CHAPTER 12: PUTTING IT ALL TOGETHER
DISCUSSION QUESTIONS

1. Generally speaking, how committed are you to running the Christian race as if to win? What is the strongest evidence of your pursuit to win in this race?

2. When thinking of the Christian life as a race to win, what are the strongest competitors you are running against?

3. Of the various disciplines essential for sustaining victory in the battle, which one(s) were most meaningful to you? Give reasons for your answer.

4. What is your current rhythm of Bible reading and prayer? Are you experiencing deeper intimacy with God?

5. What does meaningful community look like to you? How often are you engaged meaningfully with other believers? How important is it for you to know other believers and to be known by them?

6. What is the greatest obstacle you are facing today with regard to pursuing all that God has for you? Name an area of your life that is leeching passion from your walk with God. What might you do to reduce its impact so you could pursue Christ with greater abandon?

7. When have you felt most intimate with Jesus Christ? What led to feeling closer to Him?

DR. LARRY A. VOLD

PASTOR OF SPIRITUAL CARE 3CROSSES

Dr. Larry A. Vold serves as Pastor of Spiritual Care at 3Crosses in Castro Valley, CA where he previously served as Senior Pastor for more than two decades. He earned a Masters in Theology degree from Simpson University and a Doctor of Ministry degree from Bakke Graduate University.

Larry began following Jesus Christ as a young boy and matured in his faith through the mentorship of a student ministries pastor at the church where he was first introduced to the Gospel of Jesus Christ.

Larry also has served for the past twenty years as Chaplain for the Alameda County Fire Department. Larry's passion is to bring glory to God by serving others and sharing the Gospel of Jesus Christ. He and his wife Carla have raised three beautiful daughters and are blessed with two grandsons. His personal interests include family time, playing basketball, bike riding and motorcycles, ocean fishing from his kayak and playing trumpet. He is also the author of *Know His Name* and *Pray This Way* available at Amazon.com and Kindle.

RICK CHAVEZ

EDITOR

Rick Chavez enjoyed a successful career as a Bay Area TV/Radio anchor, interviewing Hall of Fame athletes, Olympic champions and Silicon Valley executives. He was Sports Director at NBC11 in San Jose and anchored at ABC7 and KRON4 in San Francisco.

Rick hosted Cisco's first international SMB webcast from The Netherlands as well as Oracle World webcasts in New Orleans and San Diego. Rick produced Silicon Valley tech reports for CNBC-Europe, was the host of "Best of the Bay" and won four Telly Awards for broadcast and documentary production excellence.

Rick was Jubilee Bible College Valedictorian in 2011 and now specializes in writing and editing for Christian audiences. He is available as an editor, proofreader or publisher. Contact rick@dreamcasters.world.